The 48th Pennsylvania
in the Battle of the Crater

The 48th Pennsylvania in the Battle of the Crater

A Regiment of Coal Miners Who Tunneled Under the Enemy

JIM CORRIGAN

McFarland & Company, Inc., Publishers
Jefferson, North Carolina, and London

LIBRARY OF CONGRESS CATALOGUING-IN-PUBLICATION DATA

Corrigan, Jim.
    The 48th Pennsylvania in the Battle of the Crater : a
regiment of coal miners who tunneled under the enemy /
Jim Corrigan.
       p.   cm.
    Includes bibliographical references and index.

    ISBN-13: 978-0-7864-2475-7
    ISBN-10: 0-7864-2475-3 (softcover : 50# alkaline paper)

    1. Petersburg Crater, Battle of, Va., 1864.   2. United
States. Army. Pennsylvania Infantry Regiment, 48th
(1861–1865)   3. Pennsylvania — History — Civil War,
1861–1865 — Regimental histories.   4. United States—
History — Civil War, 1861–1865 — Regimental histories.
5. Meade, George Gordon, 1815–1872 — Military leadership.
6. Burnside, Ambrose Everett, 1824–1881— Military
leadership.   I. Title.
E476.93.C67   2006
973.7'37 — dc22   2006001507

British Library cataloguing data are available

On the cover: Recapture the Crater, painting by Henry Kidd; hkidd@adelthia.net

Manufactured in the United States of America

McFarland & Company, Inc., Publishers
  Box 611, Jefferson, North Carolina 28640
    www.mcfarlandpub.com

For my grandfather, George, a 20th-century coal miner from Schuylkill County, Pennsylvania, who ultimately gave his life to the mines

Contents

Preface

The city of Pottsville is a quaint, friendly place nestled in the foothills of eastern Pennsylvania's Blue Mountain. The sun set on Pottsville's heyday about a century ago, when petroleum replaced coal as the premier form of energy in America. Since then, the region has never quite recovered. Even today, people seem to carry within them a faint and distant sorrow over what might have been. Reminders of the area's coal-mining past are everywhere, from the names of neighboring towns — Minersville, Coaldale, Port Carbon — to the ubiquitous hills of black refuse, which are strangely dotted with thick clumps of white birch trees.

Despite its economic struggles, the region has a rich and colorful history. Pottsville is perhaps best known as the home of D.G. Yuengling & Son, Inc., America's oldest brewery. Yuengling first began producing beer in 1829 and in recent years has earned a fashionable reputation as the nation's original microbrew. In 1877, six Irish coal miners were hanged in Pottsville for their involvement with the Molly Maguires, a violent labor group. John O'Hara, the celebrated twentieth-century novelist, was a city native. And in 1923, a band of rugged football players called the Pottsville Maroons captured an NFL championship, only to see the fledgling league revoke their title due to a petty franchise violation.

A lesser-known story from the area's past is the key role its sons played in the Battle of the Crater, which took place near Petersburg, Virginia, in 1864. I first heard of the Crater in fourth-grade history class and was intrigued by the connection between a Civil War event and my hometown. When I began researching the battle in earnest a quarter of a century later, I was struck by the lasting impression it had on its participants. In terms of size and importance, the Battle of the Crater paled in comparison to the massive engagements of Gettysburg, Antietam, and elsewhere. Yet veterans from both sides of the conflict continued to talk and write about their Crater experiences well into old age. The unusual nature and ferocity of the battle, and its many ironies, stayed with them and apparently captured a place in their hearts.

Preface

I owe a debt of gratitude to the many kind people who helped me unearth the veterans' recollections, and then organize those fragmented (and sometimes conflicting) accounts into a coherent story. Among them are: Mr. Leo Ward, curator of the Historical Society of Schuylkill County (HSSC); author Michael Cavanaugh, who spent a lifetime gathering Crater-related documents and subsequently donated much of his collection to HSSC; John David Hoptak, an expert on the 48th Pennsylvania Infantry Regiment; and Mary Beth Long of the Red Land Library in Etters, Pennsylvania, who helped me track down copies of several rare books.

I would also like to acknowledge the courteous and helpful staffs at the Petersburg National Battlefield, the Virginia Historical Society in Richmond, and the U.S. Army Military History Institute in Carlisle, Pennsylvania (particularly Mr. Cliff Hyatt and Dr. Richard Sommers), as well as the many other helpful folks I encountered while doing research. Also, special thanks go to Larry Geesaman of the Harrisburg Civil War Roundtable for his many insightful comments and recommendations.

Those deserving my deepest gratitude include my lovely wife, Connie, who trudged with me across humid battlefields and into dusty libraries without ever once complaining; my mother, who imbued in me a love of history; my father, who slogged through early drafts of the book and made many helpful suggestions; and Barry Sparks, my mentor and good friend. Lastly, I cannot forget Mr. Raymond Hinchey, the fourth-grade teacher who first introduced me to the Crater story.

To each of these people, and to those I may have overlooked, I extend my sincere thanks.

A Note on Terminology

Newcomers to Civil War history are likely to encounter a number of unfamiliar terms and expressions. Understanding the manner in which North and South organized their vast armies can be particularly vexing.

The **regiment** was the fundamental organizational unit for both sides. Ideally, it consisted of ten companies of 100 men each, but many regiments fell well below full strength late in the war. Four or more regiments usually made up a **brigade**, and two to six brigades formed a **division**, totaling roughly 12,000 men. A **corps** consisted of two or more divisions, and multiple corps composed an **army**. Union armies were typically named after rivers (e.g., Army of the Potomac) while Confederate armies were named after geographical regions (e.g., Army of Northern Virginia). A detailed listing of the specific units who fought at the Battle of the Crater can be found at the rear of the book.

Other terms from the Civil War era used in this book are defined below:

abatis a defensive obstacle made by laying felled trees on top of each other with the branches, sometimes sharpened, facing the enemy.

banquette a platform lining a trench wall on which soldiers may stand when firing.

bombproof a shelter intended to provide protection from enemy mortar shells.

breastwork a constructed fortification, usually earthen and breast-high.

canister an anti-personnel artillery projectile, consisting of a thin metal casing filled with small lead balls.

cavalier trench a shallow, hastily excavated ditch used for defensive purposes.

chevaux-de-frise an obstacle composed of spikes attached to a wooden frame, used to block enemy advancement.

covered way an enclosed passage leading to the front.

debouche to march from a narrow or confined area into the open.

fraise a defensive barrier of pointed inclined stakes.

gabion a cylindrical wicker basket filled with earth and stones used in constructing fortifications.

A Note on Terminology

grapeshot an artillery round similar to canister, but with larger iron balls.

parapet a wall or breastwork used to protect soldiers.

ultimo meaning "in or of the month before the present one."

USCT acronym for "United States Colored Troops," the Union's African-American units.

Introduction

The spring of 1864 would be different, many Northerners desperately hoped and prayed. This time the march toward Richmond would succeed, they believed. Public enthusiasm for the war had long since faded. An end to the conflict would have to come soon.

Under Lieutenant General Ulysses S. Grant, newly arrived from the West and promoted to commander of all Union forces, it would indeed be different. Grant possessed an iron determination that his predecessors lacked. He did not hesitate to attack, and he grimly accepted casualties as an unfortunate consequence of war. When heavy battlefield losses prompted some to label Grant a butcher and call for his dismissal, Abraham Lincoln flatly refused, saying, "I can't spare this man. He fights."[1]

As the Army of the Potomac set out once again for Richmond in early May 1864, Grant employed a series of swift flanking maneuvers, attempting to slip behind the Army of Northern Virginia. But each Federal movement drew a brilliant countermove from Robert E. Lee, and the two forces collided violently at the Wilderness, Spotsylvania Court House, and the North Anna River. After each encounter Grant carefully planned his next thrust at Lee's right flank, but Lee would anticipate the move and parry, and so the armies marched in lockstep through Virginia. Lee fretted over the ultimate outcome of this deadly game. "We must destroy this army of Grant's before he gets to the James River," he told a confidant. "If he gets there it will become a siege, and then it will be a mere question of time."[2]

Finally, Union and Confederate soldiers found themselves within ten miles of Richmond at the crossroads of Cold Harbor. The Southerners had arrived first, as usual, and prepared earthen fortifications with which to repel the imminent Yankee assault. That assault came on June 3, 1864, when 60,000 Federals marched headlong toward the entrenched Confederate positions. The slaughter was fearful, and by day's end more than 7,000 Union soldiers had fallen on the open ground before the earthworks. Confederate casualties came to only 1,500. The scars of this battle would stay with the Army of the Potomac until the end of the war. It was a stunning defeat, and that night a shaken Grant told his aides, "I regret this assault more than any one I have ever ordered." He decided to take a few days to reconsider his strategy.[3]

While Grant's campaign was first getting underway in northern Virginia, Federal activity was also stirring farther south. General Benjamin Butler, under orders from Grant, sailed up the James River and landed his Army of the James on a peninsula called Bermuda Hundred. As the first shots echoed in the Wilderness, 15,000 of Butler's troops were stepping ashore virtually unopposed at Bermuda Hundred and in the nearby town of City Point.

Confederate war planners were alarmed. The Army of Northern Virginia was fully occupied holding Grant at bay east of Richmond; it would be unable to stop an attack from the south. Units were summoned from distant points of the Confederacy to rush to the capital's defense. There was another concern — the vital but lightly defended rail network in Petersburg, Virginia was only a few short miles from Butler's grasp. The loss of Petersburg would be just as fatal.

The strategists need not have worried. Before the war, Benjamin Butler had been a formidable New England attorney and politician, but in uniform he was of little threat. Only through his powerful political connections did he come to command an army. Butler was among the most despised Yankee generals in the South, primarily for his heavy-handed occupation of New Orleans in 1862, where residents came to refer to him as "Beast" Butler. His military ineptitude, combined with a penchant for lining his pockets, left even his own men to hold him in low regard. (Union soldiers did not pilfer, they "Butlerized.") Rather than seize Petersburg or strike out for Richmond, the portly, cross-eyed general pitched camp at Bermuda Hundred and made some feeble probes west.

The strategic importance of Petersburg had been obvious to Southerners from the outset of the war. No less than five major railroads terminated there, including the crucial Richmond & Petersburg Railroad, which kept the Confederate capital alive with men and materiel. If Richmond was the Confederacy's brain, then Petersburg was its heart, pumping vital supplies from the Deep South northward along its steel arteries.

In the summer of 1862, the heart was given some strong ribs for protection, courtesy of Captain Charles Dimmock, an engineer assigned to construct the city's defenses. Dimmock used the Appomattox River to anchor a ten-mile semicircle that began east of the city and curved around to the riverbank on the west. The Dimmock Line, built by both slaves and paid civilians, contained 55 earthen forts to house artillery. The forts were strung together by six-foot-high breastworks for infantry. In front of the line ran an eight-foot-deep, fifteen-foot-wide continuous ditch, and the ground beyond was cleared for half a mile. Obstacles and rifle pits were scattered about this open space to further deter any aggressor. The Dimmock Line was a marvel of military engineering, yet it had one serious flaw — no less than 20,000 troops, or a full-strength Confederate corps, were needed for it to be properly manned.

For the first two years of its existence, the Dimmock Line sat quiet and empty. The North remained obsessed with Richmond, and Petersburg stayed happily obscure. The only excitement came early in the war, when a rumor spread that the Union gunboat *Pawnee* had been dispatched to sail up the Appomattox and shell Petersburg. Once proved false, the rumor mutated into a wild story of murderous Indians, unleashed by the U.S. government, roaming the surrounding countryside in search of victims. Country folk rushed to the city for safety, and some time passed before they could be persuaded to return home. Now in May 1864, as the hated "Beast" Butler consolidated his position barely five miles from Petersburg, a skeleton force of just 2,000 Virginians occupied the Dimmock Line. The city was about to be drawn into the war in a way its residents could scarcely have imagined.

1

Battleground Petersburg

Confederate General P. G. T. Beauregard was a 46-year-old Creole known for his penetrating stare and dramatic bearing. A career officer, Beauregard graduated second in West Point's class of 1838. He served anonymously in the Mexican War, but achieved instant stardom in April 1861 while presiding over the bombardment of Fort Sumter. Beauregard relished the spotlight, and was convinced that Richmond bureaucrats plotted against him.

His suspicions were bolstered by his latest assignment: the backwater command of the Department of North Carolina, a region that included southern Virginia. The war's remaining opportunities for glory, Beauregard felt, would surely take place north of the James River as the battles for Richmond raged. In his eyes, he had been sabotaged yet again.[1]

When news of a Federal landing in southern Virginia reached Beauregard in North Carolina, he wasted little time. The general gathered all available troops and headed for Petersburg, arriving on May 10, 1864 with three brigades in tow. Sensing Petersburg was in no immediate danger, Beauregard moved 18 miles north to Drewry's Bluff, a summit guarding the southern approaches to Richmond. The sluggish Benjamin Butler had ventured this far with his Army of the James, and in the early morning hours of May 16, Beauregard confronted him. With a force of 18,000 men, Beauregard attacked Butler in heavy fog and sent him reeling back toward the sanctuary of Bermuda Hundred. Upon reaching a narrow point in the 30-square-mile peninsula, Beauregard established a trench line to hold the Federal army in place.

Surrounded by water on three sides, and entrenched Confederates on the fourth, Butler and his army had, as Ulysses S. Grant disgustedly noted, "hermetically sealed itself up at Bermuda Hundred."[2] Beauregard was pleased. With an entire Federal army effectively neutralized and the 23-mile transportation corridor between Richmond and Petersburg again secure, he was free to pursue glory elsewhere. His enthusiasm quickly evaporated when Lee commandeered most of his veteran units for the defense of Richmond.

Realizing the peninsula would likely be their home for some time, the men of the Army of the James built a wooden signal tower from which to observe Confederate activity in the area. Daily reports of locomotives, laden with Southern troops, chugging away from Petersburg emboldened Butler to finally take the initiative. He arranged for 1,300 cavalrymen to cross the Appomattox on a pontoon bridge, ride south of the city, and attack Petersburg's defenses at the thoroughfare of Jerusalem Plank Road. Simultaneously, a column of infantry would assault directly from the east.

Beauregard had left Petersburg in the care of General Henry Wise, a former governor of Virginia. Like Butler, Wise was a politician turned soldier, albeit one with slightly greater military aptitude. Still, Beauregard's decision to leave Wise in charge demonstrated his confidence that Petersburg was safe. Only the local militia, a small collection of poorly trained citizen soldiers, manned the sprawling Dimmock Line.

As weeks slowly passed in the hot, dusty earthworks with no sign of the Yankees, the militiamen grew lax, taking unauthorized leaves to tend to their shops in town. On one occasion, General Wise rode out to the line in search of the militia's commander, Major Fletcher Archer. Upon hearing that Archer was in town, Wise angrily replied, "Yes, and if the enemy were to come, you would all be there in less time than it would take a cannon ball to reach there."[3]

Before sunrise on June 9, Butler's task force crossed the river. A few hours later Federal gunboats opened fire on targets in the city. General R.E. Colston, in Petersburg awaiting reassignment, described the commotion that morning: "The alarm-bell was rung in the city about 9 o'clock, and every man able to shoulder a musket hurried out to the lines." Recuperating veterans leapt from their beds in the city's military hospitals. Convicts were freed from the prisons in order to fight. Colston characterized the city's defenders as "Second Class Reserves, men exempted from active service on account of age or infirmities, and boys under conscription age, who had had no military training. Very few of them wore a uniform, and they were armed with inferior muskets and rifles...." Colston offered Wise his services, and Wise asked him to supervise the line's easternmost batteries. The commander then departed for Jerusalem Plank Road.[4]

Wise found Major Archer and about 150 of his militiamen nervously waiting at Rives' Farm, which offered a commanding view of the road. Yankee cavalry had already arrived but not yet attacked. Archer glanced at his troops, wondering how they would perform in combat. He noticed an elderly man cutting open a paper ammunition cartridge with a pocketknife, then realized that the man had no teeth with which to tear it open.[5]

Across the road, Federal cavalry commander August Kautz listened for the sound of fighting to the northeast. Once the infantry column had engaged, he would be free to destroy the motley group in front of him and ride into Petersburg without fear of Confederate reinforcements. Morning passed to afternoon with no indication that the infantry had begun their attack. Kautz grew impatient and moved forward anyway, prompting Wise to send for Colston, who quickly arrived on the scene with a howitzer and its crew. When the Federals drew within 300 yards, Colston called for the small cannon to be loaded with canister, the anti-personnel shell that sprayed dozens of lead balls. But the howitzer's caisson contained no canister, so the crew fired standard cannonballs instead, with little effect.

Archer's men opened fire and fought stubbornly against long odds. "The brave militia discharged their pieces at close range," Colston said. "Numbers of them fell killed or wounded, and before the survivors could reload the enemy turned our left flank and more of our men fell."[6] Forced to retreat, the militiamen abandoned their cannon and fled to high ground near the city's reservoir. At 1:15 pm, as Kautz's troopers closed to within 150 yards of Petersburg's streets, the wavering militiamen heard hoof beats from behind. Beauregard, upon learning of the attack, had sent a cannon battery and the 4th North Carolina Cavalry. They galloped through Petersburg's cobblestone streets and quickly unlimbered their guns. "The battery opened fire, and with rapidity and precision hurled a storm of shell and canister upon the approaching cavalry," Colston recalled. "The enemy, who thought themselves already in possession of the city, halted in surprise."[7]

Concerned that more reinforcements were on the way, Kautz withdrew his men and retreated. He was furious to learn that the Union infantry commander, General Quincy Gillmore, had been unnerved by the fearsome sight of the Dimmock Line and never actually attempted an assault. Kautz later wrote that "had the infantry been at hand to support the cavalry, Petersburg could have been taken and held at this time." He added, with an obvious measure of satisfaction, "Shortly after this affair, General Gillmore was relieved from the command of the Tenth Corps."[8] The first Federal thrust at Petersburg had failed.

Meanwhile, on June 5 at Cold Harbor, sharpshooters sporadically exchanged fire as Grant reflected on his situation. One month's fighting had brought him as far as George McClellan's Peninsula Campaign of 1862, but with ten times as many casualties—more than 50,000 men. Though tantalizingly close to Richmond, Grant's repeated attempts to flank Lee had been decisively turned away. Finally, he wired Washington. "My idea from the start has been to beat Lee's army, if possible, north of Richmond," he wrote. "Without a greater sacrifice of human life than I am willing to make, all cannot be accomplished that I had designed outside of the city."[9]

Grant then laid out a grand and radical proposal. Under the cover of darkness, he would pull his 100,000-man army from their trenches at Cold Harbor, swing south in a 40-mile arc, and capture the supply town of Petersburg. Once accomplished, he could strangle Richmond into submission, or at the very least, force Lee to engage him in the open field. Strategically, the plan was risky. Lincoln's advisor Henry Halleck pointed out that if Grant's army were discovered in transit it would be vulnerable to piecemeal destruction. Logistically, the plan was a nightmare. Two rivers lay between Cold Harbor and Petersburg — the Chickahominy and the James — the latter being a wide, tidal river running as deep as 100 feet. Moving an entire army plus its supplies across such formidable obstacles, in secret, seemed nearly impossible. Yet Grant felt it was necessary and Lincoln gave his blessings.

The next few days were marked by extensive preparation. To distract Lee, Grant sent 6,000 cavalrymen to tear up the Virginia Central Railroad northwest of Richmond at Trevilian Station. He also directed his Fifth Corps, under General Gouverneur K. Warren, to feign a flanking maneuver on Lee's army during the night of the move, hoping to convince Lee that Richmond was still his target. After staging a convincing performance, Fifth Corps would also vanish into the night and head south.

Shortly after 11 pm on June 12, Federal units quietly began withdrawing from their Cold Harbor lines for the long march down, and then across, the Chickahominy. Grant's staff described him as uncharacteristically anxious that night; the enormity of the gamble was weighing on him. Marching through the cool night air reinvigorated men who had sat idle in trenches for over a week, but those same men wilted once the sun came up on June 13. Back at Cold Harbor, Confederate troops peered across at the empty Union trenches in dismay.

Nobody was more puzzled than Robert E. Lee. He had received reports of skirmishing on his right flank throughout the overnight hours, and had positioned his forces to meet a full-scale assault at daybreak. The assault never came and now an entire Federal army was missing, presumably marching somewhere in Virginia. "It was said that General Lee was in a furious passion — one of the few times during the war," remembered a Southern officer. "When he did get mad he was mad all over."[10]

By 1:30 pm on June 14, Grant was beginning to feel confident. He sent an update to Washington: "Our forces will commence crossing the James today. The enemy shows no signs yet of having brought troops to the south side of Richmond. I will have Petersburg secured, if possible, before they get there in much force. Our movement from Cold Harbor to the James River has been made with great celerity and so far without loss or accident."[11] To this Lincoln personally responded, "I begin to see it. You will succeed. God bless you all."[12]

The first troops to reach the river were ferried across, a slow and tedious process requiring every naval ship and river transport that could be mustered. Meanwhile, 450 engineers started construction on a half-mile long pontoon bridge for the rest of the army to cross. Working from both shores, the engineers lashed together 101 wooden pontoon boats, anchoring them with three schooners for support. Five stone-filled ships were sunk upriver to deter Confederate gunboats. The bridge, which was completed in less than eight hours, rose and fell with the tide and was equipped with a swinging midsection to permit the passage of ironclads and transport ships. On the riverbank, military bands played as legions of soldiers waited for their turn to cross.

Before departing Cold Harbor, Grant had sent an advance force ahead of the army to open large-scale hostilities against Petersburg. General William F. "Baldy" Smith and his Eighteenth Corps had steamed up the James River and disembarked at Bermuda Hundred, where they were joined by Kautz's cavalry and a division of United States Colored Troops (USCT). Smith resurrected Butler's failed battle plan from a week earlier, modifying it so that this time the cavalry would merely put on a demonstration at Jerusalem Plank Road, while the infantry charged and over-ran the Dimmock Line.

General Wise again found himself sorely outnumbered. When Baldy Smith arrived shortly after noon on June 15 with 15,000 men, Wise had but 2,200 troops spread paper-thin along the first four miles of the Dimmock Line. Beyond that, the trenches were empty. But just as Gillmore had done, Smith paused at the unsettling sight of the Confederate earthworks. Wishing to avoid a repeat of Cold Harbor, where he suffered over 1,000 casualties, Smith spent the next five and a half hours reconnoitering for the best place to launch his attack. When he was finally ready, the assault was delayed another hour because the artillery horses had been taken to the rear for water.

There would be no display by the cavalry to distract the Confederates—Kautz threw up his hands and departed around 4 pm —but it was hardly necessary. At sunset, Smith finally gave the order to attack and the Eighteenth Corps surged forward like a tidal wave, sweeping the militia from their fortifications and easily capturing a mile and a half of the line.

Just when it seemed Petersburg's luck had finally run out, the Federals stopped and advanced no farther. Smith's subordinates pleaded for permission to press on into the city, but the general refused. Wary over the ease of his victory and fatigued by a bout of malaria, Smith was satisfied to spend the night in the Confederate earthworks. The error was obvious to everyone but Smith. "I swore all night," one enlisted man wrote. "I kicked and condemned every general there was in the army for the blunder I saw they were making. I only wished I could be the general commanding for one hour."[13]

Beauregard arrived on the scene and was stunned by his good fortune. "Strange to say, General Smith contented himself with breaking into our lines, and attempted nothing further that night." He continued, "Petersburg at that hour was clearly at the mercy of the Federal commander, who had all but captured it and only failed of final success because he could not realize the fact of the unparalleled disparity between the two contending forces."[14] As Smith rested, Beauregard spent the night establishing a new line along the west bank of Harrison's Creek, stocking it with veterans Lee had returned to him from Richmond.

Earlier that day, while Smith was debating where to make his charge, General Winfield Scott Hancock was undoubtedly cursing army bureaucracy. His Second Corps had been slowly ferried across the James while the mammoth pontoon bridge was being built. Once on the south side, he was forced to linger for the late delivery of food rations. Finally on the move after hours of waiting, Hancock discovered he had been handed an inaccurate map and given a destination behind enemy lines. He then received a message urging him to support the assault of Eighteenth Corps, an attack he was unaware had even been ordered.

When Hancock finally found Smith late in the evening at the Dimmock Line, he suggested that a night assault might be appropriate in order to capture Petersburg. Smith vehemently disagreed and the senior-ranking Hancock yielded to his judgement. Afterward Smith would be taken to task for his poor decisions that night. He shamelessly attempted to blame Hancock, arguing that the senior officer failed to order him to attack. The flimsy excuse failed and yet another Union general lost his command due to Petersburg. He would not be the last.

In the city, Beauregard was becoming frantic. Reports streamed in from the countryside of long, blue columns of men, all of whom were obviously massing directly in front of him. Beauregard concluded days earlier that Grant's missing army was headed for Petersburg, and he shared those conclusions with Richmond repeatedly, but without proof Lee was unwilling to expose the Confederate capital. Beauregard's telegrams grew increasingly desperate, but Lee still resisted, unsure if those reports were accurate or if the flamboyant Creole was simply exaggerating, as he had done so many times in the past.

At 11:15 pm on June 15, Beauregard forced Lee's hand. He ordered his 3,200 troops guarding Butler's army at Bermuda Hundred to abandon their lines and return to Petersburg. Then he wired Lee, explaining what he had done and concluding with, "Cannot these lines be occupied by your troops? The safety of our communication requires it."[15] Lee swiftly dispatched two divisions to Bermuda Hundred, where Butler's men were already milling around like ants released from a bottle. Lee still balked, however, at the idea of moving his army to Petersburg without further evidence of Grant's intentions.

On paper, Major General George Gordon Meade commanded the Army of the Potomac. In reality, he was little more than a conduit through which Grant's orders passed. Several months earlier, when Grant ascended to the new position of general-in-chief, he assured Meade he would not interfere with the army's operations. The

General Pierre Gustave Toutant Beauregard, the "Hero of Sumter." Richmond officials took a dim view of Beauregard's arrogance and personal ambition, but his defense of Petersburg was undeniably masterful. (National Archives and Record Administration)

promise was short-lived, and soon Grant was issuing detailed, daily instructions. Meade fumed. The tall, 49-year-old Philadelphian had led the army admirably since assuming command in June 1863, performing particularly well at Gettysburg, just a few days after taking the reins. Now Grant was constantly looking over Meade's shoulder while other army commanders operated with a free hand. Further, Grant was more aggressive than Meade, prodding him to attack before he was ready. Such was the case at Cold Harbor, after which Meade wrote, "I think Grant has had his eyes opened, and is willing to admit now that Virginia and Lee's army is not Tennessee and Bragg's army."[16]

Grant did indeed back off. After pausing a few moments to observe the grand spectacle of the river crossing, he went to establish his headquarters at nearby City Point, leaving the invasion of Petersburg to Meade. But inexplicably, Grant failed to inform Meade of his orders to Smith. While dining that evening, Meade was dumbfounded to learn that an attack was underway. He immediately ordered all supply wagons and artillery cleared from the pontoon bridge so that the infantry could cross and join the fight.[17] After a fifteen-hour march, Ninth Corps reached the front line at 10 am on June 16, easing into position on the left of Hancock's Second Corps.

Ninth Corps was something of a black sheep in the Army of the Potomac, primarily due to the poor standing of its leader, General Ambrose Burnside. Despite victories in North Carolina and Tennessee, Burnside was largely remembered for catastrophic defeats at Antietam and Fredericksburg. A decidedly dismal stint as commander of the Army of the Potomac forced Lincoln to send Burnside to the Western theater in 1863. But a year later Grant ordered Burnside and Ninth Corps back east to participate in the Overland Campaign. While in the West, Burnside reported directly to Grant, but now he was necessarily placed under Meade. Dedicated and affable, Burnside did not complain about the informal demotion, but Meade made little effort to hide his doubts about Burnside's abilities.

On the afternoon of June 16, Hancock led his Second Corps and elements of Ninth and Eighteenth Corps against a portion of the Dimmock Line still in Confederate hands. The Federals successfully took three more forts, but suffered heavy losses, including the death of Colonel Patrick Kelly, head of the legendary Irish Brigade. Beauregard's troops held their ground at Harrison's Creek. He described them as "a barrier of not even 10,000 exhausted, half-starved men, who had gone through two days of constant hard fighting and many sleepless nights in the trenches."[18] Beauregard's actual strength was closer to 14,000 men, but he faced roughly 50,000 Federals, and the disparity was growing. Despite the overwhelming numerical advantage, Meade sensed a problem. He reported to Grant, "Our men are tired and the attacks have not been made with the vigor and force which characterized our fighting in the Wilderness; if they had been, I think we should have been more successful. I will continue to press."[19]

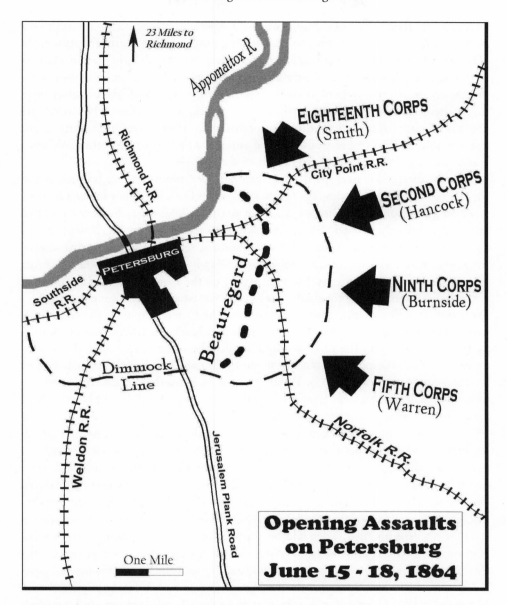

23 Miles to Richmond

Appomattox R.

EIGHTEENTH CORPS (Smith)

City Point R.R.

SECOND CORPS (Hancock)

Richmond R.R.

NINTH CORPS (Burnside)

PETERSBURG

Southside R.R.

Beauregard

FIFTH CORPS (Warren)

Dimmock Line

Weldon R.R.

Norfolk R.R.

Jerusalem Plank Road

One Mile

Opening Assaults on Petersburg June 15 - 18, 1864

Confederate General P.G.T. Beauregard managed to slow the progress of a vastly superior Federal force until reinforcements arrived.

As the attacks resumed on July 17, Beauregard recognized that his Harrison's Creek line would not hold much longer. He instructed his engineers to mark off a new line 1,000 feet to the rear, behind the marshy Taylor's Creek. He told the engineers to demarcate their new line with white stakes, which would stand out in the darkness. As night fell, Beauregard had his men build blazing campfires along the Harrison's Creek line, then ordered them to quietly fall back behind Taylor's Creek.

The ragged, weary Confederates were now less than a mile outside Petersburg's city limits. Beauregard knew this would be his last stand. Shortly after midnight, he wired Lee: "I expect renewal of attack in morning. My troops are becoming much exhausted. Without immediate and strong re-enforcements results may be unfavorable."[20] Lee was finally persuaded. The Army of Northern Virginia was marching toward Petersburg just three hours later.

As Beauregard's men spent their third straight night digging by moonlight, they were suddenly greeted by the first arrivals from Lee's army. For many, the overwhelming sense of relief brought tears of joy to their sunken eyes. Each ray of morning light seemingly carried another division into town, and by 11:30 am, General Lee himself had arrived. Beauregard was the most relieved; he promptly escorted his superior to the high ground at the city's reservoir and pointed out the situation.

The morning of Saturday, June 18, presented the frontline Union troops with a mystery — no noise or movement could be detected anywhere along the enemy's earthworks. A line of skirmishers carefully picked their way forward to investigate, reporting back that the trenches were empty. The Federals continued on, nurturing with each step the blissful thought that the Confederacy had abandoned Petersburg. Upon emerging from a forested area they spied open ground, a deep railroad cut, and the marshes of Taylor's Creek. Beyond that appeared a fresh line of Confederate earthworks. For the crestfallen Union soldiers, the sight must have seemed eerily reminiscent of Cold Harbor.

Keeping his promise to Grant to press on, Meade ordered a coordinated assault for noon. But he soon became frustrated trying to synchronize the assault with his corps commanders and, in the end, told them to attack "at all hazards and without reference to each other."[21] With this order, any remaining chance of driving the reinforced and revitalized Confederates from their breastworks was snuffed out. Over the past few days Meade's men had endured a long, dry march through the blazing Virginia heat. They had been thrown into battle with little or no rest. And now they were being asked to charge across open ground at a fortified enemy through a series of uncoordinated attacks that negated their numerical advantage.

Colonel William Bolton of the 51st Pennsylvania recalled going forward with Ninth Corps: "We charged in good order and took the railroad cut, and were followed by Raulston's brigade. The enemy's sharpshooters commanded this cut from the right. A traverse was at once built across the cut on the right of the line by tearing up the track and ties." The makeshift barricade offered only limited protection from the sharpshooters' bullets. Bolton continued, "The railroad cut was about fifteen to twenty feet deep, and the sides almost perpendicular. Steps and holes had to be made in the same so as to enable the troops to climb up on the bank, which was commanded by the enemy from his main line. Many, however, were killed and wounded here."[22]

Farther south, the newly arrived Fifth Corps made its attempt. Among the regimental commanders was Colonel Joshua Lawrence Chamberlain, the Maine professor responsible for the brilliant defense of Gettysburg's Little Round Top a year earlier. While advancing on Rives' Farm with his beloved 20th Maine, Chamberlain received a severe pelvic injury, his fifth wound of the war. Doctors declared this one fatal, and operated only at the insistence of Chamberlain's younger brother, Thomas. As a tribute to the dying colonel, Grant promoted him to brigadier general in the field. Chamberlain would surprise everyone by recovering and returning to combat five months later.

Sprinkled throughout the Army of the Potomac were the heavy artillery regiments — oversized dress parade units that Grant converted to infantry. These men had enlisted with the belief that they would spend the war quietly manning the big guns that protected Washington and the coast. They had grown accustomed to the relative comfort and safety of fortress life, and were stunned when Grant called upon them to replenish his depleted infantry. The "heavies" were completely unprepared for combat and as a result suffered dreadful losses. A captain in the 4th New York Heavy Artillery later described his experience on June 18 at Petersburg: "I shall never forget the hurricane of shot and shell which struck us as we emerged from the trees. The sound of the whizzing bullets and exploding shells, blending in awful volume, seemed like the terrific hissing of some gigantic furnace. Men, torn and bleeding, fell headlong from the ranks as the murderous hail swept through the line. The shrieks of the wounded mingled with the shouts of defiance which greeted us as we neared the rebel works."[23] Other heavy artillery units fared even worse. Of the 900 men in the 1st Maine Heavy Artillery, 632 fell within ten minutes. It was among the heaviest single-day battle losses for any regiment during the war.

By 8 pm, Meade recognized the futility of the situation and ordered his army to stand down. One of his aides put to words what virtually every officer had privately come to understand: "The men went in, but not with spirit," he wrote. "Received by a withering fire, they sullenly fell back a few paces to a slight crest and lay down, as much to say 'We can't assault but we won't run.'"[24]

Dejectedly, Meade summarized the day's events for Grant, expressing deep regret over the failure. Grant sought to ease the elder man's distress, saying, "I am perfectly satisfied that all has been done that could be done, and that the assaults today were called for by all the appearances and information that could be obtained. Now we will rest the men and use the spade for their protection until a new vein can be struck."[25] The siege had begun.

2

Unconventional Warfare

The morning light of June 19, 1864 revealed a scene appalling to everyone present, whether blue or gray, from private to general. Between the opposing lines lay hundreds of dead and dying. Two-thirds of the casualties wore Federal uniforms. A Fifth Corps major took special pity on the victims who swore no allegiance. "One sad feature of these scenes of bloodshed is the poor, wounded horses," he wrote, "whose cries are most heart-rending, as they will raise their heads and glare about them with fast-glazing eyes."[1]

Wounded men groaned and pleaded for water, their agony magnified by the blazing sun. But to step out onto the open field and offer assistance was tantamount to suicide. George Meade spent the day trying to negotiate a truce in order to collect his wounded and bury his dead. Beauregard enjoyed finally having the upper hand, and toyed with him. When the Confederate response arrived at 7 pm, it was a refusal. The stench of rotting corpses soon permeated the landscape.

Those unscathed by the past four days of carnage now embarked on a new vocation — digging. For both sides, daily work in the trenches began long before sunrise and continued well into the evening. Labor details typically worked for two hours, then rested for an equal amount of time before returning to work. Trenches were dug four to six feet deep and ten feet wide, with the excavated dirt piled up high in front to ensure protection above head level. A two-foot rise along the bottom of the trench allowed riflemen to step up and fire from loopholes in the breastworks. The whole enterprise was reinforced with logs, sandbags, and large, earth-filled wicker baskets called gabions.

Under the safety of darkness, engineers ventured in front of the trenches and built wooden barriers for added security. Devised in Europe, the obstacles retained their original French names. *Abatis* were simply clusters of felled trees connected by wire, their branches facing the enemy. Rows of large spears angled in the ground at chest height were called *fraise*. The most elaborate obstacle, the porcupine-like *chevaux-de-frise*, consisted of a log through which holes were drilled and sharpened stakes inserted. Narrow passages through the rows of obstructions gave pickets safe passage to and from their rifle pits. The hope was that any large attacking body would be blocked, or at least slowed.

Completion of a main trench line merely meant that work could begin on the secondary passageways. Recalled a private in the 49th North Carolina Regiment: "We cut deep ditches, forming covered ways, leading from the works to the rear to enable us to get in supplies and for the men to pass in and out of the trenches. One of these covered ways ran through a corner of Blandford Cemetery. In digging it we threw out old coffins and bones."[2]

The introduction of mortars to the siege presented a unique problem for both sides. While bullets and cannonballs passed over the trenches, high-arcing mortar shells could drop right in. Bunkers constructed of timber and earth, optimistically called "bombproofs," offered some protection but also presented the grim prospect of being buried alive. "We soon learned to tell by throwing up a hand where the shells were going to land," explained the private from North Carolina. "If it rose above the hand, it was going over, provided it did not burst and send the fragments down on us; if it sank below the hand, it would fall short; but if it kept hidden behind the hand, why, then look out."[3]

For the citizens of Petersburg, life changed dramatically as a result of the siege. Federal artillery shells began falling on the city in mid-June, and would continue unabated for the next nine months. Petersburg had 13 church steeples, and Union gunners used the spires to find their range within the city. The 120-foot high Tabb Street Presbyterian Church steeple became a favorite target, and cannonballs routinely dented its copper sheathing. Fire was a pressing concern and volunteers quickly organized to battle frequent blazes throughout the city. Some residents inadvertently compounded the problem by fortifying their homes with cotton bales.

Petersburg sprang into existence as a trading post during the mid-seventeenth century. Originally named Peter's Point after an Indian trader, the town was incorporated in 1748 as Petersburg. President James Madison nicknamed it the "Cockade City" to honor its rosette–capped militiamen who served so bravely during the War of 1812. In 1815, the city was rebuilt after a devastating fire.

By 1860, Petersburg was the second-largest city in Virginia, behind only the capital 23 miles to the north. Among the population of 18,000 were roughly 5,500 slaves and 3,000 free blacks. Work was readily available in the city's 20 tobacco factories and six cotton mills. No less than five major rail lines terminated in Petersburg, emanating from points in North Carolina, Tennessee, coastal Virginia, and of course Richmond. The city boasted cobblestone streets lined with gas lamps and brick sidewalks. Eight banks supported the rapid flow of commerce, while two daily papers reported the latest news and gossip.

A portion of the Federal trenchline occupied by Ninth Corps during the siege. The lush Virginia countryside quickly turned into a barren wasteland as both armies dug in. A bombproof shelter, complete with chimney, is visible in the trench (Library of Congress, Prints and Photographs Division LC-B8171-1069 DLC).

The outbreak of war altered Petersburg both socially and economically. The Union naval blockade eliminated the city's flourishing international trade, and factories retooled to manufacture war materiel. Military hospitals were established to help care for the Confederacy's wounded. Women, African-Americans, and disabled veterans replaced young white males in the work force.

The arrival of the Army of Northern Virginia in June 1864 transformed Petersburg even further. Soldiers on leave from the trenches were permitted to visit the city, although General Lee forbade them from purchasing alcohol. (Some devious traders sidestepped this rule by selling $5 cigars with a complimentary shot of whiskey.) The uniformed men were a welcomed sight to the city's young female population. As a colonel from the 8th Alabama Infantry recalled, "The soldiers married these factory girls, some for life, others for 'during the war.' Dr. J.D.D. Renfro, the Chaplain of the 10th [Alabama], informed me that he married some couples of this class every night while the army was before Petersburg."[4]

The initial euphoria of siege life soon gave way to hardship and despair. Military personnel and refugees from the countryside bloated Petersburg's population and overburdened its infrastructure. Food became scarce and rumors became plentiful. As July 4 approached, panic gripped the city. Some said that U.S. Grant intended to overrun Petersburg on Independence Day, just as he had done at Vicksburg a year earlier, then raze the city in celebration. When the Fourth of July passed without incident other rumors took hold, including an odd story about Yankee miners tunneling beneath the city.

The miles of opposing trenches snaked lazily through Petersburg's outlying hills and valleys, as each army utilized the available high ground and other topographical advantages. Accordingly, the lines did not run uniformly parallel and the distance between them varied with their curvature. In some places, trenches ran so close together that the voices of enemy pickets could be overheard. In other areas, soldiers were forced to squint to see the rival earthworks.

Foes drew nearest at a point due east of Petersburg, where Ambrose Burnside's Ninth Corps had pushed within 100 yards of Beauregard's line during the assaults of June 18. After crossing Taylor's Creek that day, Burnside's divisions started up a slight incline before intense Confederate fire forced them to halt. Unwilling to fall back, the Ninth Corps men clawed their way into the red earth, some using bayonets and tin cups, and stubbornly held their ground.

At the top of the hill lay a brigade of South Carolina troops commanded by General Stephen Elliott. Near the center of Elliott's line was an artillery battalion from Petersburg led by Captain Richard G. Pegram. While falling back during the previous night, Captain Pegram failed to take notice of the white stakes marked off for his guns by Beauregard's engineers.[5] He unknowingly entrenched his battery closer to the enemy than the engineers had intended. When the error was discovered, it was decided to have the infantry extend their breastworks forward to meet Pegram rather than pull the artillery back. Pegram's mistake proved fortuitous, as his four Napoleons bore down menacingly on the fresh Federal breastworks. The resulting bulge in the line came to be called Elliott's Salient, and the Confederates set about turning it into an earthen fortress.

A Pennsylvania regiment, the 48th Veteran Volunteers, had the distinct misfortune of facing Elliott's Salient. As they deepened their trenches, the Pennsylvanians could no doubt hear the hammering of artillery platforms atop the hill. Their stay in this location promised to be an unpleasant one.

The 48th Pennsylvania belonged to Ninth Corps' Second Division, under General Robert B. Potter. A slight, balding man in his mid-thirties, Potter was nonetheless a highly respected leader. He had been wounded during Burnside's North Carolina expedition in 1862, but returned to duty and distinguished himself at Second Bull Run and Fredericksburg. In the summer of 1863, Potter was detached from Ninth Corps to assist in the siege of Vicksburg, Mississippi. Upon his return, he briefly commanded Ninth Corps while it was stationed in Tennessee. In civilian life, Robert Potter had been a New York attorney.

Vicksburg may have been on Potter's mind as he surveyed the growing menace of Elliott's Salient on June 19, 1864. During that siege, Union forces had experimented with the use of tunnels to undermine and destroy Confederate strongholds. Those attempts had been ineffective, but the conditions here in Petersburg seemed to warrant another try. While telegraphing a routine report to Burnside that evening, Potter added the postscript: "There is a redoubt not quite 100 yards in front of our line, which I think can be approached by a sap."[6] But Burnside

Attorney Robert Potter mustered into Federal service in October 1861 as a major in the 51st New York Infantry. By early 1863, he was a brigadier general commanding the Second Division of Ninth Corps (Library of Congress, Prints and Photographs Division LC-B813-1729 B).

failed to respond to the suggestion, and Potter took no further action.

The idea of tunneling beneath Elliott's Salient soon occurred to others as well. On June 23, a cluster of soldiers from the 48th Pennsylvania struck upon the idea while idly chatting. Their conversation reached the ears of Lieutenant Colonel Henry Pleasants, the regiment's longtime commander, who was temporarily serving as brigade commander. Pleasants was intrigued by the tunnel concept, and knew that the men from whom it had come were authorities on the subject of mining. The 48th Pennsylvania had been recruited exclusively in Schuylkill County, the heart of eastern Pennsylvania's anthracite region. As a result, the regiment brimmed with experienced coal miners. In fact, Pleasants himself was a mining engineer before the war.

After consulting with two fellow engineers, Pleasants became convinced that an underground assault on Elliott's Salient was feasible.[7] He drew up a plan and approached Potter on June 24. Pleasants proposed running a 500-foot shaft under the Confederate fort, then charging it with gunpowder and blowing the Southerners into oblivion. Potter ordered a staff officer, Captain David McKibben, to accompany Pleasants to the front and identify an advantageous point within the fort to serve as the mine's target.

With renewed enthusiasm, Potter then sat down and again wrote Ninth Corps headquarters about the idea of digging a mine. He concluded with: "The men themselves have been talking about it for some days, and are quite desirous, seemingly, of trying it. If there is a prospect of our remaining here a few days longer I would like to undertake it. If you desire to see Colonel Pleasants I will ride over with him or send him up to you. I think, perhaps, we might do something, and in no event could we lose more men than we do every time we feel the enemy."[8] This time Potter received a response: report to Burnside's tent with Pleasants.

Sniping had evolved into a specialty during the war. The Northern army formed sharpshooter regiments, which supposedly received better training than the regular infantry. Southern commanders culled the top marksmen from their units for special duty. Confederate sharpshooters were required to be proficient at 600 yards. With Elliott's Salient a mere 100 yards away from the Union trenches, snipers from either side rarely missed. The thought of lying motionless for hours to kill an unsuspecting man offended the vague sense of chivalry still alive within most soldiers. Accordingly, nobody grieved when a sharpshooter fell prey to one of his own, regardless of the color of his uniform.

A popular pastime for fighting boredom in the trenches was to raise a cap on a bayonet and see how many sharpshooters' bullets it could draw. The trick also produced an instant of relative safety in which to peer over the earthworks as the snipers reloaded. It was only enough time for a swift glance, however, and Captain McKibben must have lingered a few seconds too long. While pointing out a susceptible Confederate artillery battery to Pleasants, McKibben was struck in the face by a sharpshooter's ball. His wound was severe, but proved not to be fatal. Though undoubtedly shaken by the incident, Pleasants now had a target for his mine.

Potter and Pleasants were shown into the tent of Ambrose Burnside on the morning of June 25. Burnside was a tall and imposing man with unusual facial hair. Long bushy whiskers led from his ears to his moustache — a style that, with some clever wordplay on his name, led to the coining of the term "sideburns." Burnside listened carefully as Pleasants described the plan in detail. When the colonel finished, Burnside asked several questions that revealed an understanding of engineering and explosives. He wanted to know how long the excavation would take, and Pleasants estimated 12 days with the proper tools and supplies. Burnside was particularly interested in how much gunpowder the colonel proposed to load into the mine. Pleasants anticipated needing 12,000 pounds of powder and Burnside nodded in agreement.[9]

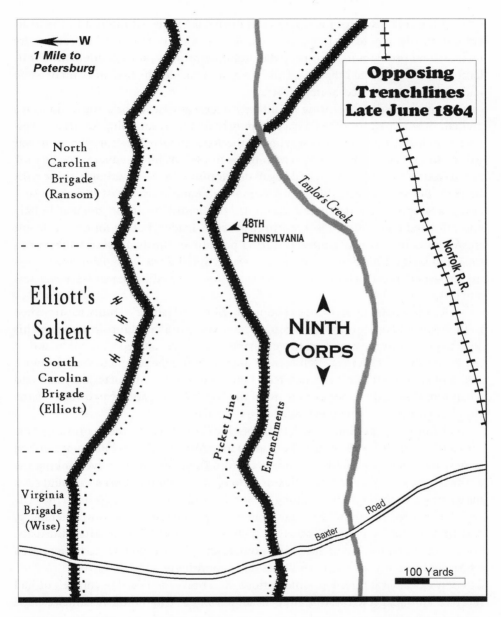

W
1 Mile to Petersburg

North
Carolina
Brigade
(Ransom)

**Opposing
Trenchlines
Late June 1864**

48TH
PENNSYLVANIA

Taylor's Creek

Norfolk R.R.

Elliott's
Salient

South
Carolina
Brigade
(Elliott)

**NINTH
CORPS**

Picket Line

Entrenchments

Virginia
Brigade
(Wise)

Baxter Road

100 Yards

The 48th Pennsylvania Infantry Regiment was situated closer to the Confederate line than any other unit.

At the conclusion of the discussion, Burnside expressed interest in the project but said he would first need to clear it with Meade. However, he said, there would be no problem in beginning the preliminary work, since it could always be halted if Meade rejected the idea. Unknown to Burnside, the first spadeful of earth had already been turned hours earlier.

Ambrose Everett Burnside's military career was cast in the same mold as his civilian life — a pattern of brief success punctuated by resounding failure. A West Point graduate, Burnside was serving in the New Mexico Territory when he was wounded in a skirmish with Apache Indians in 1849. While recuperating, he took an interest in weapons design and began developing a breech-loading carbine rifle. In 1852, Burnside resigned his army commission and moved east to pursue success as a weapons manufacturer. He founded the Bristol Firearms Company in 1855 and attracted considerable interest in his breech-loader, but he found it difficult to secure lucrative army contracts during peacetime. Burnside went bankrupt in 1857 and sold off his patents. When the war erupted a few years later, the subsequent owners grew rich on the Burnside carbine. The rifle's namesake never saw a penny.

Despite a nagging self-doubt about his ability to lead men, Burnside returned to the army and was promoted through the ranks. Abraham Lincoln respected his sincerity and integrity, and on three separate occasions offered him command of the Army of the Potomac. Reluctantly, Burnside finally accepted the job, but a string of serious strategic errors forced Lincoln to replace him after only two and a half months. He resumed command of the Ninth Corps, and scored some victories, but whispers of incompetence dogged his name.

The mining operation just laid before him could rectify those previous failures and restore his reputation. The Confederate fort that Colonel Pleasants wished to destroy was only half a mile from Blandford Cemetery, a crest overlooking the entire city of Petersburg. When Pleasants detonated his mine, Burnside could send his entire corps through the resulting breach and capture Cemetery Hill, as the Federals had started to call it. Lee would then be forced to withdraw from Petersburg, and with its vital supply line severed, Richmond would fall soon after. Burnside began drawing up a plan of attack. Of course, any plan would have to be approved by Meade, a man who was once Burnside's subordinate.

Ulysses S. Grant needed some options. The previous Tuesday, June 21, he had received an unexpected visitor at his headquarters in City Point. An aide recalled "sitting in front of the General's tent when there appeared very suddenly before us a lone, lank-looking personage, dressed all in black, and looking very much like a boss undertaker. It was the President." Lincoln had come to gauge the situation for himself. "I just thought I would jump aboard a boat and come down and see you," he told Grant. "I don't expect I can do any good, and in fact I'm afraid I may do harm, but I'll just put myself under your orders and if you find me doing anything wrong just send me right away."[10]

Grant took Lincoln on a brief tour of the area that included a meeting with Meade. As the pair returned, they rode past an encampment of U.S. Colored Troops. The black soldiers cheered and swarmed around Lincoln, hoping to touch the man they knew as their liberator. Before Lincoln departed, Grant sought to reassure him. "You will never hear of me farther from Richmond than now, till I have taken it," he said. "I am just as sure of going into Richmond as I am of any future event. It may take a long summer day, as they say in the rebel papers, but I will do it." The president expressed his confidence in Grant, as always, then said, "I cannot pretend to advise, but I do sincerely hope that all may be accomplished with as little bloodshed as possible."[11]

The message was clear — the siege of Petersburg must not drag on indefinitely. It was not news to Grant, who had dispatched his cavalry even before Lincoln's arrival. The objective was to destroy Petersburg's railroads still under Southern control. While the cavalry tore up track, two corps of infantry — the Second and the Sixth — would attempt to extend the Union line west, all the way around Petersburg. Grant wanted a noose that he could use to choke the city into submission.

Major General Ambrose Burnside, commander of Ninth Corps. Burnside served briefly as the Army of the Potomac's leader in the winter of 1862–63, with disastrous results. Accordingly, many of his peers held him in low esteem (Library of Congress, Prints and Photographs Division LC-B8172-1625 DLC).

The operation disintegrated almost from the start. Sixth Corps was forced to plod through heavy underbrush, thus lagging behind Second Corps and creating a dangerous gap. Confederate General William Mahone, a shrewd tactician who knew the ground around Petersburg intimately, promptly drove his division between the two forces and attacked each on the flank. As Mahone rolled up the panicked Federal lines, he captured six guns and 1,700 men, and touched off a retreat that bordered on stampede. At least one Union commander blamed his troops, saying they no longer possessed a fighting spirit.[12] Another quietly pointed the finger at Meade, claiming that upon learning of the developing gap, Meade simply declared, "each corps must look out for itself."[13] Regardless of the cause,

Grant would obviously have to settle for a noose that ran only partially around Petersburg's neck.

Farther west, the cavalry fared little better. Continually stalked by Confederate troopers, the arduous job of destroying railroad track became nearly impossible. Typically, the process entailed stacking ties, setting them ablaze, and laying the rails on top until they glowed red in the center. The pliable rails would then be bent around trees, into what the men called "hairpins," rendering them useless. But under a steady harassing fire, Grant's troopers merely tried to burn the ties in place, hoping the rails would at least warp. The half-hearted attempt resulted in only moderate damage, and the trains would again be running within a few weeks.

Whereas Grant still had several options, Robert E. Lee had none. He was trapped, he told Jefferson Davis, when Lincoln's counterpart visited on June 30. Lee clearly had no choice but to stay and defend the railroads of Petersburg, even though his army was starving and low on ammunition. He had thwarted Grant's efforts to encircle the city, thanks to the cunning Mahone, but there would surely be more attempts. As the Southern army slowly grew weaker, the Northern army gained strength. Rail lines were being laid to carry fresh troops and supplies directly from the wharves of City Point to the Union trenches. Meanwhile, Southern men and materiel barely trickled into Petersburg. It truly had become a matter of time, just as Lee predicted.

He could only hope to forestall the inevitable. A war-weary North would be choosing a new leader in the fall, and Lincoln's prospects for reelection looked dim. George McClellan, the former general, was gaining support on a platform of negotiated peace with the South. If Lee could drag the siege into November, and maintain the appearance of holding out indefinitely, the Northern public just might put McClellan in office. It would be a long and arduous wait.

Despite serving under Meade for two months, Burnside was still having trouble reading his new boss. George Meade was, by most accounts, a cranky and irritable man. Even Grant, who rarely spoke poorly of anyone, said Meade "was unfortunately of a temper that would get beyond his control, at times, and make him speak to officers of high rank in the most offensive manner. No one saw this fault more plainly than himself, and no one regretted it more."[14] So Burnside was relieved when Meade initially reacted favorably to the mining project, promising to "furnish you everything you want, and earnest wishes for your success besides."[15] But a week had passed since those comments and Meade's enthusiasm had faded. Burnside's daily progress reports and his requests for mining supplies largely went unanswered.

Following the unsuccessful foray west, Grant told Meade to solicit ideas from his corps commanders for ending the siege. Burnside responded that the mine, once completed, represented the best chances for success on his front. He went on

26

to say that if an attack had to be made before then, the odds of success were fair, "provided my corps can make the attack and it is left to me to say when and how the other two corps shall come in to my support."[16] Meade chafed at this last statement, interpreting it as a direct challenge to his authority. He snapped back that he alone would control all offensive operations, including the use, if any, of the mine. Burnside apologized profusely, horrified that he had inadvertently triggered Meade's temper. The Ninth Corps commander explained that he was only requesting the same support from other corps commanders that he himself had given so many times in the past. Meade told Burnside to forget the entire incident, perhaps realizing that he had overreacted. For Burnside, it was a lesson in his superior's sensitivity. He would need to exercise caution when dealing with Meade in the future.

Major General George Gordon Meade, commander of the Army of the Potomac. Meade had an engineering background, and he was skeptical of the Petersburg Mine's usefulness almost from the very beginning (Library of Congress, Prints and Photographs Division LC-B18172-1467 DLC).

Grant was less than sanguine about the prospects for a subterranean attack. The tunnels he dug at Vicksburg a year earlier had gained him nothing. The first attempt actually began as a standard approach trench aimed at a Confederate fortress. When the trench drew close enough, 36 former coal miners tunneled beneath the parapets and planted 2,200 pounds of gunpowder. Meanwhile, Grant arranged diversions in other sectors and positioned his artillery to stop any Confederate reinforcements that might try to reach the fort.

Unfortunately for Grant, the plan lacked any element of surprise. The men of the 3rd Louisiana had watched the Federal approach trench snaking toward them throughout the month of June 1863, and had deduced that an explosion was imminent. They dug a secondary trench across the rear of their V-shaped fortress and waited. When the explosion finally came on June 25, 1863, it killed only six brave Mississippians who were attempting to uncover the Yankee mine. Federal troops rushed through the trench and into the 50-foot long, 12-foot deep pit created by the detonation. Despite a withering fire from above, they held the crater for more than 24 hours. Finally, Grant recognized the situation was futile, and pulled his men out of what had almost immediately been termed the "Death Hole."

The second mine at Vicksburg was detonated a week later with little effect.

Stung by the Death Hole experience, Grant chose not to follow this explosion with an assault. He had learned that tunneling beneath an enemy's earthworks was risky business. Before committing to a similar venture a year later at Petersburg, Grant wanted his engineers to sign off on its feasibility.

The Union's preeminent engineer, General John G. Barnard, contacted Henry Pleasants on July 3 requesting specifics about the mine's construction. Pleasants dutifully prepared his response, complete with schematics. Meanwhile, Meade sent his chief engineer and his chief artillerist to examine Burnside's front and determine the likelihood of success for an offensive in that sector.

The engineers' reports were not favorable. Meade's chief engineer, Major James Duane, seemed particularly opposed to the mining project. Pleasants heard through the grapevine that Duane had called the idea "clap-trap and nonsense" and that "such a length of mine had never been excavated in military operations, and could not be."[17] Duane confidently predicted that the mine would be discovered, or it would collapse, or the miners would eventually suffocate while working in its depths. Even in the unlikely event that the mine should succeed, Duane said, a serious tactical problem remained: Another bulge existed in the Confederate line, this one located several hundred yards south, in front of Fifth Corps. Rebel artillery positioned in this salient, as well as artillery placed to the north on Cemetery Hill, would have a clear field of fire on the flanks of any attacking Union column. The men would be cut apart as they crossed the open field.

The discouraging analysis was undoubtedly the reason behind Meade's sudden change of heart. The mine was a dead end, he had been told, and not worth the resources Burnside was requesting. Meade would permit the tunneling to continue, however. Siege warfare was known to grind soldiers down, both physically and mentally. Though tactically useless, the mine was keeping the men of the 48th Pennsylvania distracted and in fighting trim. Further, Ninth Corps morale had improved since the project began. Attempts at keeping the miners' activity a secret failed miserably as word spread through the Army of the Potomac. Curious onlookers appeared, including an Ohio soldier who watched the miners "popping in and out of the hole like so many brown gophers."[18] Henry Pleasants, meanwhile, grew ever more protective of the mine, and worried that news of its existence would filter over to Elliott's Salient.

3

Tunneling Toward Destiny

Virtually every soldier in the army was accustomed to digging, but for the miners of the 48th Pennsylvania Infantry Regiment it came naturally. Burrowing into the ground was simply a way of life for them, something they had done since their adolescence. But there were no adolescents among them now. For the veterans of the 48th, the road to Petersburg had been long, hard and deadly.

The regiment was formed in the summer of 1861, following President Lincoln's call for 100,000 volunteers to preserve the Union. Colonel James Nagle of Pottsville was determined to create a regiment exclusively of Schuylkill County men, and he had little difficulty accomplishing the task. Five companies were quickly raised in Pottsville, the county seat, while five more companies came from the small mining towns and patches scattered across the countryside.

Located in the rugged mountains northwest of Philadelphia, Schuylkill County was settled by English, Irish, and German immigrants who had come either to farm the land or work the coal mines. Eastern Pennsylvania was rich in the efficient and clean-burning variety of coal known as anthracite, and the mining industry was booming. The men who volunteered to serve in Nagle's regiment were hardy laborers in their teens, twenties, and thirties who expected a swift Union victory and a quick return to their homes and families. A few had served in the Mexican-American War, but for most this would be their first military experience. Upon being mustered into service in September 1861, the 48th was presented with a gift from a prominent Pottsville attorney: a regimental flag bearing the inscription, "In the cause of the Union we know no such word as fail."[1]

The unit joined Ninth Corps during Ambrose Burnside's North Carolina expedition. At the battle for New Bern, the Pennsylvanians did not see any action but earned a measure of respect by hand-carrying scores of ammunition crates over seven muddy miles to the front. Their first taste of combat came against the fierce Louisiana Tigers during Second Bull Run in August 1862. The miners acquitted themselves well, but suffered 68 killed and wounded. They again shed blood while crossing "Burnside's Bridge" at Antietam Creek, and once more when they charged Marye's Heights at Fredericksburg. In little more than a year of service, the regiment lost over half of its original volunteers.

The 48th followed Burnside out west in 1863, landing in the turbulent town of Lexington, Kentucky. Here the regiment maintained order among a hostile mix of Union and Confederate sympathizers, and staunched the growing number of rebel incursions into the area. The 48th departed six months later over the objections of Lexington residents who had grown accustomed to the miners' protection. After a grueling 220-mile march, the regiment contributed to Burnside's successful defense of Knoxville, Tennessee by digging a moat around a portion of the city. When a majority of the men reenlisted in December 1863, they were granted a brief furlough and returned to Schuylkill County.

Although welcomed home as heroes, the veterans found Schuylkill County to be a troubled place. All hopes for a rapid victory over the South had long since vanished and public turmoil simmered below the surface. Draft riots were common. The government's shift from volunteerism to conscription in 1862 was unpopular throughout the country, but areas with a high immigrant population were hotbeds of dissent. Schuylkill County was no exception. Recent arrivals from Europe were loathe to put on a uniform and be maimed or killed for a cause in which they had no vested interest. Further, the draft laws were viewed as unfair. Men of privilege were exempted from service, and draftees with money could either pay a fee in lieu of service or hire a substitute to go in his place. To European immigrants, these rules harkened back to the societal inequality they had left behind. Schuylkill County figured prominently in many of Governor Andrew Curtin's reports to Washington about the draft resistance in Pennsylvania.

When the men of the 48th returned to service in March 1864, a different type of war awaited them. The fighting had turned into sheer butchery. Within two weeks of joining Grant's army, the regiment lost 187 men at the Wilderness and Spotsylvania. Cold Harbor took 75 more. By the time the regiment turned south toward Petersburg, it was a mere shadow of the 1,010-strong unit that had proudly marched from Pottsville in 1861. Only about 400 men remained, and any replacements would be few and far between.

Arriving at Petersburg on June 16, Robert Potter's division was led to a position across from the Shand House, a large white farmhouse overlooking a heavily wooded ravine. The division was ordered to launch a surprise attack against this Confederate base of operations before dawn the next morning. Under a full moon, each soldier secured his canteen and any other articles that might make noise, then slipped into the woods. The 48th Pennsylvania inched through the ravine with the 36th Massachusetts on its right and the 45th Pennsylvania on its left. Lieutenant

Colonel Pleasants said he and his men crept forward "like rabbits, clawing at the underbrush to keep our footing, until we felt the soft earth of the breastworks under our feet."[2]

The sleeping Confederates in and around the Shand House were caught flat-footed. Those not instantly captured bolted back toward the city in panic, leaving their muskets behind. A private in the 48th, Robert Alexander Reid, found a dozen Confederate gunners hiding beneath an artillery platform and took them prisoner. After sending them to the rear, Reid then captured the flag of the 44th Tennessee. Sergeant Patrick Monaghan of the 48th recovered the flag of the 7th New York Heavy Artillery, which had been lost a day earlier. Both men were awarded the Medal of Honor for their actions. The assault yielded four cannon, five flags, and over 600 prisoners. Meade was impressed enough to set aside his feelings against Burnside and compliment the Ninth Corps on its victory.

This engraving is perhaps the only remaining wartime image of Colonel Henry Pleasants. Following a three-month enlistment in the local militia, Pleasants helped raise the 48th Pennsylvania Infantry Regiment and became captain of Company C. Shortly after his promotion to lieutenant colonel in 1862, Pleasants suffered a leg wound at Fredericksburg. He quickly recovered and returned to service (Battles and Leaders of the Civil War).

There would be little more to celebrate that day, or for many days thereafter. The 48th and its sister regiments advanced another half mile before running into the hornets' nest of Elliott's Salient. The rest of the army encountered similar resistance up and down the line, making it painfully obvious that Petersburg would be their home for some time to come.

Despite serving with them from the very beginning, Henry Pleasants must have been something of a mystery to the men of the 48th. A mining engineer before the war with no military background, Pleasants was a fearless warrior and a tactical genius. A fellow officer in the 48th said, "He was a soldier of true grit, possessed of more than ordinary ability as an engineer — ability that he displayed many times during the campaign from the Rappahannock down to Petersburg...."[3] Though usually cordial, the colonel reportedly had a fiery temper that dwelled behind his placid brown eyes. Even his English surname contrasted with his visi-

31

bly Hispanic heritage. A serious and quiet man, few knew anything about the colonel's life.

Pleasants' father was a Philadelphia gunrunner who supplied arms to Argentine insurgents attempting to overthrow dictator Juan Manuel de Rosas in the 1830s. While in Buenos Aires, John Pleasants met and married the daughter of a wealthy landowner, and on February 16, 1833 their son was born. Before his death in 1846, John Pleasants left instructions that his son be sent to live with his brother, a Philadelphia physician for whom the boy was named. Doctor Henry Pleasants' new ward was a frightened Spanish-speaking teen who had just made a 5,000-mile sea voyage alone. The doctor spoke fluent Spanish, and helped his nephew adjust to life in America.

After high school, young Henry took a surveying job (that was arranged by his uncle) with the Pennsylvania Railroad. By 1853, Pleasants was a senior assistant engineer working on the massive Sand Patch Tunnel project, a 4,200-foot gallery carved into the Allegheny Mountains. Pleasants developed an ingenious technique for ventilation: a string of fires burning beneath vertical shafts that superheated the tunnel's stale air and carried it upward, thus creating a draft that pulled fresh air inside.

After the project, Pleasants was offered a promotion but instead resigned in protest over a friend's dismissal. He traveled east to Schuylkill County and was instantly hired as a mining engineer. In 1860 he married Sallie Bannan, whose father edited the county newspaper, *The Miner's Journal.* The couple bought a house in Pottsville and Sallie became pregnant, but a few months later she suddenly grew ill and died. Despondent over the loss, and possibly harboring the secret hope that a sharpshooter's bullet might end his suffering, Pleasants joined the army.[4]

An associate of Colonel Nagle, Pleasants joined the 48th Pennsylvania as a captain and helped recruit a company of volunteers. His creativity and leadership abilities soon became apparent. In North Carolina, he supervised the construction of a coastal fort to deter Confederate blockade-runners. Pleasants' men lacked wheelbarrows with which to move the sand, so he had them fashion makeshift stretchers by nailing long poles to discarded cracker boxes. He also displayed a gift for military tactics. During the carnage at Fredericksburg, Pleasants scouted out a location from which the regiment's sharpshooters could pick off Confederate artillerymen, quickly silencing several batteries. When the 48th's commander, Joshua Sigfried, left to command a brigade of United States Colored Troops in Ninth Corps' new division, Pleasants took over as the unit's leader. During the opening assaults on Petersburg, his superior officer was severely wounded and Pleasants was placed in temporary command of the brigade. In the coming weeks, his military career would reach its apex, and also its nadir.

3. Tunneling Toward Destiny

From its very conception, Colonel Pleasants was nothing short of obsessed with the mining project. Even before the meeting with Burnside, Pleasants had organized his miners and identified the perfect starting point for the mine. "I noticed a little cup of a ravine near to the enemy's works," he said.[5] The tree-lined gully was nestled just behind the Union's primary trench line, yet it afforded protection from minié balls and prying Confederate eyes. Pleasants had his men clear away brush from the ravine and commence digging at midnight on June 25, 1864. The work went easily and quickly on that first day, and the enthusiastic miners advanced 50 feet into the gully's western wall. The mine was to be a simple, horizontal passageway; much like the tunnels the miners had dug into countless Pennsylvania hillsides while chasing a vein of coal.

Discreetly disposing of the excavated material was an immediate and important concern. If enemy spotters were to see mounds of fresh earth piled about, they would surely deduce the existence and location of the mine. At first, the dirt was placed in sandbags and used to strengthen the line. Once the sandbags were gone, Pleasants had his men build handbarrows out of cracker boxes, just as they had done in North Carolina two and a half years earlier, and haul the dirt into the woods. Iron hoops, removed from beef and pork barrels, helped strengthen the makeshift transports.

Debris removal proved to be the single job requiring the most manpower. Each handbarrow required two men, one at each end, and as the mine lengthened so did the distance to the woods. Additionally, the mounds of dirt had to be covered with brush each night to ensure their concealment. "At first I employed but a few men at a time," Pleasants explained. "But the number increased as the work progressed, until at last I had to use the whole regiment, non-commissioned officers and all."[6] The project proceeded around the clock in shifts lasting two and a half hours. Upon completing his shift, each man was rewarded with a shot of whiskey. The practice was discontinued after about a week, when a few men who had hoarded their daily rations went on a binge and got drunk.

The tunnel was just wide enough to accommodate two miners at a time. As one man hacked with his pickaxe, the other shoveled away loose dirt. Standard-issue entrenching tools were too large and clumsy for use inside the mine's narrow confines, so Pleasants had a blacksmith transform them into the stubby, curved blades of miners' picks. On both the second and third day of digging, the tunnel advanced an additional 40 feet, bringing its total length to 130 feet by the end of June 27. Everything was proceeding just as planned.

Roughly a quarter of the 400 men in the 48th Pennsylvania were experienced miners. Among them was Sergeant Harry Reese of Company F. Born in South Wales, England in 1835, Reese took up the family vocation at the age of eight. As a young man, he left his homeland for the coal fields of Pennsylvania and settled

Colonel Joshua K. Sigfried, commander of First Brigade in the USCT division. Sigfried led the 48th Pennsylvania earlier in the war. When it was announced in the spring of 1864 that a division of black troops would be added to Ninth Corps, Sigfried volunteered his services (Roger D. Hunt Collection at USAMHI).

in the Schuylkill County town of Minersville. When it was announced in 1861 that Company F of the new regiment would be raised in Minersville, Reese was among the first to volunteer. On the enlistment roster he wrote his given name of Henry, but everyone in town knew him either as Harry or by his nickname — "Snapper." The brawny Welshman possessed sharp gray eyes and the pale complexion that was so common to men of his profession. Considering his background and demeanor, Reese was a natural choice to supervise the miners. When Colonel Pleasants put him charge of the operation, Reese set up camp at the mouth of the tunnel and rarely left.

The miners were burrowing through a combination of marine clay, sand, and silt that geologists subsequently came to call the Eastover Formation. The soft, red material yielded easily under the miners' picks, and the tunnel advanced quickly during the first week. Timber supports were required to shore up the walls and prevent a cave-in. The supports consisted of two side props capped by a heavy crossbeam, with a mudsill set along the base. These pieces were notched and fitted together outside the mine, then carried inside individually and reassembled. The props were angled outward at the bottom, giving the tunnel's walls a sloped appearance.

On July 2, Harry Reese and his men ran into trouble. Upon reaching a length of about 250 feet, they struck a deposit of heavy clay. General Potter informed Ninth Corps headquarters that the miners had encountered quicksand, but Pleasants called it *marl*. He said it was thick and wet, with the consistency of putty. Progress ground nearly to a halt as the men labored to cut through the troublesome marl. Then the mine almost collapsed under the weight of the heavy clay. Pleasants reported that, "the timbers gave way and the gallery nearly closed, the roof and floor of the mine nearly meeting."[7] A solution had to be found quickly or the project would fail. As Pleasants ruminated, the miners made the best of the situation. Discovering that the marl turned to rock after baking in the sun for a few hours, they fashioned pipes, crosses, and corps emblems. Some of the trinkets were sent home as souvenirs; others were sold to curious passers-by at a price of 25 cents each.

Upon re-timbering the subsided area, Pleasants instructed his miners to begin digging at an incline. The colonel reasoned that by following a slight angle of elevation the mine might eventually emerge from the stratum of marl. At the very least, the slope would drain off some of the excess water that had accumulated. He was right on both counts. After days of backbreaking work, the miners once again found themselves in the sandy soil they had initially encountered. But the marl had taken its toll on them physically. The heavy labor and cramped conditions caused injury and fatigue. An assistant surgeon in the 48th recalled, "I had a big job taking care of the men. Some had their backbones skinned and were laid off till they

A postwar photograph of Sergeant Harry "Snapper" Reese of Company F, 48th Pennsylvania Infantry Regiment. Reese served as the mining project's foreman, supervising virtually every detail of the tunnel's construction (USAMHI).

got well. Had they not been hardy miners, they would never have accomplished it."[8]

In reality, the Petersburg tunnel must have seemed like relatively easy work to the men of the 48th Pennsylvania. Nineteenth-century coal miners were subjected to a variety of occupational health risks. Aside from the obvious danger of being buried alive, miners had to be alert for the sudden release of naturally occurring poisonous gases such as carbon dioxide, hydrogen sulfide, and carbon monoxide. Pockets of methane hidden within a coal vein could cause spontaneous explosions when struck. Miner's asthma, later called black lung disease, was a subtle killer that resulted from the gradual accumulation of coal dust in a man's lungs. Greedy colliery owners played down the deadly side of their industry, but the laborers who went down into the shafts each day knew the dangers all too well. Fortunately, none of these perils existed in the shallow tunnel the miners were digging at Petersburg. And although the labor was demanding, the alternative was dodging bullets and mortar shells in the sweltering trenches above.

Although dangerous gases were not present in the mine, steps had to be taken to ensure a sufficient supply of oxygen. Fresh air would not naturally circulate into the narrow passageway beyond the first few dozen feet. To remedy this problem, Colonel Pleasants employed the technique he developed as a civilian during the Sand Patch Tunnel project. Specifically, he would use a fire to superheat the stale air inside the mine and force it out an exhaust shaft. Air would be drawn along the length of the mine via wooden ductwork. Pleasants explained the process for his superiors in his official report:

> The mine was ventilated at first by having the fresh air go in along the main gallery as far as it was excavated, and to return charged with the gases generated by the breathing and exhalation of the workmen, by the burning of the candles, and by those liberated from the ground, along and in a square tube made of boards, and whose area was sixty inches. This tube led to a perpendicular shaft twenty-two feet high, out of which

this vitiated air escaped. At the bottom of this shaft was placed a grating, in which a large fire was kept burning continually, which, by heating the air, rarefied it, and increased its current.[9]

The colonel had to modify his Sand Patch Tunnel technique slightly due to the unique requirements of a military mine. During the railroad project, he simply sank new ventilation shafts when needed as the tunnel progressed. He did not have the same luxury at Petersburg, since three quarters of the mine would be beneath ground either possessed or contested by the enemy. Pleasants needed to boost the efficiency of the single ventilation shaft hidden behind the Federal earthworks. His report continued:

> Afterward I caused the fresh air to be let in the above-mentioned wooden tube to the end of the work, and the vitiated air to return by the gallery and out of the shaft, placing a partition with a door in the main gallery a little out of the shaft, to prevent its exit by the entrance of the mine. The latter plan was more advantageous, because the gases had to travel a less distance in the mine than before.[10]

In other words, Pleasants reversed the airflow inside the wooden ductwork. Initially, stale air was drawn from the miners' work area into the duct and down the length of the tunnel by the oxygen-hungry fire. Fresh air then entered the mine to replace the stale air that had been eliminated. But as the miners tunneled deeper into the earth, the suction created by this process was not strong enough to pull fresh air all the way back to them. Pleasants therefore placed a partition roughly 100 feet inside the tunnel, just before the ventilation shaft, and allowed only the wooden duct to pass beyond the partition to the mouth of the mine. The burning fire continued to expel stale air from the mine, and with the partition, it created a vacuum inside. This caused fresh air to be drawn into the ductwork, travel past the partition, and flow all the way back to the men working at the face of the mine. As the miners tunneled deeper, new sections were added to the ductwork so that it advanced right along with them, thus ensuring a constant supply of breathable air.

Colonel Pleasants' makeshift ventilation system worked perfectly. Consisting of nothing more than wood, fire, and ingenuity, it safely provided oxygen to the miners without alerting the enemy to their presence. The only clue the Confederates were given was a single column of smoke rising from behind the Federal earthworks, where the fire continuously burned at the bottom of the ventilation shaft. Burnside did not want to take a chance on even this trivial evidence. He ordered nonstop campfires all along his line to mask the smoke of the ventilation shaft. The multitude of blazes throughout July's unbearably hot afternoons undoubtedly mystified anyone not aware of the mining project.

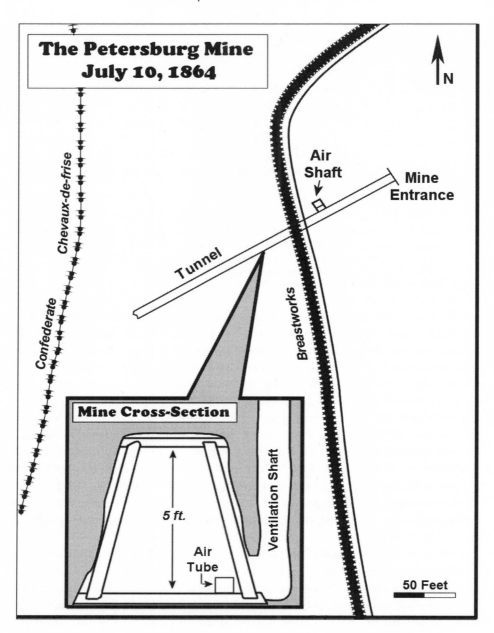

The mine progressed slower than expected due to a lack of proper equipment. After two weeks of round-the-clock labor, the miners had tunneled only about half as far as originally projected.

The next major challenge was acquiring more timber. The original source of wooden planking, a nearby railroad bridge, was picked clean during the marl incident. General Potter learned of an abandoned sawmill several miles away and requested that its contents be delivered to him, adding that, "Lumber is essential to the further prosecution of our mine."[11] Corps headquarters replied that no troops were available to transport the wood, but wagons would be made available if he wished to send his own men. He did, and the tunneling continued.

Attempts to keep the mine a secret were somewhat less than successful. The project's existence was common knowledge throughout most of Ninth Corps, although the depth of that knowledge varied widely by individual. Colonel Byron Cutcheon of the 20th Michigan said, "It had become common for the men of our command to speak of 'Elliott's Salient' as 'the mined fort.'"[12] Others knew only vague details and rumors. In a letter home, Lieutenant George Barton of the 57th Massachusetts wrote, "General Grant may pursue the same course that he did at Vicksburg. Undermine them and blow them up. I understand that something of that kind is really under way. Good if true."[13] But beyond Ninth Corps, gossip and speculation were the norm. Only Union generals and their staff officers possessed specific knowledge of the mine, leaving everyone else to hypothesize. The rumors inevitably found their way into Confederate trenches and the city of Petersburg beyond. Veterans amused themselves by telling gullible young recruits that a Yankee train ran beneath the city, and that through close observation one could see steam rising from cracks in the cobblestone streets.

For General Edward Porter Alexander, artillery chief of the Army of Northern Virginia's First Corps, an underground assault was no joke. Alexander had a longstanding interest in intelligence gathering; he had been involved with Confederate espionage operations in Washington D.C. early in the war. Even before the armies had fully settled into their trenches at Petersburg, Alexander was suspicious of the apparent lack of Federal interest in Elliott's Salient. The bulge was an obvious target for attack, and he expected to see Federal approach trenches soon appear before it. No approach trenches materialized, but Alexander noticed that the exchange of fire in this sector was more fierce and persistent than anywhere else along the line. "That indicated that some operation was going on," he said. "I became satisfied that the activity was underground."[14]

While leaving the front to report his conclusions, Alexander was struck in the hand by a sharpshooter's bullet. The wound was not life threatening, but it required a period of convalescence. Before departing for his native Georgia, Alexander stopped by the headquarters of Robert E. Lee and shared his tunnel theory with Lee's aide, Colonel Charles Venable. At the moment, Venable was meeting with *London Times* correspondent Francis Lawley. Upon hearing the hypothesis, Lawley informed Alexander that he must be mistaken. The British army tried to dig a similar tunnel in Lucknow, India a year earlier, Lawley explained. That mine had to be abandoned after 400 feet due to poor ventilation. Alexander confidently replied that, "in the Federal Army were many Pennsylvania coal miners who could be relied on to ventilate mines any distance that might be necessary."[15]

Lee heeded Alexander's warning and ordered the digging of countermines in and around Elliott's Salient. Essentially, countermining was subterranean surveillance. By boring holes into the ground at selected locations, and listening for the sound of picks and shovels, an approaching enemy mine could theoretically be detected. Successful countermining required a great deal of guesswork and good luck, but it was the only available defense against a burrowing attacker. The job fell to Captain Hugh Douglas of Virginia, an engineer who commanded a company of pontoniers. In early July, Douglas and his men turned in their pontoon boats and other bridge-building equipment for spades and pickaxes.

Captain Douglas approached his new assignment with the vigor of a man who understood its serious nature. He was charged with foiling a suspected plot undertaken by a hidden enemy. Failure to accomplish the mission could result in an unknown number of Confederate deaths and perhaps even the fall of Petersburg. Douglas began by drafting detailed procedures for his engineers to follow as they constructed the countermines. Chief among these was listening for the Yankees:

> The miners in each gallery will be very careful at intervals of not less than one quarter of an hour to stop work and, applying the ear, to listen attentively, so as to notice if the enemy are approaching with a mine (by the sound of the pick being heard through the earth), the sound can be heard a considerable distance. As soon as the officer in charge of the mine, or the miner, notices by sound the approach of the enemy he will at once stop work, remain perfectly quiet, and give the information to the officer in charge of the salient.[16]

Douglas divided his 90 men into six detachments, assigning two detachments to each of the three countermines he planned. Work was to continue around the clock, with each detachment taking a 12-hour shift. Like Colonel Pleasants, Captain Douglas initially found the Petersburg soil ideal for mining operations. The two men also employed similar techniques. Confederate sappers hauled away dirt in modified cracker boxes, just like their counterparts in blue. Douglas was, however, able to construct at least one wheelbarrow, which he said worked much better.[17] The Southerners also received a ration of whiskey following each shift. And like Pleasants, Douglas would soon encounter a number of setbacks that threatened the success of his project.

The biggest problem for Douglas was manpower. The small size of his mines meant that he did not need to worry about ventilation, as Pleasants did, nor did his mines run deep enough to hit the exasperating stratum of marl. But Douglas had to disperse his meager resources over a broad area. The Federals could potentially be digging anywhere along the salient, and Douglas had to explore all probable locations. Within a week, he had expanded the number of active countermines to seven. Scores of infantrymen from nearby regiments were assigned to help, but these men were inexperienced and poorly equipped. Douglas complained repeatedly that the soldiers being sent to him were in need of medical care and lacked the most basic field equipment.

Unlike the men of the 48th Pennsylvania, the Confederate miners did not have the natural shelter afforded by a gully or ravine. Since Elliott's Salient lay atop a slope, the countermines were located in exposed positions and Douglas' men suffered casualties as a result. The captain took every precaution, included piling up mounds of extracted soil in front of the mine entrances, but he still occasionally lost men to mortar shells and sharpshooters. Another disadvantage to being on a slope was that he had to excavate vertically to the desired depth before moving his tunnel forward toward the enemy. The perpendicular shaft made dirt removal problematic. Whereas the Pennsylvania miners could simply carry dirt out of their horizontal tunnel, Douglas' men had to hoist it up on a winch. This labor-intensive process, combined with enemy fire and a lack of qualified men, limited the progress of the countermines to just a few feet each day.

Despite the difficulties, Captain Douglas remained committed to his work. He built new covered ways and breastworks to protect his men. He drew up plans to open additional countermines. He also experimented with novel ways to discover the suspected Federal mine. On July 18, Douglas clambered down into one of his galleries and used an auger to bore deep holes into the walls. The procedure required little effort but expanded the acoustic range of his mines significantly. Two nights later, the Confederates had their first potential indication of a Yankee mine. Douglas reported:

> The officer in charge of the night detachment reports that between 9 and 10 o'clock last night he heard picking; supposed at first it was pickets in the rifle-pits, clearing them out; made inquiries and found they had not used picks or shovels, and supposed the sound proceeded from the enemy's workmen in front of our works. After half an hour — our party having stopped work — the sound ceased and was not again heard; it is quite doubtful whether this sound proceeded from the enemy's miners at work on our front.[18]

Douglas went on to say that the sound seemed to emanate from the left, so he instructed his miners to branch off in that direction. Although possible, it is unknown whether the miners of the 48th Pennsylvania produced the sounds overheard that night. But even if they had, Douglas was not going to find them. His mines were not deep enough.

4

Plan of Attack

Desertion was a growing problem for the Confederacy during the siege. Severe food shortages, squalid and perilous living conditions in the trenches, and a profound sense of futility were enough to convince some Southerners to abandon their posts and surrender to the enemy. By mid-July, Confederate officers were desperate to halt the trend. Runaways not only sapped morale and manpower, they also provided the Yankees with valuable intelligence. A journal entry by a Northern colonel exemplified the problem: "A deserter from the 59th Georgia came into our lines about 12 o'clock last night, and states that orders were issued to the pickets last evening to fire on any man seen going beyond the picket line, that his colonel said no attack would be made on our lines, as so many deserters came into our lines yesterday and told us all about it."[1]

Despite the risk of being shot in the back, the desertions continued. In the early morning hours of July 17, three desperate men from the 49th North Carolina dashed across the picket lines just north of Elliott's Salient and landed safely in Federal hands. While being interrogated, the Carolinians disclosed that their officers suspected a Federal tunnel in the area, and that a comrade with mining experience had recently been assigned to a countermining detail.

The revelation rocked Ninth Corps headquarters. Ambrose Burnside and his staff had been monitoring the mine's progress closely. They received regular reports from General Potter, and occasionally visited the work site personally to observe the miners in action. One of Burnside's aides, Colonel William Harris, was so fascinated by the project that he recorded details about it in his personal journal. Harris wrote cryptic notes so that the mine would not be compromised if his journal fell into enemy hands. On July 13, he scratched "420 feet" in the margin. Three days later he wrote "472 feet." Harris also mentioned a visit to Colonel Pleasants in order to obtain a "report of work going forward."[2] Now it seemed as if all that effort might have been in vain.

After evaluating the deserters' statements General Burnside concluded that the countermining was being conducted in the right area. However, Burnside also suspected that the Confederates were probably not digging deep enough to discover the tunnel. By all estimations, the mine was at least 20 feet beneath Elliott's Salient, considerably deeper than would be expected. Nevertheless, Burnside telegraphed Meade and warned that the mine should be charged and detonated immediately upon its completion.

Henry Pleasants wanted to investigate the reports of enemy countermining for himself. At nearly the same moment that the deserters were divulging their story, Pleasants' men were completing the mine's main gallery. The next step would be to excavate side chambers in which to pack the gunpowder. But the colonel suddenly halted all work and ordered the miners out. He and two other officers crept to the mine's terminus and stood silently for half an hour in the flickering candlelight. They listened vigilantly for any noise from above, but heard nothing. The Confederates had not yet found the right spot. Pleasants ordered his men to resume their work — albeit quietly — on the side galleries.

Burnside's telegram regarding enemy countermining was of little concern to George Meade. He merely forwarded it to Grant with a note that there would be no point in detonating the mine until a corresponding attack could be planned. Meade had vacillated over the tunnel's usefulness from the very beginning. His indecision was apparent in his discussions with Assistant Secretary of War Charles A. Dana. In a July 5 communiqué to Washington, Dana reported that Meade "favors regular siege operations where we are, and places a good deal of dependence upon Burnside's mine." But just three days later Dana informed Washington, "General Meade reports that Burnside's mine will prove of no value."[3]

Meade may have been indifferent toward the mine but his chief engineer, Major Duane, remained openly hostile. At the start of the project Colonel Pleasants had asked to borrow Duane's theodolite, a surveying tool for calculating angle and distance, but the request was refused. Pleasants bitterly recalled, "I could not get the instrument I wanted, although there was one at army headquarters; and General Burnside had to send to Washington and get an old-fashioned theodolite, which was given to me."[4] Fortunately, the antiquated device was sufficient for Pleasants' needs. On five separate occasions during the mine's excavation, he visited the front line with the theodolite in hand. During moments of relative safety, Pleasants popped above the ramparts and triangulated the distance to Elliott's Salient. In this manner he kept the slowly progressing mine on target.

At nearly 511 feet in length, the tunnel's main gallery ran beneath the Union earthworks, stretched across the open field and beneath the Confederate earthworks, then terminated under the battery of Napoleons commanded by Captain Richard Pegram. The side galleries being dug by the miners stretched from the main gallery like two deadly tendrils. The left gallery progressed rapidly and without trouble, but activity could be heard from above on the right. Pleasants suspected it was a Confederate countermine and had his men tunnel around it. Accordingly, by the time the right gallery was completed on July 23, it curved nearly into a semicircle. At 38 feet, it was one foot longer than its counterpart on the left. The exhausted miners of the 48th Pennsylvania finally set down their picks. Over the course of four weeks, they had excavated 18,000 cubic feet of Virginia soil. All that remained now was to charge their enormous weapon with its ordnance.

Pleasants installed four powder magazines in each of the side galleries. The magazines were nothing more than large crates connected to one another by narrow wooden troughs. As soon as the crates and troughs could be filled with gunpowder, Pleasants planned to run fuses out into the main gallery and down the length of the mine. The side galleries would then be sealed off with timber and sandbags, a technique known as tamping, in order to force the blast upward. But until the gunpowder and fusing arrived, Pleasants and his men could do nothing but wait.

The question of exactly how much gunpowder to use became a subject of debate. Standard military principles of the time called for 8,000 pounds, or four tons. Ambrose Burnside thought that six tons would be more effective. The former arms manufacturer felt that a larger blast would result in a broader and shallower crater, presenting less of an obstacle for his troops. But when whispers spread through Ninth Corps that the general was planning to load fifty percent more powder into the mine than necessary, some feared that the resulting blast might carry them away along with the Confederates. The consternation was so great that several officers visited Burnside and asked him to reconsider. Burnside explained that he had conducted numerous tests with gunpowder in the past and felt confident that the men would be safe. In the end, Meade insisted that the mine be charged in accordance with army standards. An order was placed with the ordnance officer at City Point for four tons of powder and 1,000 feet of safety fuse.

By July 26, the gunpowder had yet to arrive. As the mine sat idle, Colonel Pleasants fretted that the Confederates would uncover it or that it would simply collapse. "I was afraid the enemy would find me out that week," he later said.[5] The fierce drought plaguing eastern Virginia had recently broken, and two nights earlier the rain fell in sheets. Though initially welcomed, the downpour created its own problems for men in both blue and gray. Trenches and bombproofs flooded, and the exposed earth turned to sludge. Mosquitoes and other pests flourished in the standing water. Runoff poured into Captain Douglas' countermines, temporarily rendering them useless. Meanwhile, Pleasants' mine became damp and showed signs of weakening. The left gallery seemed particularly unstable, and it trembled whenever the big Confederate guns overhead fired. Finally, General Potter decided to gently remind Burnside that the tunnel would not last indefinitely:

45

> The delay in springing the mine increases continually the probability of
> its being detected and defeated, and its immediate proximity to the
> enemy's work renders it highly improbable that it can escape discovery
> any great length of time. I would respectfully represent that if the mine is
> to be exploded the earlier it can be accomplished the more likely it is to
> be attended with favorable results. The enemy are continually strengthen-
> ing this portion of their line as well as preparing a second position in its
> rear.[6]

Unknown to Potter, larger forces were at work. An expeditionary force consisting
of Second Corps and three divisions of cavalry had already departed Petersburg
and were crossing to the north side of the James River. It was Grant's latest gam-
bit in his chess match with Lee, and it was based in sound logic. Lee had no choice
but to respond; he could not permit the expeditionary force to roam unchecked.
Yet to send a force of his own across the James would weaken Petersburg's defenses.
Whichever option Lee selected, Grant would have an opportunity to strike. If Lee
kept his entire army massed at Petersburg, Grant could move on Richmond. If Lee
sent troops north to halt Second Corps and the cavalry, Grant could then move on
a vulnerable Petersburg. Robert E. Lee mulled the stark reality for himself and concluded that protecting Richmond was his first priority. He dispatched four infantry
divisions and two cavalry divisions northward, and hoped that Petersburg could
once again defy the odds. Only three divisions remained in place to protect the
city.

For the Federals, the only question that remained was where to attack Petersburg's defenses. Grant clearly wanted to take advantage of the remarkable opportunity provided by the miners of the 48th Pennsylvania. Aside from the tactical
benefits that an exploding mine offered, Grant felt it held a psychological impact
that would reverberate up and down the Confederate line. He explained:

> We had learned through deserters who had come in that the people had
> very wild rumors about what was going on our side. They said that we
> had undermined the whole of Petersburg; that they were resting upon a
> slumbering volcano and did not know at what moment they might expect
> an eruption. I somewhat based my calculations upon this state of feeling,
> and expected that when the mine was exploded the troops to the right
> and left would flee in all directions, and that our troops, if they moved
> promptly, could get in and strengthen themselves before the enemy had
> come to a realization of the true situation.[7]

Meade was far less optimistic about launching an attack from Burnside's front. His
engineer, Major Duane, had revisited the area upon learning that the mine was
finished, and once again concluded that it was unsuitable ground for an assault.
The advancing columns would be subjected to severe fire from both infantry and

artillery on the flanks. Further, Duane believed that the enemy had constructed a second line of works on the high ground behind Elliott's Salient. He conceded that if, in fact, the mine actually exploded, Ninth Corps might successfully carry the first line of Confederate works. But Duane asserted that any Federal gain would be quickly reversed as heavy fire poured in from three sides. In light of this analysis, Meade lobbied for the attack to be made elsewhere. Grant contemplated having Benjamin Butler's Army of the James try to break out from its prison at Bermuda Hundred instead, but ultimately he settled on using the mine to launch a direct assault on Petersburg. On the morning of July 27, a wagon train arrived behind Ninth Corps headquarters carrying 320 kegs of gunpowder.

The Southerners stationed across from Ninth Corps ached to learn what might be going on behind the Yankee breastworks. Every available technique was employed to satiate their curiosity, including a novel trick witnessed by Colonel Harris of Burnside's staff. Harris wrote, "The rebels raised a large mirror on the end of a pole in front of our center with a view of ascertaining what we were about behind a little crest — but it hadn't attained a very great elevation before a bullet struck it & down it came."[8]

What the Confederates were unable to see on the afternoon of the 27th was a long procession of men carrying gunpowder kegs to the mouth of the mine. The work detail consisted of laborers from the 48th Pennsylvania and other regiments in Potter's division. Two 25-pound kegs were placed in a canvas sack, which a man could then sling over his shoulder. Several points along the mile-long route from the wagon train were exposed to shot and shell, forcing the soldiers to crouch for safety. Recognizing the disastrous consequences that would result if a keg were struck, Burnside initially suggested waiting until nightfall to move the powder. But Meade overruled him, saying that the mine must be made ready as soon as possible. At the tunnel's entrance, a miner relieved each man of his burden and passed the kegs inside. Working in silence, and by the dim light of a few well-placed lanterns, the miners carefully opened each keg and poured its contents into the wooden magazines and connecting troughs. The entire process took six hours, and by 10 pm each magazine was piled high with nearly a thousand pounds of gunpowder. It was time to begin laying fuse and tamping the side galleries.

Upon prying open the crate of fusing from City Point, Colonel Pleasants received a rude surprise. Rather than the 1,000 continuous feet of safety fuse he requested, City Point had sent common blasting fuse cut into various lengths. Some of the strips were only 10 feet long. The problem with this fusing was threefold. First, the miners would need to take the time to meticulously splice the dozens of short strips together. Second, blasting fuse would be more susceptible to the moisture inside the mine than would high-grade safety fuse. And finally, Pleasants and his men knew from experience that it was not uncommon for fuses to fizzle out at a splice. Rather than dwell on the setback or lay blame, the colonel simply set about the work at hand. "I presume this fuse, like the powder, was stored at Fortress Monroe," he reflected. "They sent just whatever they had. It hardly ever happens that they require fuse for that distance."[9]

The colonel took measures to compensate for the inferior fusing he had been given. He ran a trough of gunpowder from each of the side galleries into the main gallery. Into these troughs he laid a triple line of the blasting fuse. Additional powder was placed where the two troughs converged, and from there the three lines ran 90 feet down the main gallery. With the fuse in place, the miners tamped off the side galleries and continued laying timber and sandbags for more than 30 feet into the main gallery. Small passages built into the barricade permitted air to filter through, thus ensuring that there would be sufficient oxygen for the blast. At 6 pm on July 28, Pleasants reported that the mine was ready to be detonated. All that remained was to watch the deadly effects of his work.

George Meade was suddenly feeling somewhat more optimistic about the chances for a successful assault from Burnside's front. Observers at a new signal station across from Elliott's Salient reported that the enemy did not have a second line of fortifications there as Duane suspected. Instead, it was just some "detached works" consisting of a few trenches or rifle pits. Heavy flanking fire would still pose a problem, but if Ninth Corps could rush forward immediately after the mine exploded and seize the crest known as Cemetery Hill, the Confederate line would be mortally severed. Reports from the expeditionary force north of the James indicated that the enemy was there in numbers, meaning that Petersburg was surely weakened. Meade asked Burnside to submit his plan of attack.

The Ninth Corps commander did not need long to draw up a formal battle plan. He had been contemplating his strategy ever since the mining project began. Like Grant, Burnside suspected that the mine's horrific explosion would have a powerful psychological effect on the Confederates manning the adjacent trenches. Rebel soldiers who did not flee the scene in sheer terror would for some time be too stunned to fight. To exploit this situation, Burnside wanted the leading regiments of his column to storm down the enemy's trenches on the left and right, sweeping the feeble Confederate resistance away. The remainder of his column would continue forward and capture Cemetery Hill. With both the high ground and a sizable portion of the enemy line in his possession, Burnside could safely send the rest of Ninth Corps through the breach and into Petersburg.

From the very beginning, Burnside felt that his division of U.S. Colored Troops should lead the charge. Unlike many of his peers, Burnside believed black men could make able soldiers when trained properly. In fact, Burnside had asked and received permission to add a black division to Ninth Corps when it came east to join the Army of the Potomac. Regiments were raised in Maryland, Pennsylvania,

Ohio, and Connecticut during the early months of 1864, and by spring the division was 4,300-men strong. With few exceptions, the division's white officers found the black recruits to be steadfast and eager to prove their mettle. A captain who helped raise the 23rd USCT Regiment said that, "as a rule the men were sober, honest, patriotic and willing to learn and fulfill the duties of soldiers."[10] Since most of the recruits were former slaves, they possessed virtually no education and had never before handled a weapon. So as the captain instructed them in soldiering by day, a group of civilian volunteers, including his wife, taught them to read by night.

Burnside's USCT division, designated the Fourth Division of Ninth Corps, had been present throughout Grant's Overland Campaign, but it had yet to see any significant action. As the army moved through Virginia, the black troops usually were charged with guarding the ammunition train, or given some other mundane task in the rear. At Petersburg, they were assigned to fatigue duty and spent countless hours excavating trenches and constructing earthworks. Their services were in demand not only in Ninth Corps' sector, but all along the Union line as well. Occasionally, the black soldiers had an opportunity to relieve a white unit in the trenches, but for the most part they were engaged in heavy labor.

Burnside believed it was time for the black troops to demonstrate their value on the battlefield. His white divisions had suffered terribly during the campaign, and weeks of trench warfare had mentally conditioned them to value shelter above all else. In this cruel environment, bravery and courage were rewarded with minié balls and mortar shells. The survival instinct quickly supplanted all higher notions. Burnside acknowledged that the USCT regiments were raw and untested, but he felt that even green troops were preferable to his jaded veterans, many of whom he said "had contracted a habit of covering themselves by every method within their reach."[11]

In mid-July, as it became apparent that the Pennsylvania miners would most likely accomplish their task, Burnside met with the commander of the black division, General Edward Ferrero. Burnside told Ferrero of his intention to have black units spearhead the assault, and instructed Ferrero to plan the specifics of the charge. Ferrero replied that most of his division had been parceled out for labor details along the Fifth Corps lines. Burnside had an aide look into the matter, and the work details were promptly returned to Ninth Corps.

Men of every profession volunteered to serve their country during the war, but high rank was typically reserved for those with either military experience or political connections, or both. Brigadier General Edward Ferrero was clearly an exception to that rule. Before the war, the 33-year-old immigrant had been a renowned dance instructor. He ran a successful dance school in New York City and published a book on the subject in 1859. Prior to the outbreak of hostilities, Ferrero's only military credentials were some time spent in the local militia and a con-

A solitary USCT soldier stands guard before a line of light 12-pounders at nearby City Point, Virginia. Black units were routinely assigned to guard duty and fatigue details due to the common misconception that they were unfit for combat. (Library of Congress, Prints and Photographs Division LC-B811-2583).

tract with the U.S. Military Academy to teach West Point cadets how to dance. Yet when given the opportunity to lead men into combat, Ferrero acquitted himself well and gradually climbed the ranks. Unfortunately, the intricacies of divisional command often eluded him, and the Senate declined to confirm his commission. Grant protested to the War Department, arguing that Ferrero had a knack for leading black troops, and the dance instructor was reappointed to command the Fourth Division.

Ferrero's USCT regiments had not drilled in basic battlefield movements since their induction into the service, so remedial instruction would be necessary before they could again function as an organized military force. Additionally, the regiments chosen to lead the column would need specialized training, since the battle plan called for them to make a difficult wheeling maneuver in order to sweep down the Confederate trenches. Executing such complex movements in combat posed a challenge for even the army's sharpest units.

Exactly how much preparation the Fourth Division actually received during the weeks leading up to the assault became a point of conjecture. Ferrero later claimed, "We were expecting to make the assault, and had drilled for weeks, and were in good trim for it."[12] General Robert Potter corroborated Ferrero's assertion. Potter specifically recalled watching the black troops prepare for their role in the attack.[13] But others, including some of the soldiers themselves, claimed to have received no training whatsoever during July 1864. Captain Robert Beecham of the 23rd USCT stated vehemently that he and his men had been given no opportunity to ready themselves:

Brigadier General Edward Ferrero showed great promise as a brigade commander, but he struggled at the division level, and Congress was slow to confirm his appointment (Library of Congress, Prints and Photographs Division LC-B8172-1652 DLC).

> I am prepared to say from actual knowledge derived from personal experience with the Fourth Division that the only duty assigned to the said division for more than a month before the battle of the Mine was work upon our trenches and fortifications. The Fourth Division during all that time was drilled especially in the use of pick and shovel, and in no other manner.[14]

Despite Captain Beecham's recollection, it is clear that at least a portion of the Fourth Division was schooled in battlefield maneuvers during late July. Other officers, including brigade commander General Henry Thomas remembered minute details of the affair. For example, Thomas said that after a long day of drilling, the black soldiers would gather around their campfires and proudly sing, *"We look like men a'marching on, We look like men of war."*[15] However, the degree of training appears to have varied across the division, and indeed some units may

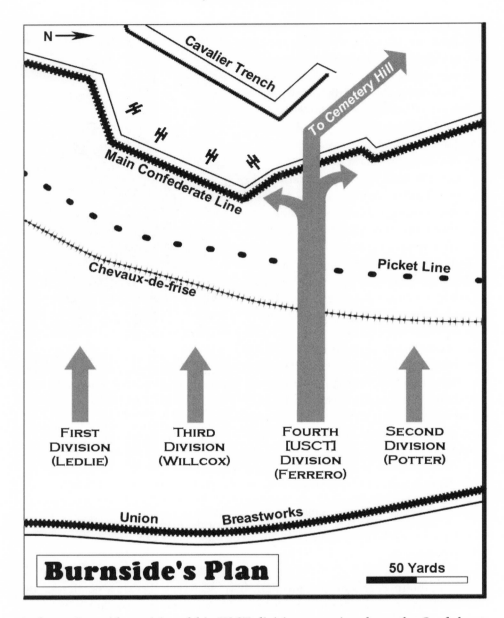

Ambrose Burnside envisioned his USCT division sweeping down the Confederate trenches and capturing Cemetery Hill. His three remaining divisions would follow and widen the breach.

have received little or no instruction whatsoever. Even the adamant Captain Beecham acknowledged that his men took part in a brigade drill "which lasted about three or four hours, and consisted of the most common and simple of brigade movements."[16]

Regiments assigned to lead the division into battle clearly received the most attention. Colonel Delevan Bates, commanding the 30th USCT, said he was informed of the mine's existence by his brigade commander on July 22. Bates then learned of his role in the impending attack. He said, "The 30th regiment was to advance immediately after the explosion, as rapidly as possible to the Crater, and then turn to the left and sweep down the line of breastworks as far as possible and hold the farthest point gained." Bates utilized every available moment to ensure that his men would be ready. "Time after time did my regiment go through the imaginary advance along the line of breastworks," he said. "Every officer and every private knew his place and what he was expected to do."[17]

Burnside had no doubt that his black division was up to the task when he submitted his formal battle plan to Meade's headquarters on July 26. He wrote first of forming up the division's two brigades in parallel columns, with "the head of each brigade resting on the front line." After the mine explosion, each column would spring forward and dash toward the Confederate line. As the leading elements peeled off to move through the trenches, the main body would continue on toward Cemetery Hill. Burnside optimistically continued, "It would be advisable, in my opinion, if we succeed in gaining the crest, to throw the colored division right into the town." He then tempered his enthusiasm by concluding, "I think our chances of success in a plan of this kind are more than even."[18]

The following morning, Burnside was summoned to Meade's tent. The two men discussed the plan in detail and Meade expressed concern about relying on the USCT division to successfully carry out the assault. He said that in an operation of such magnitude, it would be more prudent to rely on one of the battle-tested white divisions. Burnside responded that his white divisions were spent. They had endured nearly a month and a half of constant exposure to the enemy, and were losing between 30 and 60 men each day. Burnside also reminded Meade that the black regiments had been specially trained to widen the breach in the Confederate line by storming down the trenches. Meade retorted that the complicated wheeling maneuvers were unnecessary. There would be only a brief opportunity to seize Cemetery Hill before the Confederates recovered from the explosion, he said, and Burnside's entire assault force should focus on achieving that single goal. There was also the underlying consideration of appearance, Meade said. If black troops were sent in first and the attack failed, political enemies of Grant and Meade in the North would accuse them of using the Negroes for cannon fodder. Burnside continued to argue, and Meade reluctantly agreed to take the issue before Grant for a final determination. Certain in his convictions, Burnside departed the meeting confident that the general-in-chief would see things his way.

Meade's argument that exposing the USCT regiments to danger would leave he and Grant open to political criticism was unfounded. Tens of thousands of black volunteers had joined the Union army since Abraham Lincoln issued the Emancipation Proclamation on January 1, 1863. By July 1864, a number of USCT units had seen action and some had participated in major battles. Most notable was the 54th Massachusetts, the model black regiment that led the failed assault on Fort Wagner in Charleston, South Carolina a year earlier. The appalling losses suffered by that regiment did not result in public condemnation. On the contrary, the gallant charge of the 54th Massachusetts was held up as an example of what black soldiers could accomplish when properly trained and equipped.

In reality, Meade and Grant were far more concerned about the capabilities of Burnside's USCT division. Meade was correct in saying that the division was unproven, but that was only because he had chosen to exclude them from all of the heavy fighting that had occurred since May. Grant's opinion of the black troops was plainly revealed in his appeal to the War Department supporting the confirmation of Edward Ferrero. In that correspondence, Grant said that Ferrero "deserves great credit on this campaign for the manner in which he protected our immense wagon train with a division of undisciplined colored troops...."[19] Meade was hardly taking a risk by promising Burnside that he would let Grant decide the matter.

5

Twelve Frantic Hours

The siege was entering its sixth wretched week. For the weary men in the fetid, muddy trenches it was surely an eternity. Victims of the early assaults on Petersburg had been buried haphazardly, and the air was thick with the smell of decomposition. Vermin darted among the human waste and piles of garbage strewn about the trench floors. The sun's unforgiving rays forced many soldiers to burrow into the walls with their bayonets. For additional shelter, they stretched blankets or tent halves overhead as awnings. Drinking water was in short supply and, for the Confederates, food was scarce. One Southerner said, "Our rations were cut down to the lowest possible notch. We were hungry all the time; anything we could get to eat tasted good."[1] Dysentery was prevalent on both sides.

First-time visitors to the front lines were shocked by the squalor and misery. Lieutenant James Chase of Maine had enlisted in August 1863 at the age of 16. When the 32nd Maine was organized in the spring of 1864, he was made the 2nd lieutenant of Company D. Before reaching the Wilderness, Chase fell ill with fever and did not rejoin his unit until July 22 at Petersburg. Chase said that upon his arrival at Petersburg, he entered a large pine forest in the rear with little underbrush. It held the headquarters of many regiments and was used as a refuge for men on leave from the front. As he emerged from the forest, Chase saw the trench lines in the distance. An escort showed him the safest way to the front.

Four months previous, Chase had marched from Maine with over a thousand comrades. He was startled to learn that only 270 remained. And the sallow faces of the survivors bore no resemblance to those he had left behind. To Chase, the men looked more like refugees of a great catastrophe than soldiers. "Their clothes were tattered and torn," he said. "Some had no coats and some no blankets; some wore one boot and one shoe, while others had none. Officers, by their dress, could hardly be distinguished from their men, save by the sword they carried in place of a musket."[2] Chase soon understood the plight of these ragged souls; within a few days he too was exhausted, filthy, and picking lice from his clothing.

The physical discomforts of life in the trenches may have seemed almost bearable were it not for the constant specter of death. Hours of boredom concluded abruptly with moments of sheer terror as artillery rounds were exchanged. A veteran of the 49th North Carolina said that on one July day the artillery fire claimed 40 men from his regiment. "The mortar shells were sometimes thrown in volleys, landing in and on the breastworks, tearing them down and tearing up our bombproofs, killing and burying the men who were brave enough to seek refuge in them," he said.[3] Variations in the landscape occasionally gave sharpshooters firing lanes directly into loopholes in the trenches. At night, soldiers constructed stone-filled pens in an attempt to protect the exposed areas, but careless or unlucky men still fell in numbers.

No portion of the line was more perilous than that belonging to Ninth Corps and, as Ambrose Burnside had tried to explain to Meade, the men occupying that line were in no frame of mind to go on the offensive. Since June 20, the three white divisions of Ninth Corps had endured a casualty rate of more than 12 percent despite never leaving their fortifications. Burnside thought it was obvious that the steady attrition had sapped his men's will to fight. He said, "Each of the division commanders, as well as every officer in the command, who had given his attention to the subject in the least degree, was fully aware of the condition of the white troops."[4] Yet at 10:15 am on July 29, the bad news arrived by telegraph: Grant had sided with Meade. A white division must lead the attack rather than the black troops.

Forty-five minutes later, George Meade appeared at Burnside's headquarters to personally ensure that the message was understood. With him was General Edward Ord, whose Eighteenth Corps would support Ninth Corps during the engagement. When they arrived, Burnside was meeting with Robert Potter and another of his division commanders, General Orlando Willcox. Meade entered the tent and approached the trio. Eyeing Burnside, he said, "I saw General Grant, and he agrees with me that it will not do to put the colored division in the lead." With forlorn hope, Burnside asked if the decision could be reconsidered. Meade replied, "No, general, the order is final; you must detail one of your white divisions to take the advance." To this Burnside responded, "Very well, general, I will carry out this plan to the best of my ability."[5]

Meade and Ord departed to survey the ground, leaving Burnside with the unenviable task of selecting one of his tattered white divisions to send into the breach. A discussion began, and Willcox suggested that in the interest of fairness General James Ledlie, commander of First Division, should be included. Burnside summoned him, and the debate resumed. No matter which way the four men examined the dilemma a satisfactory solution eluded them. "There is a reason why either General Willcox's or General Potter's division should lead the assault," Burn-

A postwar view of the Confederate works near Elliott's Salient. Clusters of chevaux-de-frise are visible in the background (Library of Congress, Prints and Photographs Division LC-B811-322).

side said. "They are nearer to the point of assault, and it would require less time to get them into position for the work. But there is also a reason why General Ledlie's division should lead, which is, that his men have not been in such close proximity to the enemy as those of the other two divisions, and in fact have not had to do quite as hard work for the last thirty or forty days."[6] The only answer that truly made sense was using Ferrero's USCT division, as originally planned, but that option had been eliminated.

Meade returned to the tent at 1 pm and stressed that regardless of who made the attack, they must charge toward Cemetery Hill as soon as the mine exploded.

Celerity was the key to success, Meade said, because once the enemy recovered his senses after the explosion, the Union advantage would be gone. To that end, he said, Burnside should have a portion of his breastworks leveled, and the obstacles cleared from before them, in order to create a proper *debouching* point. Without an easy exit, the men would get bogged down trying to climb over the breastworks, dooming the charge to failure before it had even begun.

When Meade left, the Ninth Corps leaders returned to their discussion of which division should carry out the assault. By 3 pm, Burnside realized there was no more time for debate. The mine would be detonated in little more than 12 hours. He would have to make a decision. But in looking at the officers assembled before him, he could not bring himself to do so. Burnside stood, picked up his floppy, wide-brimmed hat, and tossed in three straws. Unbeknownst to the thousands of soldiers occupying the trenches beyond Ninth Corps headquarters, their collective fate was about to be decided by the random drawing of lots.

Burnside's unorthodox selection process was the first sign that he was rapidly losing control of the situation. Ambrose Burnside was a meticulous planner, but he did not think well on his feet. A year and a half earlier at Fredericksburg, Burnside stubbornly followed his original plan despite a delay in the construction of a pontoon bridge, which allowed the Confederates time to entrench on Marye's Heights. The disastrous result was one of the most lopsided engagements of the war. Now he was being forced to deviate from his carefully considered plan and make difficult decisions instantaneously. It was work for which Burnside was not well suited, and he knew it. With the drawing of lots, Burnside was effectively removing himself from the decision-making process. Perhaps he felt that sheer chance would make a better arbiter. Unfortunately for the men of Ninth Corps, he was quite wrong.

Brigadier General James Ledlie, possibly the most despised officer in the entire corps, chose the short lot. Ledlie was a coward and a drunkard. Many months later, in retrospect, Grant would refer to him as "an inefficient man" and "the poorest division commander that General Burnside had."[7] But on July 29, 1864, Ledlie's shortcomings were not yet readily apparent to his superiors. He was the newest of the division commanders, having only taken the reins of First Division two months earlier. During the opening assaults on Petersburg, Ledlie failed to support the attack on the Shand House as ordered, thus preventing the 48th Pennsylvania and its sister regiments from advancing farther. Later that day, Ledlie's men made an assault of their own but were forced to fall back when they ran out of ammunition. The 32-year-old general could not be found during the engagement and rumors circulated that he was drunk.[8]

The inappropriate behavior continued, and Ledlie's aides distastefully spent the next six weeks covering for him. Apparently they managed to deceive Burnside, but the officers and privates of First Division knew the truth about their leader. Their misgivings were only reinforced by the general's eccentricities. To relieve boredom in the trenches, Ledlie had his regimental bands take turns playing patriotic tunes at a spot near his headquarters. But rather than a series of varied programs with intermissions, Ledlie ordered that the music be played continuously, around the clock. The unceasing, repetitive melodies soon drew groans and obscenities from Ledlie's men, as well as the Confederates within earshot.

When Ledlie pulled the short lot from Burnside's hat on the afternoon of July 29, he made an ominous comment about being "the unlucky victim," yet a witness said he seemed almost cheerful when he left the tent.[9] The task facing him, and the other division commanders, was daunting. They had barely twelve hours to brief their

Despite a mediocre service record, Brigadier General James H. Ledlie was chosen to command the First Division of Ninth Corps on June 7, 1864. The bulk of Ledlie's experience lay in commanding artillery units, and the pressure of leading frontline infantry quickly proved too much for him (Library of Congress, Prints and Photographs Division LC-B814-1770).

brigade commanders on the new plan, and then begin the time-consuming job of moving thousands of men into position for the assault. Written orders from Burnside would have to wait until evening—he had been called to Meade's headquarters for a 5 pm meeting with Grant, presumably to discuss the final details. Upon his return, Burnside dictated the official orders for the assault to Colonel William Harris. Under the revised plan, First Division would charge forward after the mine explosion and crown Cemetery Hill. Willcox's division would move out next, establishing a defensive line south of the hill at Jerusalem Plank Road. Potter's division would establish a similar line to the north overlooking a ravine near the hill. Once the area had been fully secured, Ferrero's USCT division would proceed, with reserve elements from other corps, into the city of Petersburg.

The young Colonel Harris was both shocked and outraged by the orders he had just written on Burnside's behalf. As someone who had closely monitored the mine's construction and the preparation of the USCT division, he was appalled by Meade's last-minute interference. Later that evening, Harris expressed his frustration in his journal:

> Thus, at the eleventh hour just as the curtain was about to rise, the actors to whom had been assigned the most prominent parts were compelled to change their roles, or in less theatrical language the Negro division & its gallant commander, who believed they would be invincible & who had learned their duty by constant application to this single idea for the previous month, were informed that "it wasn't best" and they must be replaced by white troops who had already their own instructions to do an entirely different thing.[10]

By late afternoon, preparations for the impending battle were well underway. Three days of rations and extra ammunition were issued, alerting those men not current in their gossip that action was soon coming. Lieutenant James Chase, the recent arrival from Maine, grimly observed the army's arrangements to care for casualties. "A large number of surgeons arrived from City Point to render their assistance," he said. "Amputating tables and bandages seemed to be the order of the day among the surgeons. Near our brigade quartermaster's tent could be seen a wagon loaded with picks and shovels to be used in burying the dead. In the open field in the rear of the woods stood the ambulance train ready for use."[11]

Picks and shovels were also brought up for use in the attack. One regiment from each division was designated to serve as combat engineers. It was hoped that the explosion would destroy at least some of the Confederate breastworks, but undoubtedly many obstacles would still remain. The acting engineers would clear away any abatis, fraise, and chevaux-de-frise that stood in the way, as well as dig defensive works once Cemetery Hill was captured. Ledlie's regiment of acting engineers would be the 35th Massachusetts, while Potter selected the 7th Rhode Island, and Willcox chose the 17th Michigan.

Although plans had been made to deal with Confederate obstacles, virtually nothing was done to ensure that the Union's own works did not become a hindrance. Meade had given the matter forethought and made his wishes clear — the earthworks should be leveled and the obstacles removed in advance of the assault. He had stated this verbally earlier in the day at Burnside's tent, and he reiterated it later in writing. But Burnside desperately hoped to preserve the element of surprise, perhaps feeling it was the only advantage he had left, and doing what Meade ordered would almost certainly alert the Confederates. In the end, Burnside did nothing but order the construction of two sandbag stairways to the top of the parapets.

Burnside also ignored the pleas of General Henry Hunt, the Army of the Potomac's artillery chief, to cut down a stand of trees blocking his big guns. The tall pine trees obscured a Confederate battery to the south, Hunt said. He repeatedly told Burnside that the trees would have to come down, but Burnside was fearful of tipping his hand to the enemy, and did nothing. Tired of waiting for the infantry, some of Hunt's artillerists felled a few trees on their own during the night of July 28, but they did not have enough manpower to finish the job. Hunt therefore prodded Burnside once more, saying, "Don't forget the wood to be cleared away. I fear it can't be certainly cut away in one night."[12] But Burnside would not be swayed. He merely assigned a detail of black troops to wait in the woods, axes in hand, and begin chopping as soon as the mine exploded.

Before the divisions of Ninth Corps could assemble for the attack, they would first need to be relieved from their trenches. After nightfall, troops from Eighteenth Corps made their way toward Burnside's front for this purpose, but the column inched along slowly and became lost in the darkness. At 10:25 pm, Edward Ord telegraphed Burnside to say that it might be midnight or later before his men arrived. Meade told Burnside that, if necessary, he could begin forming his men before Ord arrived. In silence, the weary Ninth Corps soldiers crept from their trenches into the covered ways leading to the rear, leaving only a line of skirmishers to cover their withdrawal. Ledlie's division stayed near the front, forming in a covered way directly across from Elliott's Salient, but Potter and Willcox were instructed to mass their troops a quarter of a mile back. "It was feared that the explosion would throw up a great deal of debris and boards and everything of that kind into the air, and injure our men when they came down," Henry Pleasants explained. "I urged it upon General Burnside to mass them nearer the breastworks, still he would not agree to it for fear the men would be injured."[13]

A reserve force consisting of several thousand men from Fifth Corps was also forming in the rear, and Ord's Eighteenth Corps had finally begun to arrive. The fields and forests became choked with regiments seeking their assigned patch of ground. The 20th Michigan fell into place around 11 pm, and Colonel Byron Cutcheon told his men to get some rest. Cutcheon then observed the scene before him:

> The night was warm, the sky was clear, the men spread their blankets on the ground and lay down under the open sky, in line just as they had halted. Some slept, no doubt, but many did not. Troops were moving all about us, and artillery was rumbling along past, going into positions, before day should dawn and disclose their presence. About midnight the

company cooks were sent to the rear to make coffee for the men, and have it ready to serve before daylight.[14]

Second Corps and the cavalry that Grant had sent north would also participate in the engagement. They had quietly begun filtering back across the James River during the previous night via a straw-covered pontoon bridge. To give the illusion that Federal troops were still being sent northward, Grant had some units turn around and cross again during the daylight hours. A train of empty wagons was sent across for the same purpose, and steamboats and tugs were told to show their lights and blow their whistles at night to give the appearance of transporting troops. The ruse worked; Lee's forces north of the James made no attempt to return to Petersburg.

A tall, red brick chimney was all that remained of the home of William Byrd Taylor. Taylor and his family wisely fled their farm before the armies arrived at Petersburg, and their vacant house had burned to the ground during one of the early contests for the city. The chimney sat a thousand feet behind the Federal line, pointing skyward atop a modest ridgeline that served as the Union's high ground. No time was wasted in assembling a 14-gun battery near the Taylor House ruins, and the battery served as an effective counterbalance to Elliott's Salient. The strongpoint would eventually be christened Fort Morton in honor of Major James St. Clair Morton, the Ninth Corps chief engineer who was shot through the heart while guiding one of Willcox's brigades into position on June 17. But on July 29, it was still known simply as the Taylor House. Because of the site's excellent view, Burnside chose it for his command post during the battle. In turn, Meade moved into the Ninth Corps headquarters still farther back at Harrison's Creek. Grant would join him there in the early morning hours. The mine's detonation was scheduled for 3:30 am.

Meade's absence from the field suggested that Burnside would be the overall commander for the engagement. Yet at the same time it was clear that Meade had no intention of allowing Burnside a free rein. Meade's general orders on July 29 stated, "Headquarters during the operation will be at the headquarters of the Ninth Corps." In other words, the important decisions would be where Meade was located, not Burnside's command post at Taylor House. And although Meade would be too far away to witness the action personally, he still expected to be kept well informed. The same orders read: "Corps commanders will report to the commanding general when their preparations are complete, and will advise him of every step in the progress of the operation and of everything important that occurs."[15]

The command structure Meade had established put Burnside in a difficult spot. His men would be the primary combatants in the operation, and if all went as planned, there would be no assistance needed from the two other corps that had been designated as support. But if the enemy offered stronger resistance than expected, or if the attack bogged down for some other reason, then it might be necessary to tap the troops belonging to Warren and Ord. If Burnside had been placed in charge of the operation, he would possess the authority to decide if and when Fifth and Eighteenth Corps would be thrown into the battle. However, since Meade opted to retain direct command, Burnside could merely request that the reserves be sent to his aid. Meanwhile, as others debated about whether to grant his request, Burnside's men would continue to fight and die.

Burnside could not even suggest that Meade give him authority over the reserves. There had been that ugly incident, just a month earlier, when Meade asked about the prospects for an attack on the Ninth Corps front. Burnside's reply contained the offhand remark that, in the event of such an attack, he would prefer to say when and how the two adjacent corps came to his support. Meade's caustic reaction to that comment ensured that Burnside would never again make such a suggestion. If the mine did not have its desired effect, or if the men of Ninth Corps ran into some other trouble, Burnside could only hope that his calls for help would be answered quickly.

Outside Burnside's tent, the commotion continued as units moved into position. The ground around Taylor House was assigned to Ferrero's USCT division. These men had learned only hours earlier that they would not be spearheading the attack as planned. For some, the news was dispiriting. General Henry Thomas said that he and his regimental commanders were dejected and filled with "an instinct of disaster for the morrow."[16] Others concerned themselves with more practical matters, such as sleep and prayer. "Around us could be heard the shuffling of troops, but it was so dark that nothing could be seen," recalled Lieutenant Freeman Bowley of the 30th USCT. "Down on the picket line the rifles were flashing, and over head the bullets hummed with that peculiar droning sound of the nearly spent bullet. Most of us went to sleep as soon as we halted."[17] Men of the 27th and 28th USCT regiments who were too anxious for slumber instead participated in informal worship services, quietly praying that the coming day would bring them no harm.

The greatest anxiety no doubt belonged to the soldiers of Ledlie's division. Most of the division's 11 regiments were crammed into the covered way, making it impossible for the men to stretch out and rest. Among them was Lieutenant John Morrison of the 100th Pennsylvania, who said that he and his men had left their breastworks at midnight with no idea of their destination. They had heard only "vague rumors" about the existence of a mine previously, and were startled to learn that within a few short hours they would witness an enormous explosion and take part in a charge afterward. "The tongues of all were mute," Morrison said. "An ominous silence fell upon us, and that nervous strain so trying to soldiers— more

Despite losing a leg during the siege of Yorktown in 1862, William F. Bartlett returned to service and continued to command frontline troops. He received two more wounds in 1863, and yet another in May 1864 at the Wilderness. The following month Bartlett was promoted to brigadier general. He returned to duty just days before the Battle of the Crater (USAMHI).

trying indeed, than after actual hostilities commenced — was intense and agonizing."[18]

Few thoughts could have brought comfort to the men of First Division as they waited shoulder-to-shoulder in the dank covered way. But at least they knew that two seasoned brigade commanders would be leading them into battle. Both officers had seen their share of action, and both had shed their own blood on the field. Colonel Elisha Marshall was a West Point graduate who had been wounded at Fredericksburg and then again during the opening battles for Petersburg. General William Bartlett had been wounded a total of four times, most recently at the Wilderness. His injury sustained at the Battle of Yorktown in 1862 was the most severe, as it had cost him a leg. It was an overdue stroke of luck for First Division that both of these men had returned to duty just days earlier.

William Bartlett agonized over his missing limb. He lamented not so much the personal loss, but the burden it posed on his ability to command. At age 24, Bartlett was remarkably young for his high rank. A Harvard student before the war, he promptly withdrew from school to volunteer following the attack on Fort Sumter, but later completed his studies while recuperating from the amputation. Bartlett was the quintessential Massachusetts aristocrat. He looked down on his men and they knew it, still they could not help but admire his courage. The young general rode fearlessly about the battlefield on horseback, infecting every man with the same calm demeanor he himself carried. His gallantry was known even among Confederate soldiers, some of whom later claimed to have intentionally avoided firing on him.

Bartlett could not take his mount into the coming battle; the trenches and earthworks would prevent it. Instead, the general would have to rely on a cane for mobility. While waiting for the mine to explode, he wrote in his journal:

> We storm the works tomorrow at daylight. Our Division leads. I hardly dare hope to live through it. God have mercy.... If I could only ride, or had two legs, so I could *lead* my brigade, I believe they would follow me anywhere. I will try as it is.[19]

By 3 am, everyone was finally in position. Henry Pleasants stood at the mouth of the mine with his two closest assistants, Sergeant Reese and Lieutenant Jacob Douty. The rest of the 48th Pennsylvania was in the rear, serving as provost guard. The miners had already made their contribution to the operation, and Burnside excused them from further duty. Their only task that day would be to detain the occasional straggler or deserter trying to slip away from the battle. Regardless, many of the miners were eager to see firsthand the fruits of their labor, and they managed to find an excuse to be at the front during the appointed hour. Colonel Pleasants knew exactly how they felt. He had requested and received permission to serve on General Potter's staff for the day, thus ensuring an exceptional view of the action.

Pleasants estimated that his triple-line of fusing would take about 15 minutes to reach the powder. At 3:15 am, he entered the tunnel with Reese and Douty following close behind. They touched off the fuse and hurried back to safety.

Five minutes later, Burnside received a telegram from Meade. Since it was still extremely dark out, Meade said, Burnside could briefly postpone firing the mine if he so desired. Burnside simply responded that the mine would be detonated on schedule. He did not bother to add that the fuse was already burning.

6

"Muffled Thunder"

Thousands of eyes were fixed on Elliott's Salient as each minute slowly passed. Colonel Pleasants stood perched atop the Union breastworks, waiting in the darkness. Somewhere beneath the scarred field in front of him, a hissing fuse was creeping toward four tons of gunpowder. At last, 3:30 arrived. At any moment, the billowing flames of a massive explosion would illuminate the night sky. A waiting officer described his men, who had been on their feet since midnight, as rapt "in a feverish state of expectancy."[1]

When 3:30 passed with nothing but silence, no questions were asked. Such precision of time was not expected in 1864. But when 3:45 passed with continued silence, some concerns arose. Pleasants undoubtedly wondered how he could have misjudged the fuse's burn-time so badly. At about 4 am, Burnside asked his aide-de-camp, a Major Van Buren, to go to the front and investigate. Van Buren found Pleasants standing at the mouth of the mine. The colonel explained that Sergeant Reese and Lieutenant Douty had volunteered to go inside and determine the problem. It went without saying that the two men were placing themselves at great personal risk, since nobody knew for certain what had happened inside the mine. If the fuse had merely slowed and smoldered for a time but was now actively burning again, Reese and Douty were walking toward their own destruction.

At Ninth Corps headquarters, George Meade was becoming agitated. The first rays of dawn were not far off, and daylight would soon reveal to the Confederates a huge formation of men in blue. The element of surprise would be gone, leaving little chance for success. At 4:15, he wired Burnside at Taylor House and inquired about the delay. When Burnside did not answer, Meade tried again, but there was still no reply. Burnside would later say that he did not immediately respond because he was waiting for Major Van Buren to return with an explanation. But by 4:35, the sky had turned from inky black to slate gray, and Meade felt he could wait no longer. He told Burnside that unless the mine could be detonated at once, the assault must begin without it.

Just as Meade's message was arriving at Taylor House, Major Van Buren stepped inside the tent. He reported to Burnside that two volunteers from the 48th Pennsylvania had entered the mine, discovered that the fuse had sputtered out at a splice, and repaired it. The fuse was now burning again and Colonel Pleasants estimated that the explosion would occur in about 10 minutes.

The sky was rapidly growing brighter and Elliott's Salient was coming to life. Colonel Cutcheon of the 20th Michigan said he could hear Confederate bugles sounding reveille in the distance. Lieutenant Freeman Bowley of the 30th USCT said, "The gray of early morning appeared, and the line of Rebel fortifications could just be seen through the mist. The pickets kept up a sputtering fire, and the flashes from their rifles looked like fireflies in a meadow. Still there were no indications of an attack." Lieutenant Chase of the 32nd Maine nervously awaited the commencement of his first battle. "'What could be the cause of this delay,' was asked from one to another, no one, of course, being able to give any reason for this unaccountable delay," he recalled. "As daylight was approaching we were ordered to lie down, as a precaution from being seen by the enemy. Upon lying down a drowsiness came over me and I was soon wrapped in slumber, forgetful of what was going on around me...."[2]

In the woods outside Ninth Corps headquarters, Ulysses S. Grant waited tensely in silence. "The general-in-chief stood with his right hand placed against a tree," said an aide. "His lips were compressed and his features wore an expression of profound anxiety, but he uttered few words." A short distance in front of Grant waited the men of the 45th Pennsylvania. As part of Potter's division, they would be following Ledlie's men. "As we stood in almost breathless expectancy, a staff officer rode near us from the front going to headquarters," recalled a man from the regiment. "He stopped an instant to say that the fuse was faulty, and that the affair was a failure, but as the last word fell from his lips, suddenly a heavy sound like muffled thunder was heard...."[3]

The explosion occurred at 4:44 am. Many witnesses reported the blast's roar as far less impressive than they had anticipated. Rather than a sharp, deafening clap, most heard only a low rumble. Because the gunpowder detonated roughly 20 feet underground, its report had been stifled. Indeed, one Federal observer described it as "a heavy, smothered sound, not nearly so distinct as a musket-shot."[4]

Every other aspect of the explosion lived up to expectations. Subterranean shockwaves knocked men off their feet a half-mile away. The most fearsome element of the eruption was the tremendous amount of debris it threw skyward. A gigantic brown column shot straight into the air. Streaked with smoke and flame, it carried one quarter of an acre of Elliott's Salient upward some 200 feet. Many said the immense geyser seemed to hang suspended in the air for a moment before its tons of wreckage came crashing down.

Few Federals were nearer the blast than Major Charles Houghton of the 14th New York Heavy Artillery. Serving as infantry in Ledlie's division, Houghton and his regiment would be among the first to take the field. He wrote:

> I shall never forget the terrible and magnificent sight. The earth around us trembled and heaved — so violently that I was lifted to my feet. Then the earth along the enemy's lines opened, and fire and smoke shot upward seventy-five or one hundred feet. The air was filled with earth, cannon, caissons, sandbags and living men, and with everything else within the exploded fort. One huge lump of clay as large as a haystack or small cottage was thrown out and left on top of the ground toward our own works.[5]

Instinctively, the Federal soldiers standing just 100 yards distant began edging backward. When small bits of soil and stone rained down upon them, a panic ensued and men scattered. After several minutes, the officers managed to calm their troops, but it would take time to get everyone back into formation. In other words, the charge would not take place immediately as planned.

The dust and smoke of the explosion had not yet begun to clear when another, much louder eruption occurred. This blast emanated not from the mine, and not even from a single source, but rather from the huge collection of Union artillery that had been assembled for the battle. In the days leading up to the attack, artillery positions between Baxter Road and the Hare House had been augmented. On the morning of July 30, no less than 144 pieces stood ready, ranging from massive siege guns to diminutive Coehorn mortars. It was more heavy weaponry than either army had fielded at Gettysburg, and its purpose was to suppress all Confederate artillery protecting Elliott's Salient. The crews opened fire in unison as soon as the mine went up.

To the Federal infantrymen who were trying to reorganize, the massive artillery barrage that followed was both welcomed and unnerving. The colossal explosion they had just witnessed was disorienting. Colonel Cutcheon called it "a grand and terrible spectacle, such as none of us had ever seen before or will ever see again." Now, the surreal experience continued with an ear-splitting cacophony by the artillery. Yet as unpleasant as it was for them, they knew it would be much worse for the enemy. Those with the luxury of being able to observe from a distance marveled at the precision of the artillerists. A colonel in Willcox's division remarked, "The firing was from each piece slow, deliberate, and careful, partaking of the nature of target practice, and was very effective, taking great care in firing over our heads." Lieutenant Bowley, watching from near the Taylor House, wondered how any human could possibly survive the bombardment. "Great clouds of dust marked the explosion of the shells, and the Rebel fortifications seemed to be plowed through and through," he said. [6]

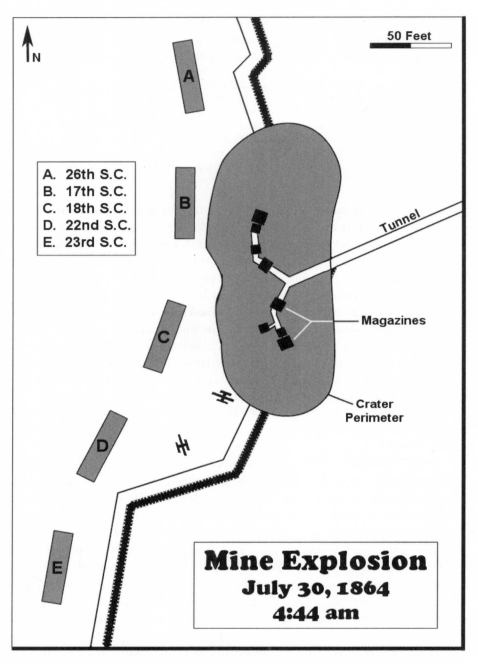

The blast obliterated the tip of Elliott's Salient and created a 200-foot-long crater. Many of the 278 Confederates killed in the explosion were buried alive by falling debris.

For the men of Elliott's Salient, the overnight hours of Saturday, July 30, seemed particularly dark and calm. The picket fire had lessened considerably, noted one Confederate officer who was enjoying the "unusual repose" afforded by the stillness.[7] Despite the relative tranquility, Robert E. Lee suspected that Grant was preparing to make a move on Petersburg. By now the existence of a Federal mine was almost a certainty, but exactly where and when the Yankees would strike still remained a mystery. Accordingly, late on July 29, Lee ordered all units to be ready for action come daybreak the following morning.

Lee's order changed nothing for the Virginians of Pegram's Battery. Elliott's Salient was so close to the enemy's line that they were required to man their four 12-pound Napoleons around the clock. At 4:30 am, the night-shift gun crews and pickets were coming off duty, and the regiments guarding the fortress were stirring to life. The 18th South Carolina was stationed directly behind the artillery platforms. On its left were the 17th and 26th South Carolina, and on its right were the 22nd and 23rd South Carolina. The latter two regiments had just swapped positions on Thursday, July 28, by order of brigade commander General Stephen Elliott. The shift moved the 23rd South Carolina away from its usual spot in the heart of the fortress and onto the southernmost fringes. A member of the 23rd would later call Elliott's inexplicable order "a merciful providence."[8]

Captain Richard Pegram was dreadfully tired. He had been watching over his battery for 48 hours straight, concerned about the threat of a Yankee tunnel. Finally, in the stillness of the night, Pegram convinced himself that Douglas' countermines would have uncovered any such menace. He turned command of the battery over to two of his lieutenants, Hamlin and Chandler, and retired to his headquarters in the city. It was the last time Hamlin, Chandler, and 20 other men from Pegram's command would be seen alive. The same was true for 256 infantrymen from the 18th and 22nd South Carolina.

Few Confederates who witnessed the blast lived to tell about it. Many who perished simply died in their sleep. For weeks afterward bodies would be unearthed, including those of "eight poor fellows lying side by side with their coats under their heads."[9] Some of the victims would never be found, including Colonel David Fleming of the 22nd South Carolina. For three days, that regiment's survivors would search for the body of their beloved commander. It was a futile effort: Fleming's bombproof had been obliterated and no trace of him remained. In the 18th South Carolina, entire companies instantly disappeared.

Despite the devastation, there were remarkable tales of survival. A lieutenant from the 18th regiment's Company F was blown clear across the Confederate earthworks and into no man's land by the concussion. Finding himself uninjured, he crawled back over the works. Two men from Company A awoke to find that their bombproof was completely buried. After clawing with a bayonet for an unknown

71

amount of time they finally reached the surface. The regimental surgeon found no injuries on the two men, but said they were so badly shaken by the experience that they seemed "more dead than alive."[10] Four of Douglas' engineers had been working in a nearby countermine when the detonation occurred. Incredibly, the tunnel's pine supports withstood the shockwave and the engineers emerged unscathed.

Just as the Federal leadership had anticipated, the explosion's psychological impact was almost as powerful as its physical destruction. Peering through the smoke and dust, Colonel Fitz William McMaster of the 17th South Carolina saw that his soldiers were rendered helpless by the blast. "Some scampered out of the lines; some, paralyzed with fear, vaguely scratched at the counterscarp as if trying to escape," he said.[11] The Confederate trenches lay virtually undefended for 150 yards in either direction.

Ten minutes had passed since the explosion, and Ledlie's men were at last ready to move out. Second Brigade, led by Elisha Marshall, was first in line, followed by First Brigade under William Bartlett. But it quickly became apparent that the brigades would not be able to advance in neat, orderly lines of battle. Burnside's refusal to create a passageway in the breastworks meant that each man would need to find his own way onto the field. Some queued up for the sandbag stairways, while others just improvised. "Our own works, which were very high at this point, had not been prepared for scaling," said Major Charles Houghton. "But scale them in some way we must, and ladders were improvised by the men placing their bayonets between the logs in the works and holding the other end at their hip or on shoulders, thus forming steps over which men climbed." A First Brigade captain said, "I tried to climb the parapet in two or three places, but was unable to do so. Soldiers with muskets and accoutrements could not get over." [12]

Once the troops managed to traverse the 8-foot wall, they were forced to navigate their own defensive obstacles. Narrow gaps had been left in the abatis for pickets to pass through on the way to their rifle pits, and the men filed along these footpaths to reach the open field. Burnside would later claim that the abatis in his sector had virtually disintegrated after weeks of enemy fire, but in reality the tangle of felled trees still made a formidable barrier. Emerging in clusters of two and three, the soldiers haphazardly made their way across the field. From a distance, Colonel Cutcheon watched with concern as Ledlie's men struggled to advance. He and his men were soon to follow. Fifteen minutes had elapsed since the explosion, and aside from some intermittent musket fire the enemy had yet to put up any resistance. Such good fortune could not be expected to last.

The first troops to cross the field ran into a 12-foot-high wall of loose earth. It was the rim of the crater created by the blast. To the left and right of this wall were Confederate abatis and chevaux-de-frise, but displaced earth had buried all of the obstacles in front. The men climbed to the top of the soft rim and peered inside. "The whole scene of the explosion struck everyone dumb with astonish-ment as we arrived at the crest of the debris," said one man.[13] A cavernous, smok-ing pit stretched before them. The oval-shaped Crater was roughly 200 feet long, 50 feet wide, and 25 feet deep. Its steep walls dropped sharply to an undulating, debris-strewn floor. Among the ruins were muskets, timber, huge boulders of clay, and half-buried, squirming bodies.

Unable to contain their curiosity, the Federals tumbled down into the Crater. Some simply milled about in amazement, while others hunted for souvenirs or began digging out the surviving Confederates. "We succeeded in taking out many," said Major Houghton. "Some whose feet would be waving above their burial-place; others having an arm, hand, or head only, uncovered; others alive but terribly shaken."[14] Another officer recalled:

> One of these [men] near me was pulled out, and proved to be a second
> lieutenant of the battery which had been blown up. The fresh air revived
> him, and he was soon able to walk and talk. He was very grateful and said
> that he was asleep when the explosion took place, and only awoke to find
> himself wriggling up in the air; then a few seconds afterward he felt him-
> self descending, and soon lost consciousness.[15]

The dazed survivors were taken to the rear and became the first prisoners of the day. Meanwhile, Ledlie's men continued to trickle across the field, bunching up at the base of the Crater's rim. The various regiments had become hopelessly inter-twined, thus destroying all vestiges of organization and command structure. Back in the Federal lines, Ninth Corps officers knew that the opportunity to seize Ceme-tery Hill was slipping away. A captain in the 45th Pennsylvania said, "Precious time was passing; 20 minutes were gone; ample time in which Ledlie's division should have cleared the enemy's line and made for and reached the coveted crest."[16]

Nobody was more alarmed than Henry Pleasants. His mine had rent an enor-mous fissure in the Confederate defenses, but rather than rushing through that breach and seizing the high ground as ordered, First Division was dawdling in and around the Crater. Suddenly enraged, Pleasants leapt from General Potter's side and dashed across the field. He implored Ledlie's men to go forward, striking sol-diers on the back with an open hand as he bellowed. But the confused mass could not be moved. When Pleasants disgustedly returned, Potter noticed that the col-onel's hand was red and blistered from pounding on soldiers' backs. A colleague from the 48th Pennsylvania who was startled by Pleasants' fury remarked, "Indeed he was more like a crazy man that day, than one in possession of his senses."[17]

Slowly, the Confederate artillery and muskets were coming to life, especially on the flanks. The North Carolinians to the north and the Virginians to the south were largely spared from the explosion. The ground trembled violently, but the blast's more deleterious effects had been localized at Elliott's Salient. Still, there were some anxious moments. A private in the 49th North Carolina who spent the entire night on picket duty had just crawled into a bombproof for some sleep. "I was suddenly awakened by a heavy jar and found myself almost buried in the dirt," he said. "I was first under the impression that a mortar shell had struck the bombproof, as the timbers overhead had been thrown apart and the dirt was pouring in."[18] He grabbed his weapon and crawled from the wrecked shelter.

Weeks earlier, when suspicions of a Yankee mine first surfaced, Confederate engineers took special precautions designed to thwart an enemy attack on Elliott's Salient. Artillery positions were established on high ground to the north and south with clear fields of fire on the salient. The engineers also excavated a shallow ditch one hundred feet behind the fortress as an emergency fallback position. This "cavalier trench" was similar to the ditch that the 3rd Louisiana had dug at Vicksburg in 1863 for protection from Grant's subterranean assault. It was part of the "detached works" that Federal observers had spotted when previously reconnoitering the salient. The cavalier trench was proving itself valuable early on the morning of July 30. Some of the terrified South Carolinians who had fled the fort were rallying there, laying down a modest but effective fire on the Crater.

With Confederate fire gradually increasing from three sides, most of First Division sought shelter inside the Crater. Ledlie's acting engineer regiment, the 35th Massachusetts, made an effort to clear away the spiny chevaux-de-frise on the Crater's flanks, but when the action intensified they also took refuge in the pit. There was no guarantee of safety once inside — a handful of enemy sharpshooters were firing from the remnants of trenches that now opened directly into the depression — but it was far safer than the open field. The Crater's steep walls provided a sense of security for men who had been conditioned to seek shelter. Instead of an obstacle through which to pass on the way to Cemetery Hill, they began to think of it as a place to be defended. The engineers of the 35th Massachusetts started digging a covered way back to the Union line. Meanwhile, with their toes planted in the soft earth, soldiers climbed to the rim and attempted to return the enemy's fire.

Some units made uncoordinated and muddled attempts to advance beyond the Crater. The 2nd Pennsylvania Provisional Heavy Artillery was the first regiment with any cohesiveness to enter the pit. Rushing across to the far side, the regiment attempted to climb out and proceed onward to Cemetery Hill. But without support, the artillerists-turned-infantry made an easy target for Confederates firing on them from nearly every direction. After advancing only a few dozen feet, the Pennsylvanians halted, dug into the ruins of the fort, and waited for assistance. Other regiments tried to push their way down the trenches that opened into the

Crater. The result was fierce, close-quarter fighting that quickly drew to a stale-mate in most instances.

Sergeant Wesley Stanley of the 14th New York Heavy Artillery decided he could best help his side by doing the work for which he had originally been trained. Two of Pegram's Napoleons had been blown straight out of the fortress toward the Union line, but the other two still sat half-buried beside the Crater. Stanley collected a group of volunteers and began freeing the pieces from the dirt. As the volunteers hauled the cannon into firing positions, Stanley managed to locate and uncover an intact magazine. Soon the two twelve-pounders were firing back at Confederate artillery that had opened up in the north and south.

Three-quarters of an hour had passed since the explosion, and First Division occupied only the Crater and some of the adjacent works. Brigade commanders Marshall and Bartlett worked feverishly to create a semblance of order, but with no success. "It was as utterly impracticable to re-form a brigade in that crater as it would be to marshal bees into line after upsetting the hive," exclaimed an exasperated major. A captain from one of the Massachusetts regiments agreed. "Any attempt to move forward from this crater was absolutely hopeless," he said. "To ask men to go forward in such a condition was useless. Each one felt as if he were to encounter the whole Confederate force alone and unsupported."[19]

Burnside's inspector general, Lieutenant Colonel Charles Loring, accompanied First Division during the assault and was present at the Crater. He described the chasm as "an obstacle of fearful magnitude," and noted, "The lines of the enemy were found to be of the most intricate nature. There was one uniform front line; then in the rear there were various lines, traverses between them, and bombproofs."[20] Loring realized that control of the division had been lost and that the collective will of the troops was to remain within the Crater. He scribbled a note for Burnside to that effect and handed it to a courier.

Given the circumstances, James H. Ledlie probably could have done little even if he were with his men in the Crater. But as First Division struggled to pull itself together under enemy fire, its commander was conspicuously absent. Shortly after the last of his regiments departed the Union trenches, Ledlie turned around and walked to a bombproof in the rear. The shelter had been converted into a makeshift aid station, and once inside Ledlie complained of being hit in the side by a spent minié ball. The general also said he was suffering from a touch of malaria. He asked the chief surgeon for "stimulants" and was given a shot of rum. Ledlie then called for General Bartlett, in order to turn command over to him, but was informed that Bartlett was in the Crater. The negligent commander of First Division would spend the entire day loitering in the rear.[21]

By 5:40 am, Meade's patience was wearing thin. Of course, he was aware that the mine had exploded nearly an hour ago, but he knew little else. Burnside never

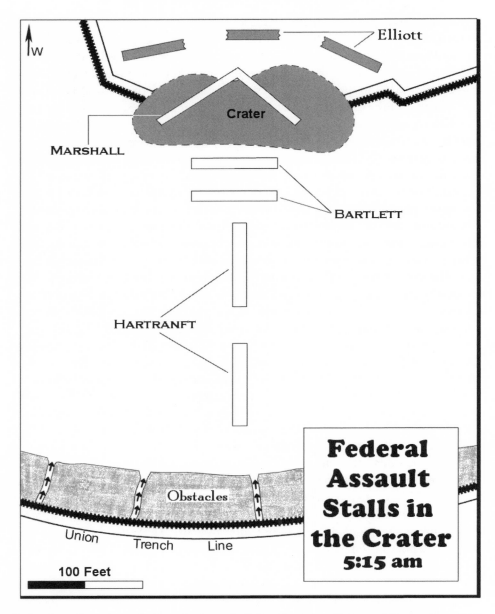

Federal earthworks and obstacles impeded the advancing Union soldiers, who subsequently became disorganized and bogged down in the Crater.

gave an explanation for the detonation's delay, and he had yet to send any updates on the progress of the attack. Unwilling to wait on Burnside any longer, Meade sent a succinct but polite message. "What news from your assaulting column?" he asked, then added, "Please report frequently." Burnside responded almost immediately: "We have the enemy's first line and occupy the breach. I shall endeavor to push forward to the crest as rapidly as possible."[22]

The report was troubling. Meade had stated repeatedly that Cemetery Hill must be taken with alacrity in order for the operation to succeed. Yet Burnside's reply suggested that Federal troops had not yet even attempted to storm the hill. Five minutes later, Colonel Loring's courier walked into the tent. The man was unaware that Burnside had moved to Taylor House for the battle, and rather than taking Loring's note there, he delivered it to Ninth Corps headquarters instead. Meade took the note, read it, and then showed it to Grant. Burnside's inspector general was reporting that First Division was hopelessly mired in the Crater. Only by sheer chance had Meade received this frank assessment, and he was going to act on it. He wired Burnside with orders to throw all remaining Ninth Corps troops toward the crest at once. He also told Burnside to have Ord send in the Eighteenth Corps.

7

Early Response

Colonel Fitz William McMaster of the 17th South Carolina was still assessing the damage caused by the blast when his brigade commander, General Stephen Elliott, arrived on the scene. Accompanying Elliott was Colonel Alexander Smith of the 26th South Carolina. To McMaster's surprise, Elliott immediately began making preparations for a counterattack. Granted, the South Carolina brigade was still adapting to Elliott's leadership style — he had only arrived in Petersburg recently from command of Fort Sumter — but to McMaster an immediate counterattack seemed "utterly impracticable."[1] A sudden, heavy loss had been inflicted on the brigade, and even those regiments that had been spared were in no condition to go on the offensive. McMaster felt that their top priority should be to organize a defense and prevent the Yankees from rushing through the breach to Petersburg. But he was not in charge; it was not his decision to make.

Elliott was busy explaining to his officers exactly what he wanted done. With great passion, the fiery young general leapt upon a mound of earth, pointing out precisely where the charge should be made. But within seconds, he fell to the ground writhing in pain. A minié ball had lodged in his left lung. With Elliott incapacitated, command of the brigade devolved to the most senior regimental commander: Colonel Fitz William McMaster. Elliott had barely been removed from the field when McMaster countermanded the order to charge. He was going to employ a defensive strategy.

For McMaster, the war to this point had been fraught with controversy, both on and off the battlefield. In 1862, he and another officer accused the notorious General Nathan Evans, then commanding the brigade, of drunkenness during battle. Evans retaliated viciously, several times arresting McMaster on exaggerated charges. When a court-martial cleared McMaster's name in March 1863, Evans went so far as to challenge him to a duel. But the rumors about Evans' indiscretions persisted, and eventually he was relieved of command for gross inefficiency and lax discipline. His successor lasted only a month before being captured in May 1864. Then came Stephen Elliott, who now lay critically wounded. Colonel McMaster surely would have preferred to ascend to command under better circumstances, but regardless he would not shy away from the opportunity now that it was here.

McMaster's first instinct on July 30 was to stretch a bandage across the gash in the Confederate line. "My apprehension was that the men in the Crater would rush down the hill westwardly and get in rear of my line in the ravine," he explained. "I ordered Colonel Smith, of the 26th, to take all of his men he could gather and immediately go down the ditch to General Elliott's headquarters, to go up this ravine and lie down, and if the enemy endeavored to rush down upon him to resist them. Smith's regiment being small, I detached three of my largest companies, under Captain Crawford, to cooperate with him, and my anxiety was very great until Smith's command got in position."[2] The entire detachment numbered only about 200 men.

With the remainder of his force, McMaster dug in behind the Crater. As he had anticipated, some Federals were starting to climb out of the pit and move into the trenches beyond. He said, "Many of the enemy jumped over the back part of the Crater, got into the rear ditch which communicated with the trench leading into Pegram's Salient and pressed me on my right flank. Nearly all of my two right companies were killed, wounded, and captured in the successive hand-to-hand fights we had here. Once, when my men retreated to the bend in the works next on their left, I was left between the enemy and my command."[3] Despite the heavy losses, the South Carolinians were holding their ground.

Major James Coit, commanding the Confederate artillery in the sector, gazed down upon McMaster's improvised defense admiringly. From his position on Cemetery Hill, Coit had an ideal view of the northernmost half of the battlefield. He praised the tenacity of the infantry below, adding that he witnessed only one tactical mistake. It happened when Smith's detachment briefly left the safety of their ravine and moved to the open ground beyond. Coit said, "The whole of this ground was swept by the enemy's artillery and musketry from their main line, not to speak of the fire from those within our works. No troops could stand a moment exposed to such a fire, and such as did not fall were immediately withdrawn." He added, "The saddest sight I saw was the wounded left in this exposed position appealing for help until they sank down in death. Any attempt to remove them would have been vain under that fire."[4]

Major Coit was among the first officers to arrive on the scene after the explosion. He had been awakened by a dull thud and the sensation of "being rocked in a cradle."[5] At the front, he quickly surmised that the artillery would need to help hold back the enemy until infantry reinforcements arrived. Coit sprinted to the four-gun battery of Captain Samuel Wright, located three hundred yards northwest of the Crater on Cemetery Hill. The battery had been placed on the hill so that it could reach Elliott's Salient by firing over the heads of the men in the trenches. Coit ordered a steady barrage of canister, which commenced roughly 25 minutes after the blast. For the remainder of the engagement, a deadly spray would greet the Federals as they crossed the field.

Five hundred yards behind the Crater, near the convergence of Jerusalem Plank and Baxter Roads, sat the Gee House. The abandoned two-story house was an unimpressive structure, but it would become the Confederate nerve center for the battle. P.G.T. Beauregard had yet to arrive, but the artillerists of Haskell's Battalion were already present and prepared. Major John Haskell had six Napoleons and 16 Coehorn mortars splayed around the house. The six cannon were stationed in front of the property, while an equal number of mortars stretched in a thin line along the Jerusalem Plank Road. The 10 remaining Coehorns were nestled in concealed positions between the Gee House and Elliott's Salient.

The Coehorn mortar was perfectly suited for trench warfare. At less than 300 pounds, the stubby bronze tube was inconspicuous and highly mobile. Three or four men could easily shuttle it between destinations by simply grasping the handles mounted on its wooden base and lifting. Despite its small size the Coehorn was a formidable weapon, capable of dropping 12-pound shells into enemy trenches at a considerable distance.

A pair of Haskell's mortars was situated in a hollow several hundred feet behind the Crater. The pieces were normally in the care of Lieutenant George Eggleston, but a day earlier Eggleston had been sent away on an errand by his commanding officer. For the first time, Eggleston's younger brother, Joseph, was placed in charge. Expecting a quiet and uneventful night, Joseph Eggleston went to sleep in his customary place — the unit's magazine. A heavy sleeper, the explosion did not even wake him, but within moments an anxious sergeant was standing over him with the report that "hell has broken loose." Eggleston collected himself and accompanied the sergeant forward. "The men, when I got out, showed panic on their faces," Eggleston recalled. "I saw that I must get their confidence, but how? I realized that I must seem calm and unconcerned."[6] He decided to climb atop the earthworks in full view of the enemy and coolly assess the situation:

> The dust and smoke were so dense that I could see nothing over towards the Crater but I decided that it would be criminal to fire that way as no one could distinguish the location of our own men fighting there. Standing there I decided to open on the different batteries in the enemy's line, the ranges of which we had perfectly, so that we could drop our shells on them in the dark. We had the range of ten of them for each of the two guns.[7]

A collection of artillery pieces from the Richmond Arsenal. In the foreground, a Coehorn mortar and a traditional siege mortar sit side-by-side. The small, lightweight Coehorn was a highly mobile and effective weapon (Library of Congress, Prints and Photographs Division LC-B811-7).

For good measure, Eggleston remained on the mound long enough to casually light his pipe before climbing down. He said that after this display of bravado, the men confidently went about their work with no sign of fear. The two mortars would keep up a steady fire all morning, cycling through targets in five-minute intervals. The other Coehorns scattered about the Confederate rear were active as well.

To the south of the Crater, all Confederate artillery remained silent. Only a single battery was capable of reaching the Crater or the field before it, and the crews of that battery were gone. Witnessing the gruesome fate of the cannoneers at Elliott's Salient, the crews had abandoned their posts for fear that a Yankee mine ran beneath them too. The battalion commander, Major Wade Gibbs, searched desperately for replacements and eventually assembled a crew of volunteers from other commands. Among the volunteers was a dust-covered private from Pegram's Battery who had miraculously survived the explosion. Ultimately, only one of the four Napoleons in the abandoned battery had an effective firing range on the Crater, the rest being out of position. But once the ad hoc crew got its lone gun into action, they added to the rapidly intensifying torrent sweeping the open field.

Gibbs' cannon caused particular aggravation for the Federal artillerists trying to silence it. The gun was thoroughly obscured by the stand of pine trees that Burnside had refused to cut down beforehand. The work crews that Burnside detailed to fell those trees once the battle began were making slow progress. General Gouverneur Warren of Fifth Corps could see the gun from his position in the Union line to the south. He notified Meade that the cannon was hindering Burnside's attack. But little could be done. Safe from Union artillery, the single gun continued its work as part of a lethal semicircle that poured canister and shell into the Crater area. Major Gibbs would eventually fall with a neck wound and be replaced by Captain Samuel Preston, an infantry commander with artillery experience. When Preston was hit with a minié ball above the eye, Captain David Walker stepped in to take his place. Both Gibbs and Preston would survive their wounds.

It was 6 am, an hour and a quarter after the explosion, and George Meade perceived that the chance for victory was slowly beginning to slip away. Reports from interrogated prisoners had filtered in, and they confirmed that most of the Confederate army was still north of the James River. Petersburg was ready to be taken, but Burnside must first push through the breach created by his mine. Trying to impress that urgency on Burnside, Meade wired the Ninth Corps commander: "Our chance is now; push your men forward at all hazards (white and black) and don't lose time in making formations, but rush for the crest."[8]

In fact, two of Ninth Corps' four divisions were already engaged. During the overnight hours, Robert Potter had mulled over Burnside's revised battle plan and saw absolutely no reason why his division could not attack at the same time as First Division. Potter's orders were to establish a defensive line north of Cemetery Hill to protect Ledlie's men from a counterattack. Why should he not begin executing that task immediately after the explosion? Around midnight, Potter called for one of his brigade commanders, General Simon Griffin. He told Griffin to deploy a skirmish line immediately following the blast. The skirmishers could give some protection to Ledlie's column as it advanced, Potter explained. They could also get a sense of how much opposition their division would face on the north. Potter said that if the skirmishers found little resistance, Griffin should move his entire brigade forward. (Weeks later, Potter would acknowledge that he had not been authorized to make this alteration in the plan, and had not even informed Burnside of it.)

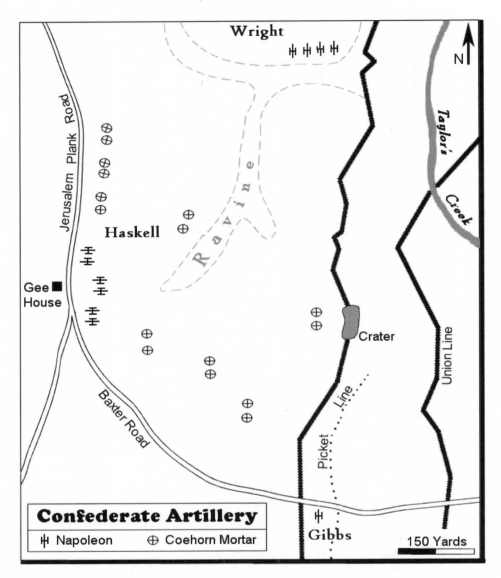

Confederate Artillery

⊩ Napoleon	⊕ Coehorn Mortar

The arrangement of Confederate artillery on July 30, 1864, enabled a steady bombard-ment of the Crater area from three sides.

Griffin assigned the skirmish duty to the 9th New Hampshire, which moved out immediately after the detonation, as ordered. The New Hampshire men encountered only light resistance, so Griffin brought the rest of his brigade onto the field. Unlike Ledlie's troops, they had little trouble climbing from their trenches and crossed the field in good order. Upon reaching the Confederate line, most of Griffin's regiments jumped into the trenches and passageways just north of the Crater, but two or three units landed inside the Crater itself. With this latter group was Lieutenant James Chase, the young Mainer, who was sickened by what he saw in the pit. "Beneath our feet were the torn fragments of men, while upon every side could be seen some portion of a man protruding from the sand," he said.[9]

Chase's colonel ordered the regiment out of the Crater and into an adjoining trench with the rest of the brigade. Some of Ledlie's troops followed as Griffin's brigade pushed northward through the trenches in the direction of Cemetery Hill. McMaster's Confederate defenders threw up barricades across the passageways to slow the Yankee advance. A maze of secondary traverses and bombproofs branched off from the main trench line, and the opposing forces became mixed in this labyrinth. One officer said, "There were so many angles and traverses there that in one there were Union troops while in the next there were Confederates. I saw myself the muskets of both sides almost crossed at the angles, while the men were obscured from each other."[10]

Eventually, a brief lull ensued after McMaster's men were overpowered and forced to fall back. Chase learned that his colonel had been shot during the melee; the bullet passed completely through the colonel and into the forearm of a nearby sergeant. Although the Confederate infantry had retreated, Griffin's brigade was being held in check by the Confederate artillery. From Cemetery Hill, Wright's Battery had turned its attention to the Federals trying to advance northward through the trenches. Small arms fire from Ransom's North Carolina brigade was also taking a heavy toll.

At the head of Griffin's brigade, Colonel Daniel White of the 31st Maine scrawled out a message for his commander: "General. We have taken the enemy's works and hold them. How are our lines doing on the right and left? We are much in advance and are getting short of ammunition. Quite a force of rebels on our right." White dispatched a runner to deliver the note to Griffin, who was farther back in line. Griffin wrote his reply on the reverse side of the paper: "We hold the fort, and are all right. Hold what you have gained. First division is now advancing. All looks well as far as we have gone."[11]

From the Union line, Potter could see that Griffin's advance through the enemy trenches had stalled. He told his other brigade commander, Colonel Zenas Bliss to send two of his regiments to support Griffin. These regiments, the 51st New York and the 2nd New York Mounted Rifles (dismounted), were ordered to dash across the field and jump into the Crater, then pivot right and sweep northward through the captured trenches. Potter hoped that by doing so they would build enough momentum to reach Wright's Battery, which he considered the linchpin to the Confederate defense. Simultaneously, Potter wanted Bliss to make a direct attack to the north with the rest of his brigade. The two-pronged assault would leave Potter with no reserve, but he knew that Confederate reinforcements would soon be on the way to plug up the hole in their line. Already, elements of the 25th and 49th North Carolina regiments were filing into the cavalier trench, substantially fortifying that barrier.

Bliss' two New York regiments followed their instructions precisely and, upon arriving at the Crater, began moving north through the enemy trenches. The New Yorkers worked quickly, mopping up pockets of Confederate resistance as they moved. But after advancing about 250 yards, they ran into a wall of blistering fire from the north. The New Yorkers stubbornly pushed ahead, drawing within 20 to 30 yards of Wright's Battery. But ultimately the canister and small arms fire became too severe to endure. Both regiments withered and fell back toward the Crater. Meanwhile, the remainder of Bliss' brigade also failed in its attack. Met by the same punishing fire from the north, those regiments drifted south as they charged across the field, with some ending up inside the Crater. Approximately 3,000 Federals were now crammed inside the 200-foot by 50-foot pit.

Regiments lost all organization upon entering the pandemonium of the Crater. New arrivals immediately became absorbed into the mass of confused soldiers, even as officers vainly tried to hold the formation together. Shouted orders could not be heard over the din, and those that were heard only confused the men further. "Every officer from colonel down to second lieutenant was giving orders of some kind, most of them being contradictory," said a frustrated captain from Massachusetts. For Captain Theodore Gregg of the 45th Pennsylvania, conflicting orders were thrown at him almost from the instant he arrived. First, General Bartlett told him to charge across the enemy's rear and capture the Gee House. Moments later, Gregg received instructions from Bliss to sweep down the trenches on his right. No sooner had these orders arrived than Griffin told him to attack on the left of the Crater. "I received so many orders from so many different commanders at that time that I did not know which to obey," Gregg exclaimed.[12]

Eventually, it was agreed by the senior officers present that Bliss' brigade, including the 45th Pennsylvania, should attack the Confederate battery in front of the Gee House, a quarter of a mile away. "The ground over which we were to charge was an open field," said one wary participant. "Fully in range of the enemy's fire, both musketry and artillery, it was easy to be seen that the task assigned us to perform was replete with difficulty and danger."[13] Not surprisingly, the ill-conceived charge was an utter failure. From such a great distance, the Confederate cannoneers had plenty of time to prepare. They loaded their guns with a double charge of canister, mercilessly peppering the Federal battle line as it came. Some regiments veered off to the right while others stayed the course, but eventually all were forced to retreat into the trenches behind the Crater.

Gregg and another captain from the 45th Pennsylvania, R.G. Richards, tumbled into a ditch with survivors from their regiment and also the 48th Massachusetts. Richards looked around and spotted a lieutenant he knew. The man's eye and a large portion of his face had been torn away by a shell fragment. Richards carefully wrapped the "ghastly wound" with his handkerchief and told the lieutenant to try for the Union lines. To Richards, the injury almost certainly seemed mortal, but the lieutenant somehow made it to the rear and managed to survive.[14]

Richards began exploring the traverse into which he and his comrades had stumbled. It was four feet wide, three feet deep, and branched off into many smaller passageways. As he was investigating, a Confederate major suddenly leapt from a side passage and leveled his pistol at Richards's chest. Both men stood frozen for an instant, unsure what to do next, when Captain Gregg sprang forward and grabbed the pistol. The major and two other Confederates were taken prisoner. Gregg and Richards realized that some other passageways were still occupied by the enemy as well. Recognizing that they would most likely be forced to remain here for some time and defend the position, Richards wrote a note requesting picks and shovels. He wrapped it around a stone and hurled it in the direction of the Crater. When no reply came, his men started digging an earthen barricade with their tin cups and bayonets.

Robert E. Lee was sitting down to breakfast at his headquarters on the north side of the Appomattox River when an aide from Beauregard's staff entered. The aide informed Lee that a mine explosion had decimated Elliott's Salient, and that the Yankees were attempting to break through to Petersburg. After hearing the scant details that were available, Lee told Colonel Charles Venable of his staff to ride to the headquarters of General William Mahone. Lee wanted Mahone to send two brigades from his division to halt the Federal advance. Normal military protocol called for Mahone's corps commander, A.P. Hill, to receive any orders first. But on this day there was no time for etiquette. Mahone's troops must begin moving without delay, Lee said. As Venable galloped away, Lee prepared to mount Traveller for the ride to Petersburg.

At five feet tall and 125 pounds, William Mahone was a strong personality wrapped in a small package. Known affectionately among his troops as "Little Billy," the 37-year-old Mahone was an alumnus of the Virginia Military Institute. Before the war, he was initially the chief engineer, and then later the president, of the Norfolk & Petersburg Railroad. Mahone's early attempts at leading men into battle produced mixed results, and his overbearing demeanor drew sharp criticism from his colleagues. The diminutive general also had an eccentric side, such as his preferred diet of nothing but fresh milk and eggs. Despite his shortcomings, by the summer of 1864, William Mahone had built a reputation as a steadfast leader and masterful tactician.

General William Mahone ascended to the command of a division in May 1864, following heavy fighting in the Wilderness. The five-foot-tall, 125-pound Virginian immediately proved his value, turning back Federal assaults at the North Anna River and Cold Harbor. At Petersburg, Robert E. Lee came to rely on him during the siege's most desperate moments (National Archives and Records Administration).

During the siege of Petersburg, Mahone's division was called upon to reinforce other portions of the line whenever threatened. On several occasions during the previous six weeks, the general had pulled some of his troops from their trenches to assist another command. The sight of Venable riding toward him, no doubt with orders from Lee, could therefore not have come as a surprise. Mahone had heard the explosion to the north and the fierce artillery duel that followed, but he knew little else of what was happening. His only clue came from a fleeing soldier who had sprinted past, wide-eyed. Mahone called to the "hatless and shoeless" man for an explanation. Without breaking stride, the soldier succinctly reported, "Hell has busted."[15]

Upon his arrival, Venable saluted and said to Mahone, "General Lee requests that you send two of the brigades of your division to the support of General Bushrod Johnson." Venable then described the situation. After a moment's thought, Mahone turned to the aide and said, "I can't send my brigades to General Johnson. I will go with them myself." Venable acknowledged the statement and sped off.[16]

Mahone's division held the extreme south of the Confederate army. His line of earthworks curved, like a comma, from Rives Salient southeast of Petersburg toward the Weldon Railroad due south of the city. Mahone chose his two most distant brigades for the job. These were the Virginia brigade, which Mahone himself commanded prior to being promoted, and his brigade of Georgians. The general knew that Federal spotters would be watching his line for signs of movement. If it appeared that units were being withdrawn to fight at the Crater, the Yankees may decide to attack. Accordingly, Mahone had the Virginians and Georgians leave their trenches a few men at a time, and then reassemble in a cornfield out of view. The men were told to shed their knapsacks and blanket rolls—an order confirming their suspicions that they were going into combat. Leaving the baggage in the care of two men on sick call, the column moved out on a circuitous route that would mask it from the enemy. Mahone stayed with the column for a short distance before riding ahead to the headquarters of General Johnson.

Bushrod Rust Johnson did little to distinguish himself on July 30, 1864, or at any other point in his military career. The Ohio native graduated in the middle of West Point's class of 1840. Seven years later, Johnson was forced to resign from the army due to accusations of bribery and smuggling. Afterward, he took teaching positions and became active in the Tennessee militia. A string of minor victories in 1862 and 1863 enabled Johnson to climb the chain of command, but he never displayed the inspired leadership of so many other Confederate generals. In fact, he was thought by many to be somewhat aloof and withdrawn. Years after the war, one of Johnson's subordinates at Petersburg spoke freely of his disdain for the general:

> He selected headquarters at a house in rear of the lines. It was tucked under the hill by the roadside, just north of Blandford Cemetery, and there he had remained, vegetative, without any friendly intercourse with his command, or communicating with it save through official channels. Seldom, if ever, was the man seen in the trenches; he was barely known by sight to his men; toward him they felt no affection, of his prowess they had no evidence, and in his ability they felt no confidence.[17]

William Mahone claimed that when he arrived at Johnson's headquarters on July 30, Johnson was unconcerned with the morning's events, and "appeared to be about ready to take his breakfast." Mahone asked him how far the enemy had penetrated, and Johnson said, "The retrenched cavalier." The reply meant nothing to Mahone. When he asked for clarification, Johnson ordered a lieutenant to show Mahone the way to Elliott's Salient. The lieutenant led Mahone along Jerusalem Plank Road until they reached a covered way that spilled into a ravine. Pointing to the top of the ravine, the lieutenant said, "If you will go up that slope there, you can see the Yankees." Mahone climbed the incline and said he could scarcely take in the reality of what he saw. The nearby trenches were "crammed with Federal soldiers and thickly studded with Federal flags." Mahone counted eleven flags within an area of less than 100 yards. Beyond that lay the Crater, the confines of which held an even greater number of Yankees. The general gave orders for his column to be brought into the ravine. He also sent for a third brigade.[18]

At 6:20 am, a signal officer posted near the southern terminus of the Union line detected movement on the Confederate side. Enemy soldiers were going to the rear of their line, he reported. An infantry column was then briefly seen traveling to the northwest. A short time later, another signal officer, Captain J.C. Paine, observed a northbound column from his station above the Ninth Corps line. He reported his observations directly to General Burnside. "The enemy are moving at least two brigades of infantry from their right," Paine said.[19] He sent another message moments later reporting that the Confederate column was moving at the double-quick. Despite all of Mahone's precautions, his force of Virginians and Georgians had been spotted. Whether the Union leadership would be able to use this information to its advantage was another matter entirely.

8

Charge of the USCT

Ambrose Burnside was struggling not only against a determined enemy, but against an agitated commanding officer as well. Meade's telegrams and hand-delivered dispatches began arriving at Burnside's command post before the battle had even commenced. Once it was underway, Meade's terse notes demanding information bombarded Taylor House like artillery fire. Many went unanswered, which only annoyed Meade further and spurred additional messages.

The cause of Burnside's failure to keep his superior informed on July 30, 1864 is unclear. Some modern historians have pointed to the absence of Burnside's long-time chief of staff, General John Parke, who suffered a relapse of malaria earlier in the month.[1] Parke had worked for Burnside since the beginning of the war, excepting those periods when he was ill, and no doubt Burnside could have used his services on July 30. John Parke's replacement, General Julius White, had assumed the job just one day earlier. White made no attempt whatsoever to answer Meade's inquiries on behalf of his boss.

As for Burnside himself, he later said that he thought one of Meade's aides was keeping the commanding general up to speed. The aide, a Captain Sanders, had been the liaison between Burnside and Meade during the opening assaults on Petersburg six weeks previous. Thus, when Captain Sanders appeared at Taylor House early on July 30, Burnside assumed it was for the same purpose.[2] Sanders did send Meade a series of short messages from Taylor House during the morning, but they were obviously based on Sanders' own observations, and not information relayed to him by Ambrose Burnside.

Compounding Meade's aggravation was the fact that when Burnside did respond, his messages seemed vague or simply irrelevant. Shortly after 6 am, in an attempt to elicit information, Meade asked if it would be an appropriate time to send the Fifth Corps reserve into the battle. Burnside's reply, which came a full 15 minutes later, said that the front line was currently too crowded to send in more troops, but it would be a good idea for Fifth Corps to assemble and get ready to move. Burnside then added the poorly chosen sentence: "I will designate to you when it ought to move."[3]

Meade's patience finally ran out. He frostily pointed out that the Fifth Corps troops had been assembled and ready for more than three hours. He then asked Burnside point blank:

> What is the delay in your column moving? Every minute is most precious, as the enemy undoubtedly are concentrating to meet you on the crest, and if you give them time enough you cannot expect to succeed. There is no object to be gained in occupying the enemy's line; it cannot be held under their artillery fire without much labor in turning it. The great point is to secure the crest at once, and at all hazards.[4]

Burnside was growing equally frustrated by Meade's grilling. With obvious exasperation he replied, "I am doing all in my power to push the troops forward, and, if possible, we will carry the crest. It is hard work, but we hope to accomplish it. I am fully alive to the importance of it."[5] Rather than mollifying Meade, the words merely fueled his rage. He shot back:

> What do you mean by hard work to take the crest? I understand not a man has advanced beyond the enemy's line which you occupied immediately after exploding the mine. Do you mean to say your officers and men will not obey your orders to advance? If not, what is the obstacle? I wish to know the truth, and desire an immediate answer.[6]

By all accounts, Ambrose Burnside was a well-mannered and agreeable man. Some who knew him doubted his battlefield skills, but nobody ever doubted his good nature. The latest message from Meade, which was placed directly in his hand by a courier, openly questioned Burnside's ability to lead men. It went straight to the heart of Burnside's nagging self-doubt, and it came at a time of great anxiety and pressure. Under different circumstances, and with more time to reflect, Burnside might have crafted a more diplomatic response to his commander. But at the moment, the best he could muster was:

> I do not mean to say that my officers and men will not obey my orders to advance. I mean to say that it is very hard to advance to the crest. I have never in any report said anything different from what I conceived to be the truth. Were it not insubordinate I would say that the latter remark of your note was unofficerlike and ungentlemanly.[7]

It was indeed insubordinate and Burnside had obviously said it. Meade answered by requesting a copy of the note he had previously sent by courier. The implication of this request was plain — Meade was collecting documentation for a court-martial.

8. Charge of the USCT

The 4,300 U.S. Colored Troops comprising Ninth Corps' Fourth Division were lying on the ground, watching the action from their position near Taylor House. Few details could be discerned from such a distance, but it was obvious that the three white divisions were engaged in a fierce struggle. The black soldiers had already piled their knapsacks and were ready to form up.

An hour after the explosion, Colonel Henry Thomas of Fourth Division was peering at the front when a voice called out behind him, "Who commands this brigade?" Thomas spun around to see Ulysses S. Grant on horseback. Jumping to his feet, Thomas replied, "I do." It appeared to Thomas that Grant was lost in thought. In the background, an aide and an orderly waited in silence. Thomas studied the commander of all Union forces with admiration. "He was in his usual dress: a broad-brimmed felt hat and the ordinary coat of a private. He wore no sword," Thomas recalled. At last, Grant said, "Well, why are you not in?" Pointing to the division's First Brigade, Thomas answered, "My orders are to follow that brigade." But feeling his response was somehow inadequate, Thomas added, "Will you give me the order to go in now?" Another moment passed before Grant said, "No, you may keep the orders you have," and then slowly rode away.[8]

Fifteen minutes after the encounter, Thomas received word to move into the covered way leading to the front. Following Joshua Sigfried's brigade, Thomas led his men into the six-foot-wide trench. At first, the black soldiers had enough room to sit, but soon the passageway became clogged with prisoners and wounded men going to the rear. "We stood there over an hour with this endless procession of wounded men passing," Thomas said. "There could be no greater strain on the nerves." Lieutenant Freeman Bowley noted that a few of the wounded men spoke words of encouragement as they passed the black troops. He also said that some Confederate prisoners expressed fear that the former slaves would bayonet them.[9]

The Southerners' anxiety was not completely unfounded. In the few instances that sizable USCT and Confederate forces had clashed previously, there were reports of atrocities on both sides. The most notorious of these events was the Fort Pillow Massacre, which occurred near Memphis, Tennessee only four months earlier. When Confederate troops under General Nathan Bedford Forrest overran the fort, they killed surrendering black and white soldiers alike, but two-thirds of the casualties were African-Americans. One week later at the Battle of Poison Spring, Arkansas, victorious Confederates refused to take black soldiers prisoner, opting instead to kill them in cold blood. Embellished accounts of actual atrocities spread throughout the North, inciting further outrage. USCT regiments adopted the battle cry "Remember Fort Pillow" and occasionally took revenge when the opportunity presented itself. On June 15, 1864, when Federal forces captured a portion of Petersburg's Dimmock Line, a detachment of black troops that took part in the attack reportedly bayoneted Southern prisoners until white officers intervened.

93

The 48th Pennsylvania in the Battle of the Crater

As Fourth Division stood waiting in the covered way, its commander, Edward Ferrero, took refuge inside James Ledlie's bombproof. Given the crowded conditions both in and around the Crater, Ferrero did not anticipate being able to advance his men anytime soon. Twice a courier entered the bombproof with orders from Burnside for Fourth Division to attack, and twice Ferrero sent the courier back with the message that there was no room for a charge. When a third note arrived from Burnside with peremptory instructions to attack at all costs, Ferrero left the bombproof to protest. Burnside's inspector general, Colonel Loring, was nearby and Ferrero showed him the orders. Since Loring had just come from the Crater, he was more aware than anyone of the awful circumstances there. "The order struck me as being so unfortunate that I took the liberty to countermand it on the spot," Loring said.[10] He then set out to find Burnside.

General Gouverneur K. Warren, commanding Fifth Corps, had watched events unfold from his portion of the Union line roughly 400 yards to the south. An engineer by trade, Warren had always viewed battles with a technical eye. At Gettysburg, his keen foresight had kept Little Round Top from falling into Confederate hands. But Warren's slow and methodical approach was not well suited for offensive operations. The unprecedented carnage at the Wilderness, Spotsylvania, and Cold Harbor made him even more hesitant and cautious. When Meade tried to coax Warren into attacking at 6:30 am on July 30, noting that signal officers had reported the Confederate earthworks in the south as only thinly occupied, Warren sent one of his officers on a lengthy reconnaissance mission. He then rode over to Burnside's command post for a consultation.

Smoke from the raging battle was obscuring the view from Taylor House, so when Warren arrived he and Burnside made their way down to the front line. The two generals were making plans for Fifth Corps to attack the lone Confederate gun wreaking havoc from the south when Colonel Loring approached. Loring felt confident that Burnside would agree to call off the attack by the USCT division. He said:

> I went up and represented to General Burnside that this colored division could not be expected to pass the lines of the old troops; that it was impossible to expect green troops to succeed where old troops had failed before them; and furthermore that, instead of accomplishing any good result, they would only throw into confusion the white troops that were already in that line and holding it. General Burnside did not reply to me, as he usually does to his staff officers, by stating his reasons for disagreeing with them, but simply repeated his previous order.[11]

Burnside would later say that he was acting on Meade's directive that all Ninth Corps troops be thrown into the fight. His hand had been forced and he no longer had any discretion in the matter, Burnside felt. Loring was dumbfounded by his commander's reaction. He returned to Ferrero and quietly explained that the order to charge stood. Meanwhile, Warren departed to prepare for his assault on the Confederate battery, but upon arriving at his headquarters he found a fresh set of telegrams waiting from Meade. He would spend the next hour exchanging messages about how to proceed. Twice Warren suggested that either Meade or his chief of staff come to the front and assess the situation firsthand, but those invitations went unanswered. Warren continued to dither. Ultimately, Fifth Corps would take no part whatsoever in the battle.

For better or for worse, Ninth Corps' Fourth Division was about to enter the fray. At the head of Ferrero's column stood the 30th USCT Regiment. Upon receiving the order to charge, the officers and men of the regiment began crawling over the Union earthworks. Lieutenant Freeman Bowley was among them. He barely reached the open field before hearing the distinctive sound of grapeshot. The iron balls made a whooshing sound as they hurtled past. Bowley turned to his right and saw a gap in his company where six men had been. He implored his soldiers to close ranks and keep moving forward. Another blast tore into the unit's color guard, instantly felling half of them. Bowley watched as a corporal took a blood-spattered flag from the hands of the color sergeant, whose head had been ripped open by a ball.

Leading the 30th USCT was a young colonel from New York named Delevan Bates. Colonel Bates later said that he was never entirely certain what he and his men were expected to do once they reached the Crater, but he was determined to accomplish something. With the rest of the brigade following, Bates and his regiment plunged headlong into the Crater. They rapidly passed through the teeming mass inside and emerged on the far side. Only one regiment became ensnared in the bedlam of the Crater, while the rest advanced into the trenches beyond.

In their inexperience and excitement, the black soldiers fired upon the first troops they came across, which happened to be men from Potter's division. A captain from the 9th New Hampshire jumped upon a parapet and frenetically waved a U.S. flag until the friendly fire ceased. Quickly recovering from the incident, Bates led his men 100 yards north and, after passing through a heavy line of abatis, the 30th and 39th USCT sprinted toward the cavalier trench. The shallow ditch was the last physical barrier before Cemetery Hill.

The mix of Virginians and Carolinians in the cavalier trench spotted the two Federal regiments coming and prepared for the onslaught. As he drew closer, Lieutenant Bowley said he saw the Southerners "bending on one knee, braced and ready to receive us on the bayonet's point."[12] Regardless, the USCT regiments swept into the trench and quickly overwhelmed its defenders, taking roughly 150 prisoners in the process. A cheer went up as the black soldiers celebrated their first victory. To their left, elements from a white regiment moved up to link with them and create some semblance of a cohesive battle line.

It had taken half an hour for the first USCT brigade to vacate the covered way behind the Union line. Accordingly, it was approximately 7:30 am before Colonel Thomas led his brigade over the earthworks and onto the field. Thomas and his men faced the same hail of fire that previous formations had endured as they charged across the open ground. Upon reaching the other side, Thomas decided not to take his column into the Crater as Bates had done. "The crater was already too full; that I could easily see," Thomas explained. "I swung my column to the right and charged over the enemy's rifle-pits connecting with the crater on our right. These pits were different from any in our lines—a labyrinth of bomb-proofs and magazines with passages between."[13] Every regiment of the brigade followed except one. The 19th USCT, which had been the last in line, huddled behind the Crater's rim and could not be moved. The rest of the column spread out in the trenches and traverses north of the Crater, joining the white regiments already there.

A steady artillery barrage coming from Cemetery Hill and Jerusalem Plank Road, combined with heavy musket fire from the Carolinians in the north, stifled all Federal attempts to move beyond the trenches. As in the Crater, the mingling of units within these narrow passageways rendered the chain of command practically useless. Individual officers gathered as many men as they could and made piecemeal efforts to advance.

In the cavalier trench, Delevan Bates was attempting to restore order among his men when a staff officer approached him. "Colonel Bates, a charge must be made on Cemetery Hill at once," the man shouted. It seemed futile, but Bates obeyed the order nonetheless. With as many troops as he could muster, the colonel climbed from the ditch. "How far we went I do not know, for a volley from our front and right disabled about one-half of our officers and one-third of the privates," he recalled. The next volley contained a bullet for him. Bates said, "An ounce of lead struck me just in front of the right ear, passed above the roof of my mouth, and came out close behind the left ear." As several men bravely helped him back to the Federal line, a dazed Bates marveled at how his wound had yet to produce any pain.[14]

Henry Thomas' brigade was not faring much better. Any endeavor to advance ended quickly and violently, and with each attempt the resolve of the men grew weaker. One of Thomas's aides, Lieutenant Christopher Pennell of Massachusetts, tried to rally the brigade. Grabbing a fallen flag, the daring young officer jumped from the trench and ran alongside. With the flag in his left hand and an upraised sword in his right, Pennell implored the brigade's men to follow him. But they merely looked on in horror as a flurry of bullets struck the lieutenant. Pennell's

Orlando B. Willcox was wounded and captured at the First Battle of Bull Run in July 1861. The Michigan native spent more than a year in Confederate custody before being returned in a prisoner exchange. Willcox was then promoted from colonel to brigadier general and given command of a division in Ninth Corps.

body whirled spastically with each impact until he finally fell dead. After the battle, Thomas would search for the body of his intrepid aide, but never find it.

Like the two divisions that had gone before it, Fourth Division had achieved some initial success that quickly evaporated under blistering flanking fire by Confederate artillery and infantry. Over three hours had passed since the mine explosion, and upward of 10,000 men from Burnside's Ninth Corps were jammed inside and around the Crater. They had been soundly denied any further gains in both the north and the west. It was time to try in the south.

Orlando Willcox's division was scheduled to immediately follow Ledlie's men forward after the explosion, and his first brigade had done exactly that. Commanded by General John Hartranft, the first brigade advanced promptly but was forced to halt on the open field while Ledlie's troops paused ahead at the Crater. Hartranft's exposed column stretched the entire length of the field, from the Crater's rim all the way back to the Union line. When the Confederate fire escalated, these men pushed their way forward and landed inside the Crater with Ledlie's troops, adding to the chaos there. Willcox's second brigade therefore remained in the foremost Union trenches, just south of the covered way, waiting for the knot of humanity to untangle.

As the hours passed, it became evident that the situation inside the Crater was not going to improve, and Willcox began looking for alternatives. At 8:12 am, he ordered Second Brigade to attack the Confederate line due south of the Crater. Just as Robert Potter had swept northward through the enemy trenches in a bid to silence Wright's Battery, Willcox was going to try to overrun the single Confederate cannon that was firing from the south. But Potter's attempt had been made hours earlier, before the Confederates had rallied from the explosion, and still it had failed. Willcox's men would have to negotiate a firestorm of lead before making their attempt.

Second Brigade consisted of seven mostly depleted regiments under the command of Colonel William Humphrey. Three veteran regiments hailed from the Wolverine State: the 1st Michigan Sharpshooters, the 2nd Michigan Infantry, and Colonel Byron Cutcheon's 20th Michigan. The 1st and 20th regiments had seen such hard service that by July 30, 1864, they numbered just 100 and 125 men respectively. Humphrey kept the trio of Michigan units together in formation, and to their left he placed the 46th New York and the 50th Pennsylvania. Since the enemy's fire would come primarily from the south, these latter two regiments would bear the brunt of it. Accordingly, Humphrey bolstered his left with the 60th Ohio and the 24th New York Cavalry (dismounted).

Colonel Cutcheon said that upon emerging from the earthworks, his regiment instantly received a heavy blast of canister. Several men fell to the ground dead or wounded, but Cutcheon noted with great pride that the rest "rushed forward without faltering, through a storm of bullets that hissed around them." The two other Michigan regiments also persevered, but the remainder of the brigade was wavering. As anticipated, the 46th New York and the 50th Pennsylvania were feeling the hottest portion of the Confederate fury. The lone cannon near Baxter Road was pouring canister into their ranks mercilessly. About halfway across the field, the New Yorkers and Pennsylvanians reached their limit. They broke and ran for the Federal lines, taking the 60th Ohio and 24th New York with them.

The few hundred Michigan men who successfully ran the gantlet had to pull apart a thick row of abatis before entering the Confederate earthworks. Once inside, they rapidly secured the trenches south of the Crater for a distance of about 150 yards, capturing two officers and several dozen enlisted men in the process. But their numbers were too small to accomplish anything more. Colonel Cutcheon said, "We lay here partly within and partly outside the breastworks for some time — it is impossible to estimate the time — perhaps half an hour."[15] As the Confederate artillery and musketry concentrated on their position, the Michigan men gradually withdrew into the Crater.

Ninth Corps was now fully engaged in the battle. It controlled the Crater and most of the surrounding trenches, but the general officers present knew that to press farther ahead was impossible. Their attention shifted from capturing Cemetery Hill to simply holding the ground they had already gained. Organizing a defense would not be easy. The partitioned nature of the trenches and the Crater's jagged interior hampered effective communication, and order among the men was nearly nonexistent. Few units were operating beyond company size, and in many instances not even that. The specter of an enemy counterattack no doubt loomed large in every man's head.

Lieutenant James Chase, the 17-year-old Mainer, decided to scale a pile of debris to see what was happening beyond his pit. As Chase reached the top, he glimpsed a deep ravine rapidly filling with gray-clad soldiers. He began to climb down from the heap in order to report this information to his captain, when Chase's world suddenly went dark. "Evidently I had been hit by a sharpshooter from a pine grove on our left," he said. "The bullet struck me near the left temple and came out through the nose at the inner corner of the right eye, throwing out the left eye in its course." Chase staggered across the trench and sat down. His comrades sorrowfully told him the truth: the wound appeared to be fatal. Chase found he could still see from his right eye, and he asked for a mirror. The reflected image seemed completely foreign to him. "My face was swollen to an enormous size," he said. "I was bleeding from my wound rapidly, which I saw was a fearful looking sight; my left eye lay upon my cheek, while my nose appeared to be shot off."[16]

Chase had resigned himself to dying when his captain approached. After calming the boy with some reassuring words and a shot of whiskey, the captain went to work on his wound. "By the aid of a penknife he now extracted some loose pieces of bones projecting from my nose into my remaining eye," Chase explained. The captain then ordered two men to take Chase to the rear. Upon being tightly wrapped in a blanket, he was carried, and sometimes dragged, across the open field as bullets buzzed past. The two men loaded Chase into an ambulance wagon and after a short but painful ride he was deposited on the ground outside a field hospital. He was not attended to until after nightfall. Chase suffered from his wound for years afterward, and at age 25 he lost the vision in his remaining eye.[17]

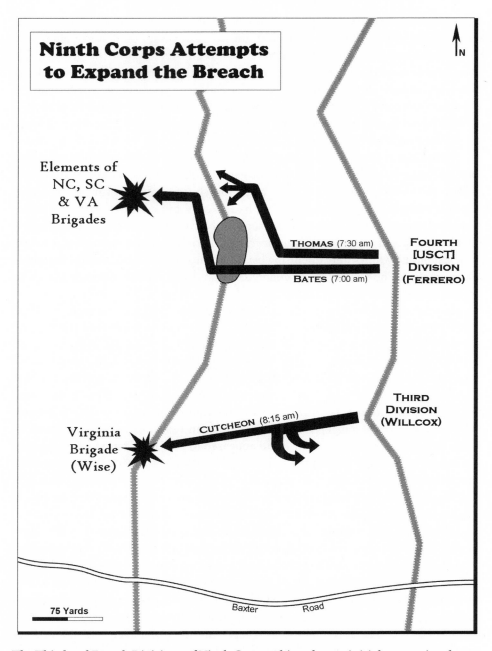

Ninth Corps Attempts to Expand the Breach

N

Elements of NC, SC & VA Brigades

THOMAS (7:30 am)

BATES (7:00 am)

FOURTH [USCT] DIVISION (FERRERO)

THIRD DIVISION (WILLCOX)

CUTCHEON (8:15 am)

Virginia Brigade (Wise)

75 Yards

Baxter Road

The Third and Fourth Divisions of Ninth Corps achieved some initial success in advancing the Union assault beyond the Crater.

8. Charge of the USCT

The Confederates whom Chase spied before being shot belonged to William Mahone's division. His Virginia brigade had passed through the covered way leading from Jerusalem Plank Road and was assembling in the ravine. Mahone stood where the covered way and ravine intersected, nodding and speaking words of encouragement to the Virginians as they filed past.

The soldiers' appearance heartened the artillerists of Wright's Battery, who were still working their guns feverishly above the covered way. "For the first time during the day, a line of infantry was between our guns and the enemy," an officer said. "The boys at the guns, knowing what reliance could be placed upon Mahone's veterans, took new heart and new courage, and pounded away with redoubled energy."[18]

The 800 Virginians formed a battle line inside the ravine and were told to fix bayonets. Mahone's aides passed the word that each man should hold his fire until reaching the trenches, and then fire into the Yankees at point-blank range. Each of the regimental commanders then stepped to the front and addressed his troops. A soldier of the 12th Virginia was so inspired by his commander's speech that years later he could recount it verbatim:

> Men, you are called upon to charge and recapture our works, now in the hands of the enemy. They are only about one hundred yards distant. The enemy can fire but one volley before the works are reached. At the command "forward" every man is expected to rise and move forward at a double quick and with a yell. Every man is expected to do his duty.[19]

For many who listened, the rousing speeches were unnecessary. They had been born and raised in the Petersburg area, so this battle, unlike any other, was personal. These men were defending more than just political ideals and heartfelt notions of right and wrong. They were defending their homes and families. Undoubtedly, the war had an urgent new meaning for them, and it motivated them more than any speech ever could. So when some tattered survivors from the USCT assault on the cavalier trench trudged by, and informed the Virginians of what had transpired during the morning, it made their blood boil. "I never felt more like fighting in my life," an officer from the 61st Virginia declared. "Our comrades had been slaughtered in a most inhuman and brutal manner, and slaves were trampling over their mangled and bleeding corpses."[20]

The Virginians would have to wait before taking their revenge. Mahone wanted his Georgia brigade to accompany them on the charge. That brigade was still filing through the covered way and getting into position behind the Virginians. The delay was taking a toll in the form of casualties. Although the men were laying prone on the ground and hidden from the Union artillery, stray shell fragments were finding their way into the ravine. Further, Federal sharpshooters perched on the Crater's

101

rim had a narrow firing lane into the depression and were occasionally finding their mark. "Every minute or two there was a call for the ambulance corps to take off a wounded man, and the situation was becoming critical," said a soldier from the 12th Virginia.[21]

The Georgia brigade still was not in place when a number of Virginians noticed a Federal officer emerge from the nearest trench. He appeared to be leading a charge directly toward the ravine. Colonel George Rogers, commanding the 6th Virginia, saw the man and was immediately concerned. Rogers said, "He seized his colors, sprang over the protecting ditch, and by every gesticulation showed the way to the front — and perhaps to victory."[22] There was no more time to wait for the Georgians.

9

Confederate Counterstrike

The Federal officer whom the Virginians saw was Lieutenant Colonel John Bross, commander of the 29th USCT Regiment, and he was indeed rallying his men for a charge. Bross's superior officer, Henry Thomas, had recently received a message from General Ferrero. From the safety of the Union lines, Ferrero wrote to his brigade commanders: "Colonels Sigfried and Thomas, if you have not already done so, you will immediately proceed to take the crest in your front."[1] Given the current state of affairs, the order seemed like sheer folly to Thomas, but he was obligated to obey it. He called his regimental commanders together and told them to do the best that they could. Bross volunteered to lead the attack.

The USCT officer corps consisted largely of skilled and dedicated men. Black soldiers were forced to tolerate inequities in pay, supplies, and medical care, but most often their leadership equaled or surpassed that of other units. The white officers who led USCT troops were usually seasoned veterans who had completed rigorous testing in order to obtain their positions. In some instances, their only goal in volunteering for USCT service was a promotion. But for most, it represented a unique challenge and an opportunity to lead men. Confederate Congress inadvertently added an extra deterrent that weeded out the slackers. In 1863, it decreed that white officers captured while leading black troops would be summarily executed for inciting servile insurrection.

History has preserved sparingly few details about John A. Bross of Illinois, but based on his actions of July 30, 1864, he stood out even among the USCT officers as a man of exceptional valor and principle. Despite the extreme heat and rigors of combat, Bross was dressed meticulously in full uniform that day. Colonel Thomas supposed that it was intended to inspire the men. Captain Robert Beecham of the 23rd USCT was stirred by Bross' poise and confidence. "He passed along our front, carrying his regimental colors, notifying the brigade that he would lead the charge in person, and giving the order for us to follow," Beecham remembered. "While I admired his lofty courage and resolved to follow his lead and do my utmost to make his daring effort a success, the thought — the conviction — was stamped upon my brain: 'It is utter madness. That grand man will throw his life into the breach and death and defeat will be our reward.'"[2]

Before mounting the earthwork, Bross made a final emotional appeal. "Boys, I want you to follow this flag," he cried. "I am going to lead you to victory. We'll show the world today that the colored troops are soldiers."[3] A handful of white soldiers from Potter's shattered division were mixed in among the USCT regiments. They also shouldered down the trenches to join the charge.

In the ravine, some of the Virginians who spotted Bross and his men bounding over the breastwork panicked and opened fire, despite their orders to the contrary. Precisely what happened next has never been factually established, and afterward the exact chain of events would become a matter of fierce debate among the Southerners who were present. At the heart of the controversy was the question of which Confederate officer gave the order to charge. For many years after the war, the debate played itself out in personal correspondence, magazine articles, and dozens of letters to the editors of Virginia newspapers. The main adversaries in the dispute were General William Mahone and Colonel David Weisiger, the commander of the Virginia brigade. Both men claimed that they issued the order to charge.

According to General Mahone, he gave the order after an aide notified him that the Yankees were attacking. Mahone was still standing at the intersection of the covered way and the ravine, watching the Georgia brigade enter. He could not see the battlefield from his position. One of his staff officers, Captain Jean Baptiste Girardey, was farther up in the ravine and saw Bross. Girardey, who was born in France but raised in Augusta, Georgia, and went by the first name Victor, was one of Mahone's most trusted aides. When Bross appeared on the rampart, Girardey yelled to Mahone, "General, they are coming!" Without hesitation Mahone shouted back, "Tell Weisiger to forward!" Mahone claimed that Captain Girardey instead lifted his sword and bellowed the command "forward," at which point the entire brigade rushed from the ravine.[4]

Colonel Weisiger contended that he had independently decided to advance his brigade in order to preempt the Federal attack. He admitted that Mahone initially told him to wait for the Georgians, but in Weisiger's estimation the Yankees would overrun the ravine before that could occur. In a letter to Mahone after the war, Weisiger said:

> I discovered that the enemy were preparing to charge me, as an officer with a stand of colors in hand sprung from the works and commenced the formation of a line of battle in my immediate front. I repeated my orders to Captain Girardey, pointed out the movement of the enemy, and suggested the propriety of charging at once, if not all would be lost. He

replied that he was directed to prolong my line to the right with the Georgia brigade and send us in together. Perceiving the rapidity with which the enemy was forming, and the imminent danger of being overrun before the Georgians could arrive on the field, Captain Girardey assented to my views. I therefore requested him to state my reasons to you for so doing, and immediately charged with my brigade....[5]

Weisiger's former aide-de-camp, Drury Hinton, corroborated the colonel's version. Hinton said he was standing with both Weisiger and Girardey when the Yankees appeared. "Just at this moment a magnificent looking Federal officer stepped out from our works, and as we could perceive by his gesticulations, was calling upon his men to form in line preparatory to a charge," Hinton recalled. "At this juncture Colonel Weisiger said to Girardey, 'Captain, had I not better go in *now*?' 'No,' said Girardey, 'General Mahone desires to annex Wright's Brigade on to you and send you in together.' A few moments later, however, Captain Girardey authorized him to charge. Colonel Weisiger then gave the word 'forward!' which was immediately communicated along down the line, and with one impulse, as it seemed to me, the whole brigade sprang forward and rushed up the hill, making the most brilliant and orderly charge I ever had the opportunity to witness."[6]

The recollections of other officers and enlisted men varied. Some agreed with Mahone and others with Weisiger, while still others said they never heard the order to charge at all. The soldier next in line began moving and they simply followed. The only man who could definitively settle the issue did not live long enough to tell his story. Victor Girardey would survive the Battle of the Crater, only to be killed in action days later. Regardless of who actually issued the order, the Virginia brigade was now free to exact its revenge.

For the inexperienced USCT troops who followed Colonel Bross over the breastworks, the sight of 800 screaming Virginians charging toward them was more than they could handle. "Their line extended beyond our right —flanking us— and to the left as far as we could see," said Lieutenant Freeman Bowley. "Company A was promptly faced to protect our right flank, and the men opened fire; but the volley was but a hurried, irregular one, and hardly a man fell from the Rebel ranks." Colonel Bross was shot and killed, at which point a frantic retreat began. The lead USCT regiments turned and the entire column collapsed back into the trenches. Then the Virginians arrived. A private in the 49th North Carolina watched their counterattack with satisfaction. He said, "They dashed up to the works, fired one volley, and sprang in among the Federals, using the butts of their guns and the bayonet. They spared the white men as best they could, but Negro skulls cracked under the blows like eggshells."[7]

Among the Confederate storming party was Private George Bernard of the 12th Virginia. Bernard was a 27-year-old Petersburg attorney. He had joined the army in the spring of 1861 but was required to take several leaves of absence due to illness. Bernard was an intelligent and articulate man who, despite his many sabbaticals, had witnessed the horrors of Chancellorsville, Gettysburg, and Cold Harbor, among other battles. Yet he was unprepared for the sheer brutality he was about to see.

Bernard's regiment was the last in line of battle, and as a result it had been the least exposed to enemy fire during the charge. Arriving at the trenches, Bernard found a black soldier lying prone in surrender. "He was the first colored soldier I ever saw, and this was my first knowledge of the fact that Negro troops were before us," Bernard explained. "I had not then fired my rifle, and I might easily have killed this man, but regarding him as a prisoner, I had no disposition to hurt him."[8] But other Virginians were far less benevolent. Bernard watched in dismay as many of his comrades clubbed, shot, and stabbed surrendering blacks. He described one such incident in detail:

> Just about the outer end of the ditch by which I had entered stood a
> Negro soldier — a non-commissioned officer (I noticed distinctly his
> chevrons) — begging for his life of two Confederate soldiers, who stood by
> him, one of them striking the poor wretch with a steel ramrod, the other
> holding a gun in his hand with which he seemed to be trying to get a shot
> at the Negro. The man with the gun fired it at the Negro, but did not
> seem to seriously injure him, as he only clapped his hand to his hip,
> where he appeared to have been shot, and continued to beg for his life.
> The man with the ramrod continued to strike the Negro therewith, whilst
> the fellow with the gun deliberately reloaded it, and placing its muzzle
> close against the stomach of the poor Negro, fired, at which the latter fell
> limp and lifeless at the feet of the two Confederates.[9]

The USCT retreat quickly turned into pandemonium. Fleeing for their lives, the black soldiers frantically pushed down through the trenches toward the Crater. Each passageway became so tightly packed with pressing bodies that it was impossible for a man to even raise his arms. Other Ninth Corps soldiers still fighting from those traverses were swept along in the rush of humanity. "If the black troops were brave in their charge, they were wild with terror, and, as a body, unmanageable in their defeat," Lieutenant Bowley said.[10] The retreat continued to snowball, rapidly gathering more men as it went. Upon reaching the Crater, it achieved stampede-like proportions as thousands bolted for the Union lines. General John Hartranft, the ranking officer present in the Crater, hastily assembled some veteran troops in an attempt to check the stampede. The thin little line of veterans, which included Colonel Cutcheon and his 20th Michigan, soon discovered that their task was tantamount to holding back the ocean. A wave of Union blue broke over them on its way out of the Crater and across the field.

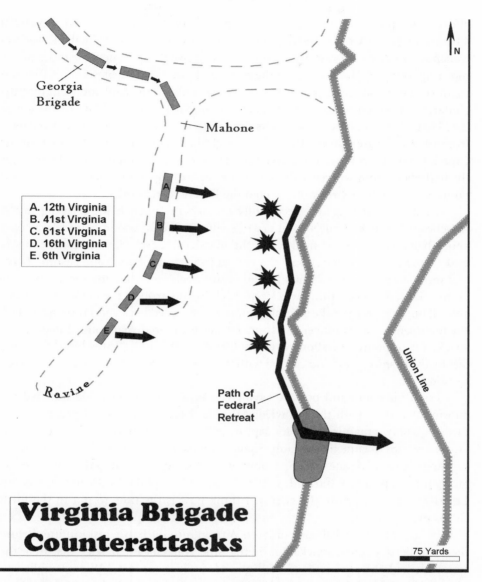

A. 12th Virginia
B. 41st Virginia
C. 61st Virginia
D. 16th Virginia
E. 6th Virginia

Georgia Brigade

Mahone

Ravine

Path of Federal Retreat

Union Line

N

75 Yards

Virginia Brigade Counterattacks

The counterattack by Mahone's Virginia brigade touched off a massive Federal retreat and shifted momentum in favor of the Confederacy.

Moments earlier, in the Federal line, General John Turner was attempting to send a second brigade of his troops into action. Turner's Tenth Corps division was temporarily attached to Eighteenth Corps under Ord. Unlike the other reserve units assigned to the engagement, Turner and his men were making a bona fide effort to support Ninth Corps. It was not easy work. The slow and piecemeal advance of Ninth Corps, starting with Ledlie's division, meant that the Federal trenches and covered ways were continually crowded with men for most of the morning, trapping the reserves in the rear. At about 7 am, Turner left his division to move ahead and scout out the battlefield. He crossed the field and went into the Crater, thus becoming the only division commander who would do so the entire day. He realized that a diversion was needed to draw the enemy's attention away from the Crater area, so he decided to attack the Confederate works north of the Crater. Upon returning to the Union line, Turner arranged for his brigades to enter the battlefield from wherever there was the slightest opening, including a narrow point where Taylor's Creek intersected the Federal earthworks.

Turner's first brigade successfully crossed the open field, arriving in the trenches prior to Mahone's counterstrike. But Turner's second brigade was only about halfway across the field when the massive Federal flight commenced. He said, "Looking to the left, I saw the troops in vast numbers come rushing back, and immediately my whole first brigade came back, and then my second brigade on my right, and everything was swept back in and around the crater, and probably all but one-third of the original number stampeded back right into our lines." An Eighteenth Corps officer assisting Turner estimated that some 2,000 panic-stricken men poured headlong over the Union earthworks. "I was lifted from my feet by the rushing mass and carried with it ten or fifteen yards in the covered way," he said.[11]

From his command post at Taylor House, Ambrose Burnside watched the enormous retreat with the knowledge that he had, in essence, played all of his cards. His only remaining hope for capturing Petersburg would be if Meade ordered Warren or Ord to launch an assault. Signal stations in the south continued to report sightings of Confederate columns moving northward, suggesting that Warren was facing little opposition. Burnside wired Meade, "Many of the Ninth and Eighteenth Corps are retiring before the enemy. I think now is the time to put in the Fifth Corps promptly."[12]

In fact, Meade had already ordered Warren into the battle just minutes before the Virginians' counterattack. But by the time Warren saw Meade's dispatch, the stampede had already occurred. "All our advantages are lost," Warren replied to Meade. The Fifth Corps commander went on to describe a bleak tactical situation which offered no further opportunities for gain. The appraisal corresponded with other incoming reports of the repulse. Meade was no doubt baffled and frustrated. He had stressed to Burnside from the outset that capturing Cemetery Hill quickly was the key to success. Yet after three and a half hours of trying, Ninth Corps was not even close to achieving that goal. The plan was a failure and Meade would waste no more men on it. He conferred with Grant, who had been to the front and personally witnessed the retreat. At 9:25 am, Meade suspended all offensive operations.

Burnside was infuriated by the order to withdraw his men. From his perspective, there was still much to be gained. Despite the rout, a sizable Federal force remained inside the Crater and in the adjacent trenches to the south. If Cemetery Hill could no longer be taken, then at least the captured ground could be held and incorporated into the Federal line. Burnside mounted his horse and left Taylor House to confront Meade.

A crimson-faced Ambrose Burnside stormed into Ninth Corps headquarters and immediately began jawing at Meade. Equally enraged, Meade fired back at his subordinate. The turbulent relationship between these two men had reached its nadir, and the sting of defeat intensified their emotions as they blamed each other for the day's setbacks. Those present were startled by Burnside's sudden transformation into a raving madman. An aide said, "Both of these officers lost their tempers that morning, although Burnside was usually the personification of amiability, and the scene between them was decidedly peppery, and went far toward confirming one's belief in the wealth of the English language as a medium of personal dispute."[13]

When the shouting finally subsided, a tense debate ensued about the best course of action. Burnside argued that victory was still attainable. His Ninth Corps had punched a significant hole in the Confederate line and currently occupied over 200 yards of it. If the hefty reserve forces that had been assembled for this engagement were utilized, Cemetery Hill could still possibly be taken.

After listening to Burnside's appeal, Meade turned to Edward Ord, who had entered the tent shortly after Burnside. Meade asked Ord if an assault by his Eighteenth Corps, or by Warren's Fifth Corps, would have any useful effect. Ord had spent much of the morning at the front, and had received a thorough description from General Turner of the chaos transpiring in and around the Crater. Ord replied that, in his opinion, such an assault could do no further good. Meade then asked Grant, who was preparing to depart for City Point, if he wished to countermand the order to withdraw. When Grant said no, there was little more Burnside could do. He left in the same fury as when he had arrived.

Outside the tent, Burnside vented his anger on Ord. "You have 15,000 men concentrated on one point," he snapped. "It is strange you cannot do something with them." Ord was a career soldier and he deeply resented being blamed for a mess that was not his making. Throwing his arms into the air, the 29-year army veteran shot back, "You can fight if you have an opportunity; but, if you are held by the throat, how can you do anything?"[14]

The Virginians' charge may have been successful, but it exacted a heavy toll from them. Casualties were incurred both during the dash to the earthworks and in the hand-to-hand combat that followed. Of the roughly 100 men from the 6th Virginia who made the charge, 80 were killed or wounded. Company K of that regiment had only one man come through the ordeal unharmed. The 16th Virginia lost half its number. In the brigade's battalion of sharpshooters, 64 of 80 men fell dead or wounded, including nine officers. The sharpshooters' commander, Captain William Broadbent, was found dead with 11 bayonet wounds in his body. So great was the carnage that an inordinate number of corpses, both blue and gray, filled the trenches and prevented passage. Officers organized details to remove the scores of bodies. A company commander in the 12th Virginia recalled, "We had orders to throw the dead out of the works, which we did, so as to get standing room. We dragged them out with gun slings around their necks, and four of our men would lift them. Others were rolled over the works toward the enemy."[15]

Among the Confederate casualties was the brigade's commander, Colonel Weisiger, who was wounded some time after the charge, and had to be helped from the field. On his way to the rear, Weisiger passed General P.G.T. Beauregard and his staff. With deep sincerity, one of Beauregard's aides approached and said, "Colonel, you all have covered yourselves with glory." In typical dramatic fashion, Beauregard endorsed his aide's compliment with a deep bow.[16]

Command of the brigade fell to Colonel George Rogers of the 6th Virginia. Rogers said that the Pyrrhic victory left he and his fellow Virginians in a tenuous position:

> The brigade for the moment was in great confusion; our loss in the charge
> had been very heavy; the work of death was yet rife in the trenches, and
> our men were suffering terribly from an enfilade fire, poured from the
> crater proper that projected far into the rear of our line, as well as from
> the fire of the main line of battle of the enemy.[17]

The thousands of Federals still remaining inside the Crater outnumbered the depleted Virginia brigade by a ratio of nearly 10 to one. If just a fraction of the Union force somehow managed to organize for a push into the trenches, they would almost certainly succeed. Mahone had originally hoped to drive all of the Yankees back to their line with one crushing blow, but the sudden appearance of Colonel Bross necessitated a change of plans. The job would now have to be done in stages. The Virginians had purged most of the trenches north and west of the Crater. Next he would call on his Georgia brigade to clear out the trenches to the south. Once accomplished, the Federals inside the Crater would be virtually surrounded. Mahone could then dispatch with them at his leisure.

Unfortunately for the general, the Georgian brigade was not at its best that day. The brigade's steadfast leader, General Ambrose Wright, was at home in Georgia recuperating from complications of wounds received at Antietam and Chancellorsville. In Wright's place was Lieutenant Colonel Matthew Hall, a New York-trained physician. Rumors swirled that the Georgians had little confidence in their temporary commander.[18] Leadership problems aside, Mahone had handed the brigade a difficult challenge under any circumstances. The Virginians had suffered mightily during their short charge from the ravine to the nearest trenches, and the Georgians' route of attack would be much longer and less direct. In making their way from north to south, a trip that would be unavoidably slowed by the broken ground behind the Crater, the Georgians' were assured of attracting much unwanted attention. And since the element of surprise had already been expended, every Yankee muzzle would surely turn to the ravine at the first sign of movement.

Not surprisingly, Hall's brigade failed to accomplish its mission. The Georgians rose from the ravine with the same spirit as their predecessors, but this time the Federal sharpshooters on the rim of the Crater were ready. The two captured Napoleons had also been moved into position to meet another charge, and they sprayed the Georgians with canister. A Virginia major watching from the trenches said that Hall's men "fell like autumn leaves" under the torrent. The survivors swerved off course and sought shelter behind the Virginia brigade.

The Georgians gathered themselves together and made another attempt less than an hour later, but the results were the same. "I am at a loss what to do with Wright's brigade," Robert E. Lee would write to Jefferson Davis after the battle. Lee's answer was to place Victor Girardey, Mahone's exemplary aide, in temporary command of the brigade. The move required an unprecedented promotion that instantly elevated Girardey from captain to brigadier. Unfortunately, the 27-year-old general was struck down by a skirmisher's bullet less than two weeks later, and the Georgians' difficulties continued.[19]

Mahone's next action would require extreme caution. His Alabama brigade had arrived, but it was the last of his reserves so he needed to ensure that it did not suffer the same fate as the Georgians. The time was shortly after 11 am, and a hot July sun was beating down fiercely from a cloudless sky. Confederate artillery had zeroed in on the Crater, greatly adding to the misery of the Federals inside. Those men would almost certainly be running low on water and ammunition. Mahone decided to let the deteriorating conditions sap their strength before making another attempt.

The supposition that the Crater's defenders were running short of supplies was entirely correct. Many of the Federal troops were entering their sixth long hour inside the pit, leaving them with dry canteens and empty cartridge boxes. Supplies taken from dead men provided temporary relief, but eventually those diminished as well. A few fleet-footed couriers managed to reach the Union line with urgent requests for supplies, but little aid was forthcoming. The murderous fire raking the open field prevented any meaningful deliveries. Burnside was finally beginning to understand the scope of the problem. "The communication between the advanced line and the crater was almost entirely cut off," he said. "Although the distance was so short, only about a hundred yards, it was next to an impossibility for messengers to reach the crater, much less to send in ammunition and water."[20]

Under such perilous circumstances, any attempt at evacuating the Crater would almost certainly result in a slaughter. Meade therefore granted Burnside permission to withdraw the men at his discretion. Burnside's plan was to pull them out after nightfall, when the casualty count would likely be lowest. But the cover of darkness was still over nine hours away. For the thirsty, exhausted Federals, nine more hours inside the pit surely sounded like a lifetime. Each man now faced a personal choice: either test the limits of his own endurance by waiting for nightfall and the safety of numbers, or sprint across the killing zone alone and in broad daylight, praying that no bullet or shell fragment found its mark. Most chose the former, meaning that the battle was to become a waiting game. During the next few hours, many would no doubt question the wisdom of their decision.

10

End Game

General John Hartranft had been in difficult places before. Perhaps his most daunting challenge was a hotly contested bridge over Antietam Creek in Maryland. As a regimental commander in September 1862, Hartranft lost 120 men taking that small stone structure, which thereafter became notoriously known as Burnside's Bridge. Now, on July 30, 1864, Hartranft was leading an entire brigade, and although the situation was growing increasingly bleak, he remained unflappable. The 34-year-old Pennsylvanian possessed a keen intellect and was accustomed to thinking his way out of thorny problems. Prior to the war he had been a civil engineer, a businessman, and an attorney. Clearly, he would need to draw heavily on his broad range of skills in order to survive the day.

Upon realizing that he was trapped in the Crater, Hartranft's first order of business was to request materials for its defense. "Will you please send us ammunition for rifle muskets," he wrote to his division commander, Orlando Willcox. "We can hold this position, but cannot advance." Back in the Union line, volunteers from Hartranft's old regiment, the 51st Pennsylvania, took it upon themselves to help. They gathered up cartridges in tent halves, and then scurried across the field with their bundles in tow. Remarkably, some of these men reached the other side, delivering 10,000 much-needed rounds to the pit. Their bravery bought the Crater's defenders some additional time, although it would not be nearly enough to last until nightfall. Meanwhile, Orlando Willcox was working on an evacuation route. He organized labor details to dig three separate trenches from the Union line toward the Crater. His hope was that at least one ditch would reach its destination by evening, affording the trapped men a safe means of escape.

Hartranft supervised the defense of the roughly 50 yards of Union-occupied earthworks immediately south of the Crater. The two other brigade commanders present, Simon Griffin and William Bartlett, tried to organize the mob of soldiers inside the depression itself. The most important task was to keep up a steady rate of suppressing fire on the enemy. An officer recalled, "All in the crater who could

John F. Hartranft was a Ninth Corps veteran who had been promoted to brigadier general during the early stages of Grant's Overland Campaign. After the war, Hartranft would remain in public service for most of his life, including two terms as Pennsylvania's governor.

hang on by their elbows and toes lay flat against its conical wall and delivered their fire; but not more than a hundred men at a time could get into position, and these were only armed with muzzle-loading guns, and in order to reload they were compelled to face about and place their backs against the wall."[1] Men on the Crater floor scavenged among the dead for weapons and ammunition, and passed loaded rifles up to the shooters.

Among those clinging to the rim were roughly a dozen Ottawa Indians from the 1st Michigan Sharpshooters. Company K of that regiment consisted almost entirely of Ottawas from Michigan's lower peninsula. They had mustered into service in January 1863 and saw heavy action during Grant's Overland Campaign. The Ottawas chose to support the Union out of concern that a Confederate victory would lead to their enslavement. They also hoped that their loyal service would persuade the Federal government to amend some of the inequitable land treaties signed in the 1850s.

From the very beginning of their enlistment, the men of Company K displayed an aptitude for the art of warfare, combining their formal military training with the tribal customs they had learned as braves. Some of their more unusual practices, such as camouflaging their blue uniforms in dirt and mud before combat, were eventually adopted by the entire regiment once the benefits became apparent. On the Crater's rim, the sharpshooters of Company K ignored the chaos behind them, firing with a steady hand at carefully chosen targets. "They seemed to bear charmed lives, and escaped the many bullets shot at them," remarked an observer.[2]

The Ottawas were not the only Native Americans engaged in the fight. An Iroquois serving in a USCT regiment was killed in the Crater, while a Pequot also from the USCT division suffered a shoulder wound. On the Confederate side, more than a dozen Catawbas from South Carolina were serving in Elliott's brigade.

Confederate artillery was having a deeply demoralizing effect on the Crater's defenders. The episode would become a shining example of accuracy and effectiveness for the oft-maligned batteries of the Confederacy. To the south, a lone cannon continued to spray canister onto the slope between the Union line and the Crater. Captain David Walker, who directed that gun after other officers had fallen, said that it was "sweeping the open field like a tornado." By late morning, grisly evidence of the artillery's efficiency littered the field. "There was a gradual accumulation of dead and wounded, until, from our position, it looked like an inclined plane of dead men," Walker said.[3]

To the west, Confederate gunners focused their attention on the Crater and its adjoining trenches. A line of Napoleons stretching from Gee House to Cemetery Hill pounded the Crater's rim, while concealed batteries of Coehorn mortars dropped shells directly into the pit. An infantryman with the 23rd South Carolina watched with glee as the mortars found their range. "The first and second shells thrown bursted over the Crater," he said. "But each succeeding shell fell into the Crater, resulting in the upheaval into mid-air many blue fragments as the shells exploded." Joseph Eggleston, the young man temporarily commanding a pair of Coehorns in his brother's absence, complimented the precision of the Napoleon batteries along Jerusalem Plank Road behind him. Eggleston marveled as the big, low-trajectory guns found a way to reach the Crater's interior. He said, "The distance was so short and the skill of one and all so great that the shells tipped the crest of the Crater and burst over the mass of men filling the inverted cone in the ground with deadly effect."[4]

From its elevated position in the north, Wright's Battery was hurling grapeshot into the southern half of the pit. In order to inflict even greater damage, a cannon was rolled down into one of the trenches that intersected with the Crater. The gun was positioned to fire straight down the traverse and into the unsuspecting mass of Federal troops. After the horrific arrival of the first few shells, General Bartlett realized that something had to be done. He ordered the immediate construction of a protective barricade across the 8-foot mouth of the trench. A detail of black soldiers frantically began tossing debris into the opening, but the stones, boards, and chunks of clay proved inadequate against the heavy blasts. "A few moments showed them that their work could not be accomplished in this manner," explained Lieutenant Freeman Bowley. "Someone cried out, 'Put in the dead men,' and this suggestion was instantly acted upon. There were plenty of dead, and the men piled them across the gap, as cordwood is piled. White and black, Union and Rebel, officers and privates, were heaped on top of each other, and formed a solid barricade of human flesh. Some of the working party were killed, and their comrades threw them in with the rest."[5]

The macabre barrier had yet to be completed when a new threat emerged. Under the direction of General Mahone, a Confederate artillery officer named John Haskell brought two of his Coehorns within 20 yards of the Crater. At such short range, the compact mortars required a gunpowder charge of just one and a half ounces in order to deliver their ordnance. For the terrified Federals inside the pit, there was virtually no warning. Haskell said that the shells rose so slowly and lazily into the air that he initially wondered if they would clear the Crater's rim. His doubts were answered a second later by the screams of Federal soldiers. Men inside the pit quickly learned to watch for the slow-moving projectiles and flee those that were headed their way. Accordingly, the majority of Haskell's victims were those already immobilized from their wounds.

By noon, the atmosphere within the Crater was one of outright anguish and desperation. Dead sharpshooters, most of them shot through the head, rolled down the walls and collected at the base. Casualties from the shelling covered the Crater's uneven floor. "It was a sickening sight," recalled one officer. "Men were dead and

116

dying all around us; blood was streaming down the sides of the crater to the bottom, where it gathered in pools for a time before being absorbed by the hard red clay." A dire lack of water exacerbated the misery. "Wounded men died there begging piteously for water and soldiers extended their tongues to dampen their parched lips until their tongues seemed to hang from their mouths," another officer said.[6]

As the situation worsened, one able-bodied soldier approached his commander and offered to fetch water from the Union lines. The request appeared to be little more than an honorable way to attempt escape, but it was nonetheless approved. Soon other soldiers caught on and requested permission to do the same. As the men clambered over the rim, each with a collection of empty canteens, no one truly expected them to return. Surviving a one-way trip across the field would be difficult enough. Voluntarily tempting fate with a return trip, while loaded down with gallons of water, seemed beyond the scope of human capacity.

Yet some of the men did indeed return, and others perished trying. As onlookers cheered, each runner started back across the field toting his precious cargo. Those who made it leaped over the rim and tumbled into the Crater, where they were promptly relieved of their burden. The less fortunate volunteers lay sprawled on the open field among the other corpses. On at least one occasion when a canteen-laden soldier fell dead, another man jumped from the Crater and risked his own life to complete the delivery. A captain from the 9th New Hampshire praised the water carriers, saying that their work was "the most striking exhibition of heroism and true courage that I saw during the whole war."[7]

At 12:20 pm, Burnside's order to withdraw reached the Crater. Before dispatching the order, Julius White, Burnside's chief of staff, argued that an attempt should be made to hold the Crater permanently and incorporate it into the Union line. Burnside explained that the order to withdraw came directly from Meade and was peremptory. The only subject that remained open to debate was the best method for minimizing the loss of life. It was decided that the senior officers inside the Crater should make that call, and Burnside's withdrawal order solicited their recommendations.

With the battle raging around them, Generals Hartranft, Bartlett, and Griffin exchanged opinions on how to handle the evacuation. Bartlett preferred trying to hold out until nightfall. "It will be impossible to withdraw these men, who are a rabble without officers, before dark, and not even then in good order," he said. Hartranft agreed that the men were in disarray, but he pointed out that the water and ammunition supplies would not last long. Accordingly, both he and Griffin favored an immediate evacuation. The generals requested a heavy artillery bombardment to cover their withdrawal, plus a demonstration by skirmishers in the north and south to further distract the enemy. They were totally unaware that

Meade had already ordered the rest of the army to stand down. Ninth Corps was on its own, and Meade was no longer even monitoring the situation. He considered the engagement to be all but over, and was on his way back to Army of the Potomac headquarters.

The three generals in the Crater were also unaware, although they must have suspected, that another Confederate assault was only moments away. Satisfied that the artillery's destructive fire had softened up the Federals, William Mahone now readied his Alabama brigade for one last push. Additionally, General Bushrod Johnson had finally appeared on the field and offered the support of his brigades. The final attack was scheduled for 1 pm.

Mahone gathered together the five commanders of his Alabama regiments and explained the plan. He still felt it essential to capture the trenches south of the Crater before moving into the pit itself. But this time measures would be taken to ensure that the Alabamians would not be cut down during their charge, as had the Georgians. Specifically, an artillery barrage would be directed at both the Crater and the Union line in order to keep Federal heads down and distract the Yankee batteries. Once the big guns ceased, the Alabamians would rise up from the ravine and dash about 200 yards to the Crater's western rim. There they would be sheltered from Federal artillery and could concentrate all their attention on the infantry. Mahone concluded his address by noting that Robert E. Lee had arrived at the Gee House. He reminded his officers of the subterranean treachery committed by the enemy that morning, and said that General Lee would be observing their charge most eagerly.

As artillery fire from both sides gradually escalated, the roughly 630 men of the Alabama brigade readied themselves for action. A few men from other outfits volunteered to join them. Captain John Featherston of the 9th Alabama recalled being approached by a dust-covered South Carolinian who requested permission to go along. Featherston looked over the tattered fellow and asked him his motivation for wanting to go. In a level tone, the man replied, "I was blown up in that fort, and I want to even up with them."[8] Featherston gave his assent.

Shortly before 1 pm, the artillery bombardment reached a crescendo. The Alabamians lay flat on the ground, as far up the ravine as they dare, peering over its lip. Federal cannon were busy pounding away at the Confederate batteries, just as planned. At once, all of the Confederate artillery ceased fire; it was the signal for the Alabamians to move out. With a fearsome yell, each man sprang to his feet and charged forward. The brigade emerged from the ravine swiftly and began its race to the safety of the Crater's western wall. "When we came within range, we saw the flash of the sunlight on the enemy's guns as they were leveled above the walls of the wrecked fort," Captain Featherston said. "The heavy guns joined in the awful din, and the air seemed literally filled with missiles."[9]

In the trenches to the west of the Crater, small groups of surrounded Federal troops were still fighting desperately. The Alabama brigade promptly overran these pockets, killing the Yankees and taking prisoners. Among them was Captain R.G. Richards of the 45th Pennsylvania, the company commander who had holed up inside a ditch with his men after their failed charge on the Gee House. When Richards' request for assistance — a note tied to a stone tossed back toward the Crater — went unanswered, he and his men had hunkered down and waited. They spent the entire morning successfully defending their little sanctuary in complete isolation, but the arrival of the Alabamians was more than they could handle. "Further resistance was impossible and could only result in the useless sacrifice of the lives of the few men under my command," Richards said.[10] He and his men dropped their weapons and stood. A Confederate officer jumped into the ditch and accepted their surrender.

Federal troops in the trenches to the south were also overwhelmed. Those not killed or captured retreated into the Crater, which became the last remaining Union stronghold. Before taking on that challenge, the Alabamians first needed to regroup. "When we got to the walls of the fort, we dropped down on the ground to get the men in order and let them get their breath," Featherston said. Quite a few discarded rifles were strewn about, and somebody had the idea of pitching them into the Crater javelin-style. Shell fragments, clods of earth, and other debris were tossed over the wall as well. "The rebels threw over muskets with bayonets attached, and a number were severely wounded by this harpooning style of warfare," said Lieutenant Freeman Bowley. "We could hear the commands of the Rebel officers, and knew that they would soon charge us."[11]

The remaining Union leadership in the Crater gathered together one final time to discuss their limited options. They met in the relative safety of a triangular pocket created by two intersecting earthen walls. The officers agreed that the only reasonable alternatives were retreat or surrender, and the majority said they would prefer to take their chances in a retreat. An urgent message was dispatched to General Burnside requesting artillery cover for the withdrawal, and officers spread the word that each man should be prepared to go as soon as the barrage began.

One officer, General William Bartlett, would be staying behind with the wounded. Bartlett's wooden leg had been smashed when a shell landed nearby, killing the man next to him. Although the general was unhurt, a clay boulder had landed on his prosthesis and shattered it to splinters, leaving him completely immobilized. With no hope of escape, Bartlett perched himself on a mound of earth and directed the final defense of the Crater.

Few men were fighting now. The ammunition had been largely expended and a sense of hopelessness permeated the scene. Only a few sharpshooters still clung to the rim, plugging away. The rest were either dead or wounded. Lieutenant Bowley noticed that even the Ottawas of the 1st Michigan Sharpshooters had succumbed. "A number of them were fatally wounded, and, clustering together, covered their heads with their blouses, and commenced chanting their death-song," he said.[12] The two captured cannon that had been so effective were finally silenced as well. Sergeant Wesley Stanley, the man who found the half-buried guns and put them into service, was dead.

Shortly before 2 pm, a row of Confederate caps appeared along the rim of the Crater. Reflexively, the Union troops still possessing loaded rifles fired a volley. But the caps were merely decoys raised on muskets, and in an instant the Alabamians came bounding over the wall. According to John Featherston, the caps had not fooled all of the Yankees. He said:

> As we went over the embankment into the fort one of my sergeants,
> Andrew McWilliams, a brave fellow, was shot in the mouth, and the ball
> did not cut his lips. It came out the top of his head. He was evidently
> yelling with his mouth wide open. He fell on top of the embankment with
> his head hanging in the fort.[13]

The sight of enemy troops pouring into the Crater triggered the last stampede of the day, as nearly one thousand Federals bolted from the pit and ran for their lives. They were easy targets as they crossed the open field *en masse* and without protection. An 18-year-old private from Michigan said that as he ran he lost his cap, felt the odd sensation of bullets passing through his clothing, and had the sole of his shoe ripped back by a shot. Miraculously, he reached the Union lines unharmed.

General Bartlett shouted for the hundreds of Union soldiers still remaining in the Crater to surrender, but his voice could not be heard. Another officer tied a handkerchief to a ramrod and waved it overhead, hoping that soldiers from both sides would see the surrender and cease hostilities. But the fury and bloodlust of hand-to-hand combat could not be extinguished so easily. A deep hatred, caused by six straight weeks of impersonal trench warfare against a distant enemy, boiled up inside each man. That distant enemy had just been given a face in the soldier who now grappled at arm's length. Within the Southerners, a rage burned over the invasion of their homeland, the employ of armed slaves against them, and the devious manner in which their comrades had been slaughtered as they slept. To the Northerners, the fight boiled down to a simple matter of survival. For eight hours the tide of battle had steadily turned against them, with each moment becoming more miserable and deadly than the last. The Southerners' frenzied ire, coupled with shouts of "No quarter!" convinced them that they must either fight or die.

The melee continued for about 15 minutes until sheer exhaustion forced a return to reason. According to at least one account, an officer named Morgan Cleveland of the 8th Alabama yelled to a nearby Union colonel, "Why in the hell don't you fellows surrender?" The colonel shouted back, "Why in the hell don't you let us?" Afterward, the fighting tailed off and officers on both sides regained control of their men.[14]

For the black soldiers of the USCT regiments, the flag of surrender did not necessarily guarantee their safety. Witnesses in both blue and gray reported that some of the black prisoners were executed where they stood. The remaining Federals were formed into a double line and marched out of the Crater, but they too would face one final danger. Distant Union artillerists mistook the column for a Confederate unit and opened fire. Ironically, although they had survived a protracted battle and intense hand-to-hand combat, as well as endured the humiliation of defeat and capture, some of the Federal prisoners ultimately fell victim to the fire of their own guns.

During the battle's last moments, a ring of protectors had surrounded General Bartlett and shielded him from harm. As Bartlett was carried from the Crater, the Confederate guards marveled at this stoic Yankee general who had lost his leg but refused to show any expression of pain. When it was later learned that Bartlett had lost only a wooden leg, the guards recounted their story with much amusement and it became a staple of campfire yarns.

Bartlett and the others were taken to a rocky field outside Petersburg where they would spend the night. They received no food and were relieved of their personal possessions by Confederate visitors. When asked for personal information, some of the USCT officers gave a false regiment for fear of retribution, but Lieutenant Freeman Bowley proudly identified himself as an officer of the 30th United States Colored Infantry. He noted that next to his name the words "Negro officer" were written. As for the black soldiers, it was soon discovered that many of them hailed from eastern Virginia. A notice was posted in Petersburg that owners of missing slaves could go to the POW camp and claim their property.

Inside the Crater, Confederate troops began the arduous task of burying the dead and restoring the scarred area into defendable ground. The scale of the carnage shocked even those who had participated in the fight. "The slaughter was fearful," observed Captain Featherston of the 9th Alabama. "The dead were piled on each other. In one part of the fort I counted them eight bodies deep. There were but few wounded compared with the killed." Most of the dead were simply buried where they lay and, as a result, manning the Crater quickly became a dreaded assignment. Lime was spread about in an attempt to cover the stench but it did little good. "Green flies without number buzzed audibly all around us and added to the hideousness of the scene," said a private in the 23rd South Carolina. "Every attempt to eat or even open one's mouth caused nausea."[15]

More than 26,000 soldiers participated in the battle, roughly two-thirds of whom swore allegiance to the Union. In total, the engagement claimed approximately 900 lives and inflicted 2,600 injuries. As usual, a significant number of those wounds would eventually prove lethal. Another 1,800 men were either captured or declared missing. The Union bore the brunt of the losses with 500 dead, 1900 wounded, and 1400 captured or missing. All but 300 of the Federal casualties belonged to Ninth Corps. The black regiments of Edward Ferrero's division suffered the most deaths, accounting for four out of every ten Union fatalities. On the Confederate side, Stephen Elliott's brigade endured the most casualties with 700, including Elliott himself. More than a third of those men were lost instantly in the mine explosion. Mahone's brigade accounted for about 600 of the total Confederate casualties, or 40 percent.

The affair was far from over. A cease-fire had to be arranged to bury the dead and recover the wounded lying between the opposing lines. Given that nearly all of the bodies on the open field wore blue uniforms, the Southerners felt no urgency to negotiate such a truce. For the Union, there was also the tactical issue to consider. Ninth Corps had lost nearly a quarter of its strength, leaving it in disarray. A third of its regimental commanders were gone. Two brigade commanders— Bartlett and Marshall — had been taken prisoner. Robert Potter's division no longer had enough troops to safely man its own trenches. Meade fretted that the disaster might embolden Lee to launch a counteroffensive against his left flank. (The attack never came; Lee's aggressive days were behind him.) And finally, there would be political ramifications for the Northern army. Such a debacle required an investigation and the leveling of blame. Before it was over, reverberations from the mine explosion would be felt in Washington and beyond.

11

Aftershocks

Afternoon turned into evening, and the Union wounded remained stranded helplessly on the battlefield. Meanwhile, some Confederate victors celebrated by harassing their foes in the opposing earthworks. Hundreds of Federal muskets were left behind in their trenches. The Southerners amused themselves by loading a weapon with its own ramrod and firing it across the field, thus producing a horrific screech.

George Meade had departed for his headquarters long before the battle ended, assuming that Burnside would withdraw Ninth Corps from the Crater as soon as possible and then furnish him with a full report. But, as had been the case throughout the day, Burnside's report was not forthcoming. By 7:40 pm, Meade grew tired of waiting and asked Burnside for an update. He asked if Ninth Corps still held the Crater, and inquired about what steps were being taken to remove the wounded. He reminded Burnside that General Beauregard had toyed with them six weeks earlier when a cease-fire was requested to care for casualties. In essence, Meade simply wanted to know what was happening.

Burnside's reaction to the message demonstrated just how profoundly the day's tragic events had affected him. Rather than taking the request for information at face value, as he normally would have done, Burnside suspected that Meade was goading him. By his own account, Burnside tossed the telegram aside and vented his feelings to an aide:

> [I] said to my staff officer, who was with me, that I would not answer such a message; that if General Meade felt disposed to cease offensive operations on the right and left, and leave us to get out of the crater as best we could, and had taken so little interest in the matter as not to know late in the evening that we had been driven from the crater before two o'clock, I certainly would not give him the information, and I believed he knew all about it.[1]

Meade tried again three hours later, but once more he received no reply. It wasn't

123

until a third request arrived the following morning, Sunday, July 31, that the Ninth Corps commander finally replied. Burnside reported that about 100 living men still remained on the battlefield, and he asked for permission to send out a white flag. Meade forwarded an official letter of truce, addressed to Robert E. Lee, but told Burnside only to use the letter if the local Confederate commander would not agree to an informal cease-fire. The letter was tantamount to an admission of defeat, and although it was obvious to all, Meade hoped to avoid making such a formal concession, if possible.

As might be expected, the ploy failed. A staff officer from Mahone's Alabama brigade met the Federal white flag half way across the field and returned to his line with the Yankee request for an informal truce. Several hours later, officers from both sides again marched out onto the field under a white flag. The Southerners politely advised that the informal request had been declined, thereby forcing Burnside's men to produce the official letter addressed to Lee. Several more hours would be needed to determine if this request could be honored.

While the lengthy exercise in military protocol played itself out, injured men lying on the field agonized and died. "The soldiers who are badly wounded, lay exposed to the fire of friend and foe alike," said a lieutenant in the 115th New York. "One moves painfully towards our works an inch at a time, but the heartless rebels give him a volley of bullets for his pains. Another, unable to move, piteously begs to be saved, and motions to some friends imploringly with his hand."[2] The lieutenant added that among the pitiful groans and pleas for help were appeals by some men to instead be put out of their misery. The scenes of dreadful suffering tugged at Confederate heartstrings as well, and the Southerners encouraged some of the nearest wounded to crawl into their line for assistance. Colonel William Stewart of the 61st Virginia described one such incident:

> I remember a Negro, between the lines, who had both legs blown off. He crawled up to the outside of our works, struck three muskets with bayonets in the ground and threw a piece of tent cloth over them to shelter his head from the hot sunshine. After awhile, in an interval, when the shots from the enemy had slackened, one of our soldiers managed to push a cup of water to him, which he drank and immediately commenced to froth at the mouth, dying in a very short time after.[3]

As Meade's letter made its way to Robert E. Lee, permission was granted for civilian volunteers from the U.S. Sanitary Commission to step onto the field and comfort the wounded where they lay. Meanwhile, Lee read Meade's request and decided to delegate it to P.G.T. Beauregard. It was nearly nightfall before Beauregard received the document and agreed to the request, so the truce was put off until the next morning. By this point, the matter had become almost moot — only two dozen souls still suffered on the battlefield. The rest were already dead.

11. Aftershocks

At 5 am on August 1, almost exactly two full days after the battle began, a large white flag was planted in the center of the field. Roughly 20 wounded men had somehow managed to survive and they were at last carried away and treated. One soldier, however, needed no medical assistance; he had lain completely still on the battlefield, feigning death, for nearly 40 hours. Only after he was certain that a cease-fire was in effect did he pop up and scurry back to the Federal lines.

Next came the grisly task of burying more than 200 corpses that had spent two days putrefying under the hot Virginia sun. Confederate work details carried out dead Union soldiers from behind their earthworks. A 40-yard-long, 10-foot-deep common grave was dug for the decaying bodies. "Men were swollen out of all human shape, and whites could not be told from blacks, except by their hair," remarked a Maine officer. "So much were they swollen that their clothes were burst, and their waistbands would not reach halfway around their bodies; and the stench was awful."[4]

Each side sent out a brass band to distract the laborers from their work, and for two hours Northern and Southern tunes alternately wafted across the field. The lively music and the temporary absence of danger created an oddly festive atmosphere. "Both sides came over their works, and, meeting in the center, mingled, chatted, and exchanged courtesies, as though they had not sought in desperate effort to take each other's lives but an hour before," recalled Captain Featherston.[5] The Alabamian was introduced to Robert Potter, and the two men conversed casually on a variety of subjects. Featherston revealed to General Potter that after the battle he found some papers left behind in the Crater by a Federal officer. When Potter asked for the documents, Featherston took some from his jacket and handed them over, but others he kept as a souvenir.

Once all of the dead were finally gathered up, Federal labor details covered over the mass grave with a mound of dirt and began to trudge off the field. But their work was not yet finished: General Mahone noticed that the dirt had been piled several feet high on top of the long grave, essentially creating a breastwork in the middle of the field. Since the mound could conceivably be used as cover for another Yankee assault, Mahone demanded that it be leveled. The laborers grudgingly complied. Mahone was not the only Southern general to remain mindful of the tactical situation. P.G.T. Beauregard was also on the scene, using the cease-fire to his advantage. According to a young North Carolinian, Beauregard donned a private's uniform in order to deflect attention from himself and made an extensive survey of the Union defenses.

As the truce expired, two Federals were discovered to have strayed too far into Confederate territory and were therefore detained. The first was Colonel Henry Thomas of the USCT division. Thomas had been searching vainly for the bodies of Colonel Bross and Lieutenant Pennell, the two daring men who had given their

125

lives trying to rally his black troops. Thomas spent the rest of the day in Confederate custody but was eventually released. The second man, Private James Meyers of the 43rd USCT, was less fortunate. As a result of wandering too far from the burial detail, he spent the remainder of the war performing heavy labor for the Confederacy.

A different type of ritual had occurred inside Petersburg a day before the cease-fire. At 8 am on Sunday, the Federal prisoners were roused by their captors and assembled into an unorthodox formation. White officers were placed in rows of four by rank. Between each row of soldiers, a row of black soldiers was inserted. The odd assembly was designed to amuse the townspeople, who had suffered mightily under the Federal siege. To complete the joke, the one-legged General Bartlett was propped up on a lame old horse and placed at the front of the column.

The gag had the intended effect. Dressed in their Sunday best, Petersburg's residents jeered and cackled as the Yankee prisoners were paraded through town. Lieutenant Freeman Bowley said that he and his dispirited comrades "were assailed by a volley of abuse from men, women and children that exceeded anything of the kind that I ever heard."[6] The procession ended at the Appomattox River, where the POWs were placed on a small island. A day later, they were loaded into boxcars and taken south to Confederate prison camps.

The Crater fiasco came at a particularly inopportune moment for the North. Confederate cavalry under General Jubal Early had just entered Pennsylvania and burned the town of Chambersburg. Increasingly, Washington was being perceived as vulnerable to invasion. Siege artillery was hurriedly pulled from Petersburg and shipped north for the capital's defense. The struggle for Petersburg itself seemed deadlocked, a perception that the Crater defeat strongly reinforced. Yet another Union general had failed in his mission, the rumors said of Grant. Meanwhile, the presidential race was nearing its bitter end, and Lincoln's reelection seemed in doubt. On Wall Street, the price of gold soared to new highs.

The wasted advantage of the mine explosion was particularly distressing to Ulysses S. Grant. Just as in mid-June, Petersburg could have been taken with ease if only his subordinates had acted promptly and cooperatively. But unlike past failures, Grant could not dismiss this loss so easily. "It was the saddest affair I have witnessed in the war," he brooded in a report to Washington. "Such opportunity for carrying fortifications I have never seen and do not expect again to have."[7]

Meade and Burnside were equally disheartened over the defeat, and spent the next few days exchanging thinly veiled accusations of blame. While reporting a tally of his casualties, Burnside included the unsolicited observation that most of his losses were inflicted after Meade's order to withdraw had been issued. As intended, the statement irritated Meade, and he asked Burnside to clarify its meaning. Burnside replied that the withdrawal order demoralized the men in the Crater by showing them that their generals had lost all confidence in them. He implied that had the order not been given, the engagement might have ended differently or, at the very least, with a less severe loss of life. To these allegations Meade simply replied that a court would investigate the matter and determine who was at fault.

For Lieutenant Colonel Henry Pleasants and the miners of the 48th Pennsylvania, the Crater disaster was an astounding disappointment. Despite the ominous predictions of so-called experts, Pleasants and his men successfully produced the longest military mine to date, and did so without being discovered by enemy sappers. Their ingenuity and backbreaking labor had been rewarded with an early-morning explosion that sent the Confederates reeling and presented the Army of the Potomac with a golden opportunity to capture Petersburg. But rather than a glorious victory, the mismanaged attack that followed resulted in a resounding defeat.

The 48th Pennsylvania suffered no casualties during the battle, having been excused from frontline duty as a reward for its work, but the regiment's morale sank to new depths nonetheless. The news that Confederate raiders had razed Chambersburg, just 100 miles from their homes, only added to the miners' despair. Their spirits would be given a slight boost on August 3, when Meade's headquarters issued a general order commending the regiment for its efforts. It read:

> The commanding general takes great pleasure in acknowledging the valuable services rendered by Lieut. Col. Henry Pleasants, Forty-eighth Regiment Pennsylvania Veteran Volunteers, and the officers and men of his command, in the excavation of the mine which was successfully exploded on the morning of the 30th ultimo under one of the enemy's batteries in front of the Second Division of the Ninth Army Corps. The skill displayed in the laying out of and construction of the mine reflects great credit upon Lieutenant-Colonel Pleasants, the officer in charge, and the willing endurance by the officers and men of the regiment of the extraordinary labor and fatigue involved in the prosecution of the work to completion, is worthy of the highest praise.[8]

For Colonel Pleasants, the accolade did little to relieve his frustration over the botched assault. He was disillusioned with the army's leadership in general, but later it would become clear that he reserved a special blame for George Meade. Pleasants' immediate superiors, Generals Potter and Burnside, had supported the mining project, while Meade and his staff scoffed at it and withheld much-needed equipment. Then, when the mine was at last completed and charged, Meade stepped in and interfered with Burnside's battle plan, throwing all of Ninth Corps into confusion just hours before the attack.

On August 1, as Ninth Corps struggled to reestablish a chain of command following its losses, Pleasants was placed in charge of Second Brigade in Potter's division. His tenure in this position would not last long. A special board of officers was being assembled to investigate the Crater disaster, and Pleasants recognized that he would be called upon to testify before the committee about what he had witnessed. No doubt he would also be asked for his opinions regarding the cause of the attack's failure. The colonel understood that revealing his true feelings on the matter could be detrimental to his military career. "I did not want to go before the board," Pleasants later explained. "I thought no good would come of it; it would only make me enemies, and I thought it better, as long as I remained in the army, that I should not go before the board."[9] Accordingly, Pleasants applied for a leave of absence. It was granted and he returned to Pennsylvania.

Henry Pleasants was not the only officer who wished to avoid the impending political firestorm. Brigadier General James Ledlie, the inept and inebriated commander of Ninth Corps' First Division, also departed Petersburg. Ledlie knew that even the most cursory investigation would reveal his gross negligence during the battle. He therefore obtained an extended medical leave and left for his New York home. Nobody was sorry to see Ledlie go, and Grant saw to it that he never led troops again. "His removal from command was a heavy loss to the enemy," wrote a Massachusetts lieutenant.[10]

For the Confederates at Petersburg, the initial euphoria following the Crater victory was short-lived. A realization quickly set in among the troops that there was a new front in the war — the ground beneath their feet. Dodging Yankee shells from the air was no longer good enough. From now on, they would also have to be vigilant of attack from below. In describing the events of July 30 to Jefferson Davis, a weary Lee noted that although the Federal advance had been checked, the "demoralization of the troops was great."[11]

Despite the Southerners' perceptions, the thrashing received at the Crater had soured Federal interest in underground attacks. For many Confederates at Petersburg, especially the engineers, tunneling became a subject of great interest. For one such engineer, a lieutenant colonel named William Blackford, locating a remnant of the tunnel dug by the miners of the 48th Pennsylvania became an ambition that bordered on obsession. Finding the original mine might reveal clues for unearthing other Yankee tunnels in the area, Blackford felt, and he searched relentlessly.

Unfortunately for his men, the subterranean work was most unpleasant. Finding the Pennsylvanians' mine naturally meant digging in the vicinity of the Crater, and the Crater had become a mass grave. An unimaginable stench from dozens of decaying corpses followed Blackford and his men wherever they labored, and on more than one occasion the excavation had to be temporarily halted as a result. Eventually, Blackford found his prize, but the remains of the Federal mine yielded little useful information, and no signs of other attempts were ever uncovered.

Six hundred yards to the north, another Confederate mining project was underway. This one had actually started prior to the explosion of July 30, and it was offensive, rather than defensive, in nature. Captain Hugh Douglas, the man who had established the initial countermining operations at Elliott's Salient, was running a tunnel toward the Union trenches of Eighteenth Corps. But Douglas lacked the manpower and resources that had been available to Colonel Pleasants. His project was therefore much smaller and less precise than that of the Pennsylvanians. Without the aid of a theodolite, Douglas was forced to estimate the distance to his target. And whereas four tons of gunpowder had been loaded into the Union mine, the Confederates could muster only 850 pounds.

At 9:15 am on Monday, August 1, Douglas reported his mine as charged and ready to be sprung. But he would have to wait; the cease-fire to bury the Yankee dead was still underway. When the fighting resumed later in the day, Douglas received orders to detonate his mine. He touched off his four fuses and, just as Colonel Pleasants had done two and a half days earlier, waited anxiously for the fruits of his labor. And just like Colonel Pleasants, he was disappointed. After 45 tense minutes, Douglas realized that something had gone awry. A miner named Black cautiously entered the tunnel and discovered that three of the fuses had gone out, while the fourth sputtered aimlessly. Black was unable to relight the fuses as his Federal counterparts, Sergeant Reese and Lieutenant Douty, had done. Captain Douglas examined the fusing and declared it "very defective and perfectly valueless."[12]

While awaiting the delivery of replacement fusing, Douglas decided to extend his mine farther toward the enemy. He removed the powder and advanced the main shaft another 25 feet, also adding side galleries of a similar length. However, the extra distance was not enough and the 850-pound gunpowder charge was insufficient. Douglas successfully detonated his mine at 6:30 pm on August 5, but the only result was a disappointing plume of earth that shot into the evening sky some 40 yards short of the Federal line.

The previous squabbles between Meade and Burnside proved almost cordial when compared to their final showdown. The Crater debacle convinced Meade that Ambrose Burnside was unfit for command, and he set the wheels in motion for Burnside's removal even before the last casualties were carried from the battlefield. Meade's assault would be two-pronged. First, he would file formal charges against the Ninth Corps commander. Second, he would establish an investigative board to determine the cause of the attack's failure. The latter move was designed to exonerate Meade of any culpability as well as to implicate Burnside.

The formal charges accused Burnside of "disobedience of orders" and "conduct prejudicial to good order and military discipline." In justifying these charges, Meade cited several specific examples of Burnside's failure to keep his superior officer (i.e. Meade) informed of events during the battle despite direct orders to

The entrance to a Confederate mine that was intended to destroy Fort Sedgwick. Following the Battle of the Crater, Petersburg's defenders experimented extensively with mining operations, achieving little success (Library of Congree, Prints and Photographs Division LC-B8171-3195 DLC).

do so. To illustrate Burnside's poor conduct, Meade attached a copy of the dispatch in which Burnside called him "unofficer-like and ungentlemanly." When submitting the charges to Grant's chief of staff, John Rawlins, Meade added that this was not the first time Burnside had been insubordinate. He said, "my patience and forbearance are exhausted, and I think the time has arrived when General Burnside should understand disrespectful and insubordinate language cannot be used in official communications with impunity."[13]

Meade next created the board that was to investigate the Crater fiasco. For this job, he selected only men that he knew well, including his inspector general, Colonel Edward Schriver. The other members were General Romeyn Ayres of Fifth Corps, General Nelson Miles of Second Corps, and Miles' commander, General Winfield Scott Hancock, who served as the board's president. Meade made it clear to the group that theirs was more than just a fact-finding mission. They should also determine whether "any party or parties are censurable for the failure."[14]

To their credit, the board members felt uncomfortable with the latter task. They were being asked to assign guilt to fellow officers, much like a military tribunal, despite having no real legal power or legitimacy. Their findings could potentially end at least one high-profile military career, and perhaps even be used as evidence in a court-martial. Before walking into a potential quagmire, the board wanted some reassurance that it was on solid legal ground. When the four men convened for the first time at 10 am on August 2, they prepared a brief statement outlining their concerns, and then quickly adjourned.

Meade could do little but forward the board's concerns on to Grant, who was essentially left with two options. He could either order the board to gather factual data only and not render an opinion, or he could ask President Lincoln to designate the board as an official Court of Inquiry, thus giving it the authority to find fault. Meade lobbied for a Court of Inquiry. "I am desirous that my conduct, as well as that of all others concerned, should be thoroughly examined," he wrote. "This examination should be immediate and prompt. There is the broad fact, that well-laid plans, executed under the most favorable circumstances, have failed."[15] Grant sent the request to Washington and it was approved.

Ambrose Burnside was more than slightly alarmed by the transformation of Meade's handpicked board into an official Court of Inquiry. He openly acknowledged that his "unofficer-like and ungentlemanly" comment had been insubordinate and said that he regretted it. But Burnside still fervently believed that Meade's actions were largely responsible for the battlefield defeat. He felt that an impartial panel would certainly agree with him, once they saw how Meade had capriciously altered his battle plan at the eleventh hour, and then issued arbitrary commands from afar throughout the engagement. Obviously, Meade's group would be far less likely to arrive at the same conclusion, and far more likely to blame Burnside. He cabled Washington and asserted that, "if an investigation is to be had, I feel that I have a right to ask that it be made by officers not in this army and not selected by General Meade."[16]

Lincoln was fond of Burnside, recognizing him as a loyal and trustworthy man, qualities that the president valued. But this was strictly an army matter, and if Grant was content with the current state of affairs, then Lincoln would not interfere. Secretary of War Edwin Stanton responded to Burnside that the president "does not see that any evil can result to you. The action of the Board of Inquiry will be merely to collect facts for his information."[17] Burnside surely doubted the veracity of this response but there was nothing more he could do. He had appealed to the highest authority and been turned away. Now he would have to make his case before a decidedly biased court and hope to sway them with his presentation of the facts.

12

Censure and Commendation

After some gentle prodding from Grant, George Meade agreed to drop the charges of disobedience and bad conduct against Burnside. But he still insisted that Burnside could not remain under his command, so it was decided that instead of a court-martial, Burnside would be sent away on indefinite leave. Prior to departing, Burnside was required to appear before the Court of Inquiry and explain his role in the failure of July 30. He would not be the first to testify, however; that honor belonged to Meade.

The court convened at 10 am on August 8, at which time General Meade was sworn in. He began with a lengthy statement that ultimately set the tone for all subsequent proceedings. Throughout his narrative, the general bluntly blamed Burnside for every element of the Crater disaster. Meade stated that he never liked the location of Burnside's mine for an assault because of the enemy's command of the flanks. He complained extensively that Burnside provided him with virtually no information during the engagement, and then he delved into the details of Burnside's insubordination. To document each point, Meade provided the court with copies of telegrams and orders. In the back of the room, Burnside sat stone-faced as he listened to Meade's testimony, waiting for his turn to speak. When the four-man panel wearily adjourned late in the afternoon, Meade still had not finished his statement.

Early the next day, before any further accusations could be made against him, Burnside petitioned the court to disallow a portion of Meade's testimony. He noted that the court was charged only with investigating the battle, and that the insubordination issue was therefore beyond the court's purview. Burnside's request was denied. The panel ruled that his objections should have been made at the time the evidence was submitted, not afterward.

When Meade finally concluded his statement, Burnside was given the opportunity to question him. Like a trial lawyer, Burnside grilled his superior about inconsistencies in his testimony. Meade was forced to acknowledge that he was over a mile away from the action and had never ventured toward the front the entire day. To counter Meade's assertion that he was kept in the dark as the battle raged, Burnside asked why Captain Sanders of Meade's staff was dispatched to Taylor House if not to keep him informed. Meade replied that Sanders' purpose was merely to "facilitate the transmission of information" and that his presence did not entitle Burnside to ignore incoming telegrams.

Meade stepped down, and Burnside was sworn in so that he could continue his defense as a witness. To the court's chagrin, Burnside launched into a rambling statement that lasted even longer than Meade's epic address. Burnside defended his decision not to level the earthworks before the attack, saying that had he done so, the element of surprise would surely have been lost. He spoke at length of Meade's interference in his battle plan, and explained his reasons for wanting the USCT division to lead the assault. Burnside also tacitly criticized Meade's choice to direct the battle from the rear and base his decisions solely on the reports of others. After three days of testimony, Burnside was excused. He returned to his tent and packed his belongings for home. He had been told that he was being put on a 20-day leave, but it proved to be a permanent dismissal. Ambrose Burnside's military career was over.

Following Burnside's departure, the Court of Inquiry did not meet for nearly three weeks due to more pressing matters. In a strange bit of irony, Burnside's judges would suffer a humiliating battlefield setback of their own. In mid-August, Grant succeeded in severing the Weldon Railroad—a vital Confederate supply line—at a point six miles south of Petersburg. But he discovered that the railroad was still being used to transport supplies from the South. Trains simply rode north as far as they dare and then offloaded their freight onto wagons for the short ride into the city. On August 23, Grant ordered Winfield Scott Hancock to take two of his Second Corps divisions and destroy 40 miles of track. Hancock, the court's president, chose the divisions of Generals John Gibbon and Nelson Miles, the latter also being a court member.

On the first day of its mission, Second Corps succeeded in tearing up eight miles of the Weldon line. That night, Hancock's men rested in a small, unfinished earthen fortress near Reams' Station. By this point, word of the Yankee foray reached Lee and he sent a sizable task force, including William Mahone's division, to stop it. Hancock had adequate warning that the Confederates were coming, but he underestimated their strength. On the morning of August 25, the men of Second Corps were caught by surprise and driven from their work on the railroad. They fell back to the tiny fort at Reams' Station and tried to establish a defense, which soon buckled under the weight of the heavy Confederate attack. Unlike Burnside, Hancock realized when he was beaten. He withdrew to the safety of the Union lines after losing nine cannon and 2,700 men, the majority of whom were taken prisoner. It was an embarrassing defeat for Second Corps, and it may have somewhat tempered Hancock's opinion of Burnside.

The court returned to its work in earnest on August 29 and heard testimony from General Gouverneur Warren, commander of Fifth Corps. Warren said frankly that he believed the assault was hindered by an ambiguous chain of command, and by delays "to await the transmission of dispatches and corresponding answers" from the rear. He said that there should have been a single officer present at the front on July 30 with authority over all of the amassed forces. The court adjourned shortly after Warren's comments. When it reconvened the following morning, Meade was present. He told Warren to clarify his previous

Major General Winfield Scott Hancock was labeled "Hancock the Superb" by his countless admirers, but during the Petersburg siege his leadership abilities often fell short. The Second Corps commander was in poor health, the result of a thigh wound he suffered a year earlier at Gettysburg (Library of Congress, Prints and Photographs Division LC-B8172-1877 DLC).

remarks about the chain of command. Sarcastically, Meade asked, "Were you not aware that the commanding general of the Army of the Potomac was in the field and in telegraphic communication with yourself and the other officers alluded to?" Now backpedaling, Warren stammered his way through a vague response, ultimately conceding that the physical presence of a single commander at the front may not have changed the outcome of the battle. But before his testimony was finished, Warren rallied and restated his opinion that a "controlling power should have been there and nowhere else." He was then excused.[1]

Ulysses S. Grant was the next witness to appear before the court. He immediately stated at the outset that he was too far away from the front on July 30 to render an opinion about the assault's failure. The excuse was typical of Grant, who as a rule avoided publicly criticizing his officers, no matter his own personal feelings. Naturally, the court was unwilling to press him, and Grant departed after answering three innocuous questions.

After Grant came a procession of two dozen additional witnesses, ranging from line officers to regimental surgeons, each offering their own account of what occurred that day. Engineers offered technical assessments on issues such as the placement of troops prior to the attack, the impact of not leveling the earthworks, and the overall suitability of Elliott's Salient as an assault point. Artillery officers complained about Burnside's refusal to clear the stand of trees that shielded the Confederate battery in the south. The court made a point of asking certain officers, such as General Edward Ferrero of the USCT division, to clarify their whereabouts during the battle. Ferrero said he spent much of the day directing his troops from the front line. He made no mention of his visit to Ledlie's bombproof; that fact would come to light from the testimony of subsequent witnesses.

The court deliberated for three days before issuing its findings. The panel noted that the potential for success most certainly existed during the early morning hours of July 30. The mine explosion, and the Federal artillery barrage that followed, stunned enemy soldiers and created mass confusion within their ranks. The enemy's bewilderment was so great that a full 30 minutes passed before any significant resistance was offered. During this time, the numerically superior Federal force could have easily pushed through the enemy's line and captured Cemetery Hill.

The court found that poor leadership and an utter lack of preparation had negated all Federal advantages. Proper exit points from the Ninth Corps trenches should have been prepared in advance. Assault columns should have been formed behind the Federal line prior to the explosion. If that was not possible, then unit commanders should have instead formed their men on the open field and proceeded in unison, rather than letting them straggle across independently. The absence of several brigade and division commanders from the battlefield merely compounded the effects of this mistake.

When naming the officers deemed responsible for the failed assault, the court placed Ambrose Burnside at the top of the list. Burnside's refusal to level his earthworks was in direct violation of an order from Meade. Further, he neglected to ensure that Ninth Corps was properly formed prior to the assault, and the panel said he should have acted sooner to relieve Ledlie's men once it became apparent that they had bogged down inside the Crater. The court chastised Generals Ledlie and Ferrero for loitering in a bombproof rather than leading their men, and General Orlando Willcox for not pressing the assault with "more energy." Robert Potter was the only Ninth Corps division commander to escape the court's ire, although one of his brigade commanders, Colonel Zenas Bliss, was censured for not going forward with his men.

As an aside, the court noted that even if Cemetery Hill had been successfully taken, it might not have been held for very long. Without adequate exit points from the Ninth Corps trenches, artillery pieces could not have been promptly moved up onto the hill. Additionally, the panel found that Burnside had failed to properly equip his acting engineer regiments, an oversight which would have hindered the construction of defensive works on the crest. The court made no comment about Meade's last-minute revisions to Burnside's battle plan. However, it did condemn his hazy command style, saying that "explicit orders should have been given assigning one officer to the command of all the troops intended to engage in the assault when the commanding general was not present in person to witness the operations."[2] Having presented its report, the court permanently adjourned on September 9, and the matter was considered closed.

The siege of Petersburg carried on through late summer and into the fall. Grant continued to probe for weakness and occasionally found it. Although Robert E. Lee remained in control of the city, it was slowly being wrestled away from him and he periodically entertained plans to abandon it. In other theaters, the tide of war was turning distinctly in favor of the North: September saw the fall of Atlanta, and Confederate General Jubal Early's forces no longer threatened Washington. In November, the political atmosphere stabilized when President Lincoln was reelected by a handsome majority, winning all but three states. But despite a growing confidence in the nation's capital that the war would soon be over, the Crater disgrace was not yet forgotten. Congressional insiders said that the War Committee was planning to investigate the disaster.

The Joint Committee on the Conduct of the War was established in late 1861 to "inquire into the conduct and expenditures of the present war." The standing committee of seven legislators investigated a variety of war-related issues, including the treatment of Federal POWs, fraud by private military supply contractors, and accusations of inept leadership within the Union army, particularly the Army of the Potomac. On this last subject the committee spent an inordinate amount of time. Most of its members were fervent Republican abolitionists, and they tended to judge a general more by his political leanings than his military capabilities. As a result, men such as George McClellan and George Meade were routinely subjected to harsh criticism for their losses, while the blunders of incompetents such as Benjamin Butler were usually overlooked.

Lacking any military background of their own, the congressmen also distrusted career officers, viewing them as overly cautious or just plain cowardly. The intricacies of battlefield tactics eluded the committee, as did the impact of technological change. The defensive advantage afforded to the Confederacy by the proliferation of the rifled musket, for example, was lost on committee members. They were unable to grasp how a ragtag Southern army could hold off the much larger and better-equipped Northern war machine. A protracted standoff, such as that which was transpiring at Petersburg, was simply unfathomable to them.

Even before Petersburg became a battlefront, the committee had tried and failed to have George Meade — that cantankerous professional soldier — removed from command of the Army of the Potomac. During that attempt, the committee solicited testimony from disgruntled Meade subordinates, most notably General Daniel Sickles, who previously drew Meade's ire for disobeying his orders at Gettysburg. These men were obviously fulfilling a personal vendetta against their former boss, a fact that mattered little to the committee. But Lincoln saw through the scheme and refused to be swayed by it.

The Crater affair offered the politicians fresh ammunition against the ill-tempered army commander. Not only was Meade directly involved in the defeat, he had personally assembled the military tribunal that found others to blame for it. Some Washington politicians no doubt smelled a cover-up. Additionally, Burnside had personal friends in Congress and was a committee favorite due to his political views. Therefore, on December 15, 1864, Senator Henry Anthony of Rhode Island, Burnside's home state, moved that the Joint Committee on the Conduct of the War should investigate the failed attack of July 30. Hearings commenced two days later with the testimony of none other than Ambrose Burnside.

As he had done previously, Burnside recounted the entire series of events that preceded the engagement. He again talked about his battle plan, explaining how the black soldiers of the USCT division were specially trained to execute it. He told the committee of the confusion caused by Meade's last-minute revisions to that plan. He complained about Meade's order for the rest of the army to stand down at a time when the men of Ninth Corps were still trapped inside the Crater. Not surprisingly, the congressmen showed far more interest in these matters than had the Court of Inquiry. When Burnside was finished, the committee traveled from Washington to Petersburg in order to interview officers in the field.

Unlike the initial investigation, when he was the accuser, George Meade this time found himself squarely on the defensive. The committee members asked him pointed questions and frequently challenged his answers. Meade repeatedly referred them to the documents compiled by the Court of Inquiry for a more thorough explanation, but the politicians insisted on hearing the details firsthand. They asked Meade why he had denied Burnside's request to let his black troops make the charge.

Meade said that it was merely out of concern that the USCT regiments were green and unproven. When asked why he remained so far in the rear during the battle, Meade said that he chose Ninth Corps headquarters because it was "a central position where I could be in prompt communication with the several corps commanders."[3] Meade was obviously dissatisfied with his responses to the War Committee; he later forwarded a copy of his testimony before the Court of Inquiry, requesting that it be made part of the committee's records as well.

Ulysses S. Grant sat down before the committee with the air of a man who refused to make excuses. He would not blame Meade for the debacle. Grant said that if Meade's orders had been followed properly, "we would have captured Petersburg with all the artillery and a good portion of its support, without the loss of 500 men." Grant felt that Burnside should have leveled his earthworks as instructed, in order to permit an organized assault. He also felt that Burnside's division commanders should have gone forward with their men in order to maintain control and press the attack on Cemetery Hill. Grant said he did have one regret, which was not stepping in to prevent James Ledlie from leading the assault. Grant was aware that Burnside had chosen a leader by the random drawing of straws. "It happened to fall on what I thought was the worst commander in his corps," Grant said, referring to Ledlie. "I knew that fact before the mine was exploded, but did nothing in regard to it. That is the only thing I blame myself for."[4]

When questioned about Meade's decision to keep the USCT division from making the charge, Grant answered frankly:

> General Burnside wanted to put his colored division in front, and I believe if he had done so it would have been a success. Still I agreed with General Meade in his objection to that plan. General Meade said that if we put the colored troops in front (we had only that one division) and it should prove a failure, it would then be said, and very properly, that we were shoving those people ahead to get killed because we did not care anything about them. But that could not be said if we put white troops in front.[5]

The committee returned to Washington and adjourned for the holidays. Only a few witnesses remained to be interviewed when it reconvened in January 1865. Among them was a civilian named Henry Pleasants. The lieutenant colonel had dutifully returned to Petersburg following his leave of absence, but he found that military life no longer appealed to him. The squandered opportunity of his mine had permanently soured Pleasants' faith in the army. A promotion to full colonel in October failed to restore that faith. Two months later he was placed in charge of Fort Sedgwick, a miserable outpost located a mile and a half south of the Crater. The fort was so close to Confederate lines that it was commonly referred to as Fort Hell. Thus, when his term of service expired, Henry Pleasants chose not to extend his military career any further. He was mustered out of the army on December 18, 1864. One of his closest friends, Lieutenant Colonel George Gowen, assumed command of the 48th Pennsylvania.

Four weeks later, Pleasants was testifying before the War Committee. As an officer, he had been reluctant to talk about the Crater fiasco, but as a civilian he did not hesitate. Pleasants described how he constantly had to scrounge for tools and materiel during the mine's construction because the army's chief engineer, Major Duane, considered the project to be "clap-trap and nonsense." Pleasants estimated that had his requests for supplies been filled, the tunnel could have been completed in as little as 12 days. He railed against Ledlie's division for not advancing beyond the Crater, which both allowed the enemy adequate time to recover from the explosion and also obstructed other Federal divisions as they attempted to pass. The resentment Pleasants felt toward Meade was obvious in his words, but he never directly criticized the army commander.

The War Committee's 12-page report on the Crater affair opened with praise for the officers and men of the 48th Pennsylvania. In commending Colonel Pleasants, the congressmen said, "he labored under disadvantages in the successful accomplishment of this important work, which would have deterred a man of less energy and determination." They went on to laud "the zeal, energy and persistence displayed on that occasion by Lieutenant Colonel Pleasants and the men of the 48th Pennsylvania regiment, under his command." The committee criticized "the evident lack of faith in the success of the enterprise" by the Army of the Potomac's leadership, saying, "that lack of faith was accompanied by an entire failure to furnish the assistance and implements necessary to the success of the undertaking within a reasonable time."[6]

Concerning the failed assault, the politicians came to an entirely different set of conclusions than had the Court of Inquiry. The court had blamed the defeat on inadequate preparation and leadership by Burnside and his officers, but the politicians looked beyond Ninth Corps to George Gordon Meade. They felt that "the first and great cause of disaster was the change made on the afternoon preceding the attack," when Meade ordered Burnside to replace his black troops with another division. The committee agreed with Burnside's assessment that six weeks of trench warfare had mentally conditioned his three white divisions to seek cover whenever possible, whereas the USCT division was fresh and eager. "The conduct of the colored troops, when they were put into action, would seem to fully justify the confidence that General Burnside reposed in them," the committee stated.[7]

The congressmen also criticized Meade for ceasing offensive operations too early, leaving Ninth Corps to fend for itself in the Crater. The only criticism they had for Burnside was the random manner in which he chose a replacement for the

USCT division. Otherwise, predictably, the burden of defeat was placed entirely on Meade. The committee's report concluded:

> [T]he disastrous result of the assault of the 30th of July last is mainly attributable to the fact that the plans and suggestions of the general who had devoted his attention for so long a time to the subject, who had carried out to a successful completion the project of mining the enemy's works, and who carefully selected and drilled his troops for the purpose of securing whatever advantages might be attainable from the explosion of the mine, should have been so entirely disregarded by a

Colonel George W. Gowen of the 48th Pennsylvania Infantry Regiment. In December 1864, he succeeded Henry Pleasants as the regiment's commander. Gowen would be killed four months later as the war drew to a close (Roger D. Hunt Collection at USAMHI).

general who had evinced no faith in the successful prosecution of that work, had aided it by no countenance or open approval, and had assumed the entire direction and control only when it was completed, and the time had come for reaping any advantages that might be derived from it.[8]

In the end, the War Committee's investigation had the same impact as most of its other undertakings—nothing. Meade continued to command the Army of the Potomac and Burnside remained banished from it. If anything, the congressional report assured that Burnside would never return. Grant was furious over the public vilification of Meade, a man with whom he frequently disagreed but always respected, and he held Burnside accountable for instigating the investigation.

Burnside was therefore left in a state of limbo. He could not resign from the army; he had tried while in Washington but Lincoln refused to accept it. But clearly he would not be permitted to return to service, either. As the war slowly wound down, Burnside remained quietly in Rhode Island and pondered a political career.

Epilogue

By March 1865, the patience and persistence of Ulysses S. Grant was finally being rewarded. Throughout the winter, his army had gradually grown stronger while Lee's grew weaker. Grant's forces successfully pushed south and west, stretching the Confederate defenses of Petersburg and severing the city's supply lines from the Deep South. By late March, Lee recognized that Petersburg could no longer be protected. He therefore ordered an attack aimed at the center of the Union siege line. Lee's hope was that the Federal line would instinctively contract in order to defend its threatened center, therefore allowing him to slip away to the south and regroup in North Carolina.

In the predawn hours of March 25, a massive Confederate assault force lay in wait, just as Burnside's troops had done nine months earlier. Their target was Fort Stedman, an earthen fortification to the north of the Crater area, which Confederate General John Gordon perceived as the weakest point in the Union center. At 4 am, more than 11,000 Southerners led by Gordon swarmed on Fort Stedman and the adjoining trenches, taking its Ninth Corps occupiers completely by surprise.

Gordon's men quickly captured a thousand yards of Union line, but the victory would be extremely short-lived. By 7 am, the overwhelming Federal forces in the area had rallied and surrounded the fort. Previously, on July 30, 1864, General John Hartranft had learned the futility of trying to hold a tenuous position within the enemy's line. Now he would play the opposite role in that scenario. At 7:45 am, Hartranft launched a heavy counterattack on the Confederates still occupying Fort Stedman and sent them reeling back toward their own lines. Gordon lost over a quarter of his men, roughly half of whom were taken prisoner. Even worse, the brief engagement had failed to open an escape route for the rest of the Confederate army.

Following the repulse at Fort Stedman, Lee's defenses unraveled rapidly. Grant sensed the end was near and pressed ahead on all fronts. The badly depleted Army of Northern Virginia was dealt a decisive blow at Five Forks on April 1, and less than 36 hours later it was forced to evacuate the city. The siege of Petersburg was finally over. Within a week, Lee would agree to surrender at Appomattox Court House.

The miners of the 48th Pennsylvania had remained at Petersburg for the duration of the siege, spending its final long months at Fort Hell. On April 2, in some of the last fighting of the war, the regiment assaulted Fort Mahone. Although successful, the Pennsylvanians suffered 90 casualties, including 10 killed. Among the dead was Henry Pleasants' friend and successor, Colonel George Gowen. The next day the regiment marched into Petersburg with the rest of the Union army. Four months later it returned victorious to Schuylkill County.

Very few of the original volunteers from 1861 remained, most having been killed, wounded, or simply discharged. But Harry "Snapper" Reese was still present, although he now sported the shoulder straps of a second lieutenant. He would forever be remembered as the foreman of the Petersburg Mine, and one of the two volunteers who risked life and limb to repair the mine's defective fusing. Reese remained in Pennsylvania's coal regions and worked at a number of jobs during his postwar years. For a time, he was the bodyguard to a particularly unpopular mine boss. He was also a butcher and a barkeep. In later life, Reese held an official position in the small town of Shamokin. It was there that he died at age 57 from complications of a tooth infection. His tombstone reads, "The Hero Who Touched The Fuse At Petersburg, Va." The man who accompanied Reese into the mine that night, Lieutenant Jacob Douty, had mustered out of the service just two months after the battle. He died in Philadelphia in 1895.

Other men would also forever be associated with the Battle of the Crater. Most notorious was General James Ledlie, who cowered in a bombproof as his division floundered on the battlefield. Following his dismissal, Ledlie managed to overcome both the disgrace of an abysmal military record and his struggle with alcoholism. In the years after the war, he performed valuable engineering work for the Union Pacific Railroad and the city of Chicago. Ledlie's cohort in the bombproof, General Edward Ferrero, also managed to land on his feet. Despite being publicly chastised by the Court of Inquiry, Ferrero not only remained in command but was brevetted a major general in December 1864. He subsequently returned to New York City and resumed his dance instruction business, opening a chain of successful ballrooms.

Likewise, General Orlando Willcox was not permanently scarred by the court's admonishment. After a brief interlude as a civilian in 1866, Willcox resumed his military career and participated in campaigns against the Apache and other Native American tribes. He retired in 1887 as a brigadier general. Robert Potter, the immediate superior of Colonel Pleasants and the only Ninth Corps division commander to emerge from the Crater hearings unscathed, was less fortunate. Potter was seri-

A dead Confederate soldier and a section of chevaux-de-frise lay in an abandoned trench, shortly after the fall of Petersburg in April 1865 (Library of Congress, Prints and Photographs Division LC-B8171-3183 DLC).

ously wounded during the Confederacy's death throes on April 2, 1865. He later attempted a railroad career but found that his poor health would not allow it. For years, Potter traveled Europe seeking remedies for his ills. He lived out his final years in Rhode Island, where he died in 1887.

As he had done so many times before, Ambrose Burnside shook off failure and went on with his life. He was still extremely popular in Rhode Island, and a year after the war he became that state's governor. Later, Burnside traveled to Europe and helped mediate an end to the Franco-Prussian War. In 1875, he began the first of three terms in the U.S. Senate, serving in that body until his death at age 57.

For Edward Ferrero's green USCT division, the Battle of the Crater was a dreadful baptism of fire. Nearly a third of the black soldiers who participated became casualties. The black regiments had acted with more courage and valor than some of the white units that went before them that day, yet many in the army simply assumed that they were the cause of defeat. The assumption was based solely on prejudice, and it prevailed only among those who had not personally witnessed the engagement. Some who actually fought alongside the black troops at the Crater subsequently heaped praise on them. A captain in the 9th New Hampshire said, "I never saw men fight better than the colored division, but they came too late to avail us."[1]

There was an additional sign that the black soldiers had earned a degree of respect for their bravery and sacrifice at the Crater. An African-American noncommissioned officer, Sergeant Decatur Dorsey of the 39th USCT, was awarded the Medal of Honor for his actions on July 30, 1864. With colors in hand, Dorsey had charged across the field at the vanguard of his regiment and planted the flag atop the Confederate earthworks. Later, when the entire division was retreating in panicked disarray, Dorsey managed to rally a sizable group of men at the Union line and restore a measure of order. Twenty-three white Union soldiers also received the Medal of Honor for gallantry at the Crater, and 24 Southerners were named to the Confederate Roll of Honor.

While the animosity between Confederate and USCT forces continued unabated, the encounter at the Crater may have slightly dulled their razor-sharp intolerance for one another. When they clashed again a few weeks later at Second Deep Bottom, there were no reports of Southerners murdering their black prisoners or vice versa. But the most telling change came in early 1865, when Lee's troops voted to allow black men, both free and slave, into their army. Although the move was obviously borne from desperation, the performance of USCT forces at Petersburg, beginning with the Battle of the Crater, must have been on some of the Confederates' minds as they cast their votes.

William Mahone is the Southerner most closely associated with the Crater triumph. The diminutive general tallied many victories in his storied career, but the 10-month defense of Petersburg was clearly his crowning achievement. Even as the end drew painfully near, Mahone fought on with tenacity, fiercely defending the army's path of retreat to Appomattox. After the war, Mahone applied that same energy to the railroad industry and built a small empire for himself. During the 1870s, he parlayed his power into a formidable political machine that took control of the state legislature, and in 1880 he was elected to the U.S. Senate. Mahone died in 1895 and was laid to rest in Blandsford Cemetery, on the very same hill he had denied the Yankees over three decades earlier.

The general's postwar rival, Colonel David Weisiger, was buried on Cemetery

Hill as well. Evidence suggests that Mahone was highly annoyed by the controversy over who gave the order to charge from the ravine on July 30, 1864. Like most Southern participants, Mahone relished his role in foiling the devious Federal plan to capture Petersburg. He enjoyed chatting with war veterans—Northern and Southern alike—and frequently showed off a large oil painting of the battle that hung in his library. The disagreement with his former subordinate was therefore an embarrassment for the general, especially when Weisiger accused him of never having left the safety of the ravine that day. Mahone responded by publishing a pamphlet containing his own account of the battle. He carefully detailed his actions during the engagement, including his order to the Virginia brigade to charge, and his subsequent presence in the recaptured trenches. Regardless, the dispute continued until some time after Mahone's death.

Although it has been speculated that the controversy was prolonged by Mahone's political enemies, it seems just as likely that the old war veterans simply took pleasure in recounting one of their finest hours. For years, they also hotly debated whether the bulk of the credit for repelling the Yankee assault should go to the infantry or the artillery. Representatives from each side waged a polite war of words on the pages of *Confederate Veteran*, the *Southern Historical Society Papers*, and other publications. George Bernard, a Petersburg attorney, author, and veteran of the 12th Virginia, finally tried to settle the matter in 1892. He wrote, "The fight was one in which *both* infantry and artillery took part and in which *neither* could have accomplished much without the efficient aid of the other, and it is believed that this is a conclusion which will be reached by any impartial student who will read the details of this memorable engagement."[2] Bernard's eloquent appeal did not keep the veterans from continuing with their fun.

Henry Pleasants remained bitter about the Crater fiasco for the rest of his life. Years later, while corresponding with an old friend from the 48th Pennsylvania, he described the mine as, "A project, the success of which was perfect, and which, had it not been for the want of harmony between the generals commanding the Ninth Corps and Army of the Potomac, and the bad conduct of the commander of the First Division, would have broken through the thin shell that separated us from the heart of the Confederacy and ended the war then and there." Pleasants claimed that shortly after the battle the chief engineer of the army, General John Barnard, approached him. Barnard suggested that they walk the Petersburg line together and search for suitable places to begin new mining operations. But Pleasants declined; he wanted nothing more to do with West Point-trained engineers.[3]

As a civilian, Pleasants quickly built a happy life for himself. He found that the death of his wife no longer haunted him. In 1863, while the regiment was on garrison duty in Kentucky, Pleasants met a young woman named Anne Shaw, and the two stayed in contact throughout the war. They married in 1867 and settled in Pottsville, where Pleasants was working for the Philadelphia and Reading Coal and Iron Company. Within a few years he ascended to the title of chief engineer, and in 1873 he became active in fighting the Molly Maguires, a labor group that used violence to draw attention to miners' abysmal wages and deplorable working conditions.

During the summer of that year, while vacationing in Cape May, New Jersey, Pleasants met by chance with Ulysses S. Grant, who had just begun his second term as president of the United States. According to family legend, Grant recognized Pleasants from across a crowded hotel dining room and asked to speak with him. Over cigars, the two men reminisced about common friends and wartime experiences.[4]

Henry Pleasants' success as an engineer afforded him the opportunity to travel, and in 1879, he toured Europe with his wife and their three children. It was during this time that Pleasants began suffering from severe headaches. Upon seeking treatment, he was informed that he had an inoperable brain tumor. Pleasants returned home and lived out his final months in Pottsville. The architect of the Petersburg Mine died on March 26, 1880 at age 47. Pleasants had been brevetted a brigadier general by President Andrew Johnson shortly after the war, but his gravestone bore no indication of military service.

The Crater itself still exists today, though not in its original form. When the armies finally left Petersburg in 1865, farmer William Griffith returned to his land and began covering over the scars of war. But many of those scars ran too deep, and Griffith could reclaim only a small portion of the area for farming. Breastworks and trenches remained, as did the Crater, and thousands of shallow, unmarked graves lay sprinkled everywhere. The same problem existed throughout the entire Petersburg region.

In 1866, the federal government established Poplar Grove National Cemetery four miles south of the city to properly bury its fallen warriors. A spot was chosen where the 50th New York Engineers had assembled pine logs into a small church during the siege. A burial corps was organized to begin the arduous task of recovering the scattered bodies. Workers would form a long line, each man standing a yard apart, and slowly march across the battlefield searching for signs of a burial. In some instances it was easy: the dead man's comrades had left behind a marker. Some soldiers had been buried with such haste that the head and feet protruded above ground, while others had not been buried at all. More challenging to the searchers were proper interments, where the only evidence might be a suggestion of disturbed earth. The entire line of workers halted whenever a grave was found, not resuming their march until the body was dug up and removed. It was foul, tedious work, and although the government paid a respectable $5 for each collec-

Blandford Church and its adjacent graveyard, situated atop the coveted high ground that was dubbed Cemetery Hill. It was the primary objective for the Union assault of July 30, 1864. The cemetery became the final resting place for most of the siege's Confederate victims (Library of Congress, Prints and Photographs Division LC-B8171-1090 DLC).

tion of bones that included a skull, the laborers reportedly contracted dysentery and other ills from handling the dead.

Excavations inside the Crater began on July 30, the battle's second anniversary. The pit quickly yielded 300 corpses, which the work crews found to be remarkably well preserved. These too were permanently laid to rest in the rapidly expanding national cemetery. Of the more than 6,000 Union soldiers interred at Poplar Grove, little more than a third could be positively identified. Even worse was the identification rate at Blandford Cemetery — barely 2,000 of the roughly 30,000 Confederates buried there were identified. After three long years, the burial corps concluded its work in the summer of 1869.

What seemed like a tragedy to William Griffith ultimately proved to be a significant financial opportunity. Within a few years, strangers were showing up at the farmer's door asking to see the mysterious Crater they had heard and read so much about. For some reason, the peculiar little episode from recent history captured the public's imagination. Perhaps it simply stood out as something unique on a lengthy roll call of conventional Civil War battles. In any case, scores of tourists were soon arriving to see the magnificent hole rent in the earth by Burnside's mine explosion. In true entrepreneurial spirit, Griffith erected a fence around the Crater and charged a 25-cent admission fee for those who wished to go inside and have a look. Bolstered by his success, Griffith later added a souvenir shop and the Crater Saloon. The war had robbed him of his first vocation, but it created for him another.

In 1931, long after William Griffith's death, the ground once known as Elliott's Salient was being developed for inclusion in a new golf course. Landscapers were startled to unearth 29 skeletons that the burial corps had missed over six decades earlier. The remains were taken to Poplar Grove National Cemetery and buried with full military honors. A few years later the Crater was incorporated into the newly established Petersburg National Military Park. A dedication ceremony in the spring of 1937 included a grand reenactment of the Battle of the Crater, complete with oil-soaked balls of rags that were set afire and hurled through the air to simulate cannon shot.

The existing remnants of the Crater today are carefully preserved, but they may nevertheless disappoint the visitor to Petersburg National Battlefield. Time and human activity have severely degraded the site, leaving only a small, grassy depression where once was a great, gaping chasm. But the location of the mine's entrance can still be seen, as can a long trail of sinkholes left behind by the collapsed tunnel. Evidence of Confederate countermining still exists as well. These landmarks, and a few granite monuments, bear testament to the unlikely chain of events first set into motion by Henry Pleasants and the miners of the 48th Pennsylvania.

Conclusions

No study of the Crater affair would be complete without at least a cursory analysis of its causes and effects. Whether the engagement is viewed as a colossal Federal blunder or a brilliant Confederate achievement, or both, the fundamental reasons for its outcome are nonetheless debatable. At the time, the battle was given close scrutiny by the Court of Inquiry and the Joint Committee on the Conduct of the War, but political considerations obviously clouded the judgement of both those bodies. Furthermore, their members did not have the benefit of nearly a century and a half of subsequent military history with which to put the battle into context.

The decision to excavate the Petersburg Mine was made by Ambrose Burnside. Preliminary work on the tunnel was already underway when Pleasants and Potter met with the Ninth Corps commander to discuss their idea, but had Burnside disapproved, all work no doubt would have ceased. However, Burnside did not disapprove; he embraced the idea and encouraged his subordinates to proceed with haste. Initially, George Meade also reacted favorably to the proposal. It was only after his engineers concluded that such a mine would most likely fail did Meade sour on the project.

Meade's engineers condemned the mining concept for two reasons. First, they believed that the distance to Elliott's Salient was too great for a tunnel. On this count, they obviously underestimated the men of the 48th Pennsylvania. Colonel Pleasants and his miners were familiar with the latest techniques for extracting coal from the ground, and their expertise in tunneling far surpassed that of the army engineers. The Pennsylvanians proved that fact throughout the month of July 1864. The second objection the engineers raised was the location of the mine. Elliott's Salient was flanked on either side by smaller bulges in the Confederate line that would enable the enemy to pour enfilading fire into any attacking column. This assertion was correct; the flanks were indeed a major problem. However, the same could be said of almost any point in the Petersburg defenses. Both the Union and the Confederate lines endlessly coiled and curved along the entire battlefront. Flanking fire would be a concern for almost any head-on assault, whether the target was Elliott's Salient or elsewhere.

Ultimately, the opportunity to undermine Elliott's Salient was too great to be ignored. By chance, a regiment of experienced miners occupied the Union's closest position to the enemy lines. The miners happened to be located at the bottom of a gradual incline, meaning they could bore into the slope and tunnel their way deep below the enemy position. In purely strategic terms, the project carried little risk. If the mine collapsed or was discovered by the enemy, the total loss could not exceed a few dozen miners— men who would otherwise be risking their lives anyway in the trenches. Even if the Federals ultimately chose to forego an assault and simply detonate the mine to kill as many enemy troops as possible, the decision to go ahead with the project was still a good one. The tunnel's vindication came at 4:44 am on July 30 when 278 Confederates suddenly met their fate.

The War Committee harshly criticized Meade for failing to support the mining project as it crawled along. Colonel Pleasants testified that many of his requests for supplies and equipment went ignored, forcing him to cobble together tools out of discarded materials and scrounge lumber from wherever he could find it. Pleasants estimated that with proper support he could have completed the job within two weeks, instead of the 33 days actually needed. It is difficult to imagine that Meade or his staff purposely withheld any available equipment from the miners. With the possible exception of a theodolite, which Burnside was forced to acquire from Washington, the items that Pleasants wanted were most likely unavailable at the time. As the miners labored underground, the rest of the army was engaged in digging trenches and constructing fortifications. Lumber, picks, and wheelbarrows would naturally be in short supply, and the essential task of entrenching an entire army would obviously take priority over a small project of dubious value. If the mine had been excavated three months later, in the fall of 1864 when the nearby docks of City Point teemed with supplies, perhaps the miners would have received more aid. But in the early summer of 1864, difficult choices about the allocation of limited resources still had to be made.

It is interesting to suppose what might have happened if, in fact, all of Henry Pleasants' requests had been promptly filled. Would there have been a different outcome to the battle had the miners been provided with everything they needed? In that instance, the mine would have been completed by July 7, assuming that Pleasants' estimate was accurate. Of course, it is impossible to judge whether an attack made early in the month would have been any more successful than the one of July 30. However, it obviously would have permitted the Southerners less time to fortify Elliott's Salient. Specifically, the cavalier trench behind the fort and the strategic placement of Confederate artillery — both of which proved instrumental in thwarting the Federal advance — were not yet completed. On July 30, a warren of Confederate trenches and passageways hindered the Union attackers. Three weeks earlier, that labyrinth would have been far less intricate.

The sluggish pace of the excavation had another penalty: it created doubt and hesitation among the Union leadership. Throughout the month of July, Meade remained ambivalent about the mine's value and Grant searched for other options. Burnside used the time to formulate a battle plan and train his USCT division, but he did not share his intentions with Meade until he was asked to do so on July 27. Had the two men discussed the matter beforehand, Burnside would have learned about Meade's reluctance to rely on the USCT soldiers, and had adequate time to alter his plan accordingly. But the slowly progressing mine remained a question mark until late in the month, allowing the Union's decision-makers to be easily distracted by other matters.

The lack of communication between Burnside and his commander was a recurring theme at Petersburg. Meade, like others within the officer corps, harbored reservations about Burnside's military capabilities. Those suspicions were not unfounded. Burnside's brief tenure as head of the army in 1862–63 was an undeniable failure. The man performed well enough when events unfolded as anticipated, but he lacked the ability to adjust and improvise. Additionally, a small but persistent stubborn streak lurked beneath his outwardly helpful demeanor. Burnside would never admit it, perhaps not even to himself, but the occasional comment or mildly rebellious action suggested that he resented reporting to Meade, a former subordinate whom Burnside himself had once promoted.

Burnside's shortcomings no doubt grated on the short temper of Meade, a man commonly known as the "old snapping turtle." The Ninth Corps commander often unwittingly touched off that temper with a poor choice of words. The exchange of telegrams between Meade and Burnside on July 3 was a prime example. That incident began when Meade inquired about the chances of success for an attack launched from the Ninth Corps front. Burnside innocently replied that the odds were fair, provided that he could call in the two adjacent corps to his support if necessary. The stipulation greatly annoyed Meade — issuing orders to corps commanders was his job — and he let Burnside know it. From that point on, their tense relationship precluded effective communication. Burnside was forced to select his words carefully, and Meade cast a wary eye on everything he suggested. One cannot help but wonder if the mining proposal would have been more welcomed in Army of the Potomac headquarters had it come from a general other than Ambrose Burnside.

The same could be said of Burnside's battle plan. His choice of the USCT division for the attack's vanguard may have been controversial, but it was also logical. The black regiments were inexperienced to be sure, but they were also fresh and at full strength. Conversely, the three other divisions of Ninth Corps were depleted, both in terms of numbers and morale. Meade also dismissed Burnside's idea for the leading regiments to sweep down the Confederate trenches in order to widen the breach. Capturing Cemetery Hill should be the sole objective, Meade said, since there would be precious little time for anything else. But Burnside had intended all along for the bulk of his troops to charge directly for the crest. Only a handful of specially trained regiments would be diverted to secure the flanks. Tactically, the idea made sense. Clearing the trenches to the north and south would help protect the lodgment on Cemetery Hill. It would also open the way for the rest of Ninth Corps to march on Petersburg. Yet Meade would not hear of it. His only concern was getting troops to the top of the hill as quickly as possible.

Just as Meade could not resist altering Burnside's battle plan, he also could not bring himself to let Burnside direct the engagement. Grant's feign to the north of the James River had successfully drawn away most of Petersburg's defenders. This was a one-time opportunity, since Robert E. Lee would not be fooled in such a way again. Burnside could not be allowed to squander it. Regardless, Meade chose to remain a mile to the rear, at Ninth Corps headquarters. He may have done so out of consideration for Burnside, who had championed the mining project when others scoffed, and whose men would be making the assault. More likely, Meade was trying to establish a more efficient command and control system. Under this arrangement, he would remain in the rear, well away from the confusion of battle, and make decisions based upon the information that streamed in from his subordinates.

With the advent of the field radio in the twentieth century, Meade's "command center" approach would become the norm in most battlefield situations. But in 1864, it simply did not work because communications technology had not yet advanced far enough to permit it. The telegraph worked well for routine communications, but it was too slow to keep up with the ever-changing dynamics of battle. By the time a message was composed, transmitted, and delivered to its recipient, it may have already become obsolete. General Gouverneur Warren made it clear in his testimony that the telegraph was a hindrance on July 30, requiring him to waste valuable time drafting messages and waiting for replies as the battle raged and opportunities were lost. His pleas for Meade to come to the front for a firsthand view proved that he did not believe in the "command center" arrangement. Burnside's reaction was even worse; he found the system so foreign that he was either unwilling or unable to do what Meade expected of him. The result was a near complete breakdown in Federal communications.

Meade's absence from the field also created confusion about who was in command. Generals Warren and Ord appeared willing to follow Burnside's lead, but Burnside did not feel he had the authority to give them orders. The rebuke Meade had given him earlier in the month for suggesting that he be permitted to call in supporting troops was still fresh in Burnside's mind. (Indeed, Burnside later presented those telegrams to the War Committee as proof that he had no authority to direct Warren and Ord on July 30.) As a result, the three corps commanders periodically conferred with one another during the engagement, but acted independently. Their feeble attempts at the Confederate line were made without any planning or coordination, and in Warren's case, no attempt was made at all. Meanwhile, Meade remained in the rear, demanding to be told what was happening. Had he been present at the front, perhaps at Taylor House with Burnside, Meade could have assessed the situation for himself and issued timely orders to his corps commanders. Otherwise, he should have granted one of those men supreme authority over all of the assembled forces. On that score, both the War Committee and the Court of Inquiry hit the mark.

Meade's errors should not overshadow the many mistakes made by Ambrose Burnside in the days leading up to, and during, the battle. The Ninth Corps commander made virtually no preparations along his front for a major offensive, despite the urgings of others. The artillerists who would protect his infantry requested that Burnside remove a stand of trees blocking their guns, but he declined. Meade ordered Burnside to level some of his earthworks and the corresponding obstacles so that assaulting columns could pass, but it was not done. Burnside used the excuse that any such activity would alert the enemy that an attack was imminent. He may have been correct, but there were of course ways of masking the intent of those actions. Weeks earlier, Burnside had disguised smoke from the mine's ventilation shaft by burning decoy fires all along his line. A similar effort involving the felling of trees and leveling of ramparts would have had the same camouflaging effect.

Burnside also displayed a lack of forethought when he failed to adjust to Meade's revisions to his battle plan. In his testimony, Burnside often stated or implied that Meade's changes were handed down to him mere hours before the battle. In reality, Meade stated his objections to the plan when the two men met on the morning of July 28. When Burnside protested, the Army of the Potomac commander agreed to refer the matter to Grant. But rather than returning to his headquarters and prepare for the very real possibility that Grant would concur with Meade, Burnside did nothing. Thus, an entire day of planning and preparation was lost.

When the bad news finally arrived on July 29, Burnside was unable to recover. Rather than working feverishly to accomplish as much as possible within the limitations placed upon him, Burnside seems to have resigned himself to defeat. He would let fate decide the outcome of the battle. Emblematic of that attitude was the manner in which he chose a leader for the assault. Instead of making that agonizing decision himself, as a good commander should, Burnside deferred to the random drawing of straws.

Whether Burnside was aware of James Ledlie's deteriorated mental condition is not known; Ledlie's aides went to great lengths to hide his drinking binges and spells of cowardice. Either way, it does not reflect well on Burnside. Ulysses S. Grant later acknowledged that he himself was aware of Ledlie's problems. If the rumors had spread that far up the chain of command, then Burnside should have known too. His apparent ignorance in the matter casts further suspicion on his leadership abilities. If he was, in fact, alive to Ledlie's condition but permitted him to lead the attack anyway, then Burnside was even more culpable.

Grant remarked that his only personal regret for the Crater debacle was not intervening when he learned that Ledlie was chosen. However, it appears that he was remiss in another matter as well. Grant had experimented with subterranean warfare during the siege of Vicksburg in 1863, and there he learned that the crater created by a mine explosion could trap charging troops. The painful experience of the "Death Hole" could not yet have faded from his memory, but it appears that neither Grant nor anyone from his staff warned Ninth Corps of the danger. Armed with that knowledge, some officers may have been more careful to steer their men clear of the pit and its deceptive appearance of safety.

The Crater's irresistible lure to the onrushing Union troops was a direct result of intense psychological conditioning from trench warfare. Seeking cover had become second nature for these men. Without effective leadership to spur them along, the urge to obtain shelter prevailed. The mental conditioning was not limited to privates. The arrangement of Federal units prior to the assault shows that high-ranking officers fell victim to it as well. Rather than forming traditional battle lines, entire brigades were jammed into trenches and covered ways. The narrow ditches filled up quickly, and units for which there was no room were stationed half a mile to the rear. Darkness would have permitted troops to form up safely on the open ground immediately behind the Union trench line. But for the previous six weeks this area had been thought of as an exposed and dangerous position, so it was overlooked. A habitual inclination toward using only sheltered passageways left the assault force strung out over a wide area. Once the shooting began, no unit could advance until the one in front of it moved. The result was a piecemeal attack that fully negated the Union's numerical advantage.

Despite the missteps, a Federal victory was still possible, and perhaps even probable, at the moment the mine exploded. The massive fireball sent most Southerners fleeing in terror. A few Confederate commanders subsequently claimed that their men stood their ground, undaunted by the blast. However, most evidence indicates that the majority obeyed their natural instincts to run away. The much more important point is that once rational thought reasserted itself, the seasoned

Confederate veterans returned to their posts. As an immense Federal artillery barrage raged, the Southerners gradually came back to the line and prepared to mount yet another defense.

Unlike their counterparts in blue, Confederate leaders excelled at the Crater. Colonel Fitz William McMaster of the 17th South Carolina stepped in for his fallen brigade commander without hesitation, organizing his scant forces into a temporary resistance. Artillery officers hurried their guns into action, providing a critical bulwark for the shaken infantry. Aiding both the infantry and the artillery was the foresight of the engineers. Weeks earlier they had established the cavalier trench behind Elliott's Salient as a fallback position, and identified the most effective firing locations for the big Confederate guns.

The Confederacy's upper-echelon leaders also made good decisions on July 30, 1864. Robert E. Lee was many miles away when the initial reports of the mine explosion first reached him. Sensing urgency, Lee bypassed the normal chain of command and dispatched orders directly to William Mahone. When Mahone arrived on the scene, he immediately comprehended the tactical situation and utilized the terrain to form his men for a charge. Enemy movement forced the general to launch his counterattack sooner than planned, but he did not panic. Nor did he panic when his Georgia brigade was driven off. Mahone patiently allowed events to unfold, not committing his last reserves to battle until they had a better chance of success. Meanwhile, neither Lee nor P.G.T. Beauregard interfered with their subordinate's actions. Instead, they observed from a distance and permitted Mahone the freedom to execute his plan as he saw fit. Their restraint was rewarded just a few hours later with an uplifting victory and the complete restoration of the Petersburg defenses.

The siege of Petersburg signaled a new era in the history of warfare. Technological progress, particularly the invention of the rifled musket, had shifted battlefield advantage in favor of defense, thus making a protracted standoff almost inevitable. The same scenario would be played out on a much larger and more horrific scale in Europe half a century later. With neither side able to achieve a permanent breakthrough, armies of the First World War were also forced to entrench and wage a grinding war of attrition.

As in Petersburg, mines were employed during World War I as a means of initiating a breakthrough. Although British forces achieved more success with underground attacks than did their American Civil War predecessors, a permanent solution to trench warfare would not emerge until the 1930s with the evolution of the armored tank. Within this historical framework, the nature of the Battle of the Crater can be more readily understood. It was an early, imperfect attempt at a fundamental military dilemma, and an important lesson from America's past.

Appendix A: Organization of Engaged Forces

(C= Captured, K = Killed, W = Wounded, MW = Mortally Wounded)

FEDERAL FORCES AT THE BATTLE OF THE CRATER

COMMANDER IN CHIEF
Lt. Gen. Ulysses S. Grant

ARMY OF THE POTOMAC
Maj. Gen. George G. Meade

Chief of Artillery — Brig. Gen. Henry J. Hunt
Chief Engineer — Maj. James C. Duane
Chief of Staff — Andrew A. Humphreys
Volunteer Engineer Brigade — Brig. Gen. Henry W. Benham
Battalion U.S. Engineers — Capt. George H. Mendell
Provost Guard — Brig. Gen. Marsena R. Patrick
Signal Corps — Capt. Benjamin F. Fisher

NINTH ARMY CORPS
Maj. Gen. Ambrose E. Burnside

Aide de Camp — Lt. Col. James L. Van Buren
Assistant Inspector General — Lt. Col. Charles G. Loring
Chief of Staff — Brig. Gen. Julius White
Escort — 3rd New Jersey Cavalry (detachment), Lt. John S. Hough
Provost Guard — 8th United States, Capt. Milton Cogswell

Appendix A: Organization of Engaged Forces

First Division
Brig. Gen. James H. Ledlie

First Brigade — Brig. Gen. William F. Bartlett [C]
   21st Massachusetts, Capt. William H. Clark [MW]
   29th Massachusetts, Lt. Col. Joseph H. Barnes
   35th Massachusetts, Capt. Clifton A. Blanchard
   56th Massachusetts, Capt. Charles D. Lamb
   57th Massachusetts, Maj. Albert Prescott [K], Capt. George H. Howe [K]
   59th Massachusetts, Col. Jacob Parker Gould [MW], Lt. Col. John Hodges Jr. [K]
   100th Pennsylvania, Maj. Thomas J. Hamilton [W & C]

Second Brigade — Col. Elisha G. Marshall [C]
   3rd Maryland Battalion, Lt. Col. Gilbert P. Robinson
   179th New York, Maj. John Barton [K]
   14th New York Heavy Artillery, Maj. Charles Chipman
   2nd Pennsylvania Provisional Heavy Artillery, Lt. Col. Benjamin Griffin Barney [W]

Second Division
Brig. Gen. Robert B. Potter

First Brigade — Col. Zenas Bliss
   36th Massachusetts, Capt. Thaddeus L. Barker
   58th Massachusetts, Capt. Everett S. Horton
   2nd New York Mounted Rifles, Col. John Fisk
   51st New York, Maj. John G. Wright [W]
   45th Pennsylvania, Capt. Theodore Gregg
   48th Pennsylvania, Lt. Col. Henry Pleasants
   4th Rhode Island, Maj. James T. P. Bucklin
   7th Rhode Island, Lt. Col. Percy Daniels

Second Brigade — Brig. Gen. Simon G. Griffin
   31st Maine, Capt. James Dean
   32nd Maine, Capt. Joseph B. Hammond
   2nd Maryland, Lt. Col. Henry Howard Jr. [MW]
   6th New Hampshire, Capt. Samuel G. Goodwin
   9th New Hampshire, Capt. John B. Cooper
   11th New Hampshire, Capt. Arthur C. Locke
   17th Vermont, Lt. Col. Charles Cummings

Third Division
Brig. Gen. Orlando B. Willcox

First Brigade — Brig. Gen. John F. Hartranft
    8th Michigan, Lt. Col. Ralph Ely
    27th Michigan (1st & 2nd Companies Michigan Sharpshooters attached),
    Capt. Edward S. Leadbeater
    109th New York, Capt. Edwin Evans
    51st Pennsylvania, Col. William J. Bolton [W]
    37th Wisconsin, Col. Samuel Harriman
    38th Wisconsin, Lt. Col. Colwert K. Pier
    13th Ohio Cavalry (dismounted battalion), Lt. Col. Noah H. Hixon

Second Brigade — Col. William Humphrey
    1st Michigan Sharpshooters, Capt. Elmer C. Dicey [C]
    2nd Michigan, Capt. John L. Young [K]
    20th Michigan, Lt. Col. Byron M. Cutcheon
    46th New York, Capt. Alphons Serviere
    60th Ohio (9th & 10th Companies Ohio Sharpshooters attached), Maj. Martin
    P. Avery
    50th Pennsylvania, Lt. Col. Edward Overton, Jr.
    24th New York Cavalry (dismounted), Lt. Col. Walter C. Newberry
    Acting Engineers—17th Michigan, Col. Constant Luce

Fourth Division
Brig. Gen. Edward Ferrero

First Brigade — Lt. Col. Joshua K. Sigfried
    27th U.S. Colored Troops, Lt. Col. Charles J. Wright [W]
    30th U.S. Colored Troops, Col. Delevan Bates [W]
    39th U.S. Colored Troops, Col. Ozora P. Stearns
    43rd U.S. Colored Troops, Lt. Col. H. Seymour Hall [W]

Second Brigade — Col. Henry Goddard Thomas
    19th U.S. Colored Troops, Lt. Col. Joseph G. Perkins
    23rd U. S. Colored Troops, Col. Cleveland J. Campbell
    28th U.S. Colored Troops, Col. Charles S. Russell
    29th U.S. Colored Troops, Lt. Col. John A. Bross [K]
    31st U.S. Colored Troops, Capt. Thomas Wright

Artillery Brigade
Lt. Col. J. Albert Monroe

Maine Light, 2nd Battery (B), Capt. Albert F. Thomas

Appendix A: Organization of Engaged Forces

Maine Light, 3rd Battery (C), Capt. Ezekiel R. Mayo
Maine Light, 7th Battery (G), Capt. Adelbert B. Twitchell
Massachusetts Light, 11th Battery, Capt. Edward J. Jones
Massachusetts Light, 14th Battery, Capt. Joseph W. B. Wright
New York Light, 19th Battery, Capt. Edward W. Rogers
New York Light, 27th Battery, Capt. John B. Eaton
New York Light, 34th Battery, Capt. Jacob Roemer
Pennsylvania Light, Battery D, Capt. George W. Durell
Vermont Light, 3rd Battery, Capt. Romeo H. Start
Mortar Battery, Capt. Benjamin F. Smiley

FIFTH CORPS ARTILLERY
Col. Charles S. Wainwright

1st New York Light, Battery B, Lt. Robert E. Rogers
1st New York Light, Battery E, Lt. James B. Hazelton
1st New York Light, Battery H, Capt. Charles E. Mink
5th United States, Battery D, Lt. William E. Van Reed

SIXTH CORPS ARTILLERY
Capt. William Hexamer

Maine Light, 4th Battery D, Lt. Charles W. White
New York Light, 3rd Battery, Capt. William A. Ham

ARMY OF THE JAMES
Maj. Gen. Benjamin Butler

Siege Artillery — Col. Henry L. Abbott
  1st Connecticut Heavy Artillery, Col. Henry L. Abbott
    Company A, Capt. Edward A. Gillett
    Company B, Capt. Albert F. Booker
    Company M, Capt. Franklin A. Pratt

EIGHTEENTH ARMY CORPS
Maj. Gen. Edward O.C. Ord

Chief Engineer — Capt. Francis U. Farquhar

TENTH ARMY CORPS
(Attached to Eighteenth Corps)

Second Division
Brig. Gen. John W. Turner

First Brigade — Col. N. Martin Curtis
  3rd New York, Capt. George W. Warren
  112th New York, Lt. Col. John F. Smith
  117th New York, Lt. Col. Rufus Daggett
  142nd New York, Lt. Col. Albert M. Barney

Second Brigade — Lt. Col. William B. Coan
  47th New York, Capt. Charles A. Moore
  48th New York, Maj. Samuel W. Swartwout [K]
  76th Pennsylvania, Maj. William S. Diller
  97th Pennsylvania, Capt. Isaiah Price

Third Brigade — Col. Louis Bell
  13th Indiana, Lt. Samuel M. Zent
  9th Maine, Capt. Robert J. Gray
  4th New Hampshire, Capt. Frank W. Parker
  115th New York, Lt. Col. Nathan J. Johnson
  169th New York, Maj. James A. Colvin

CONFEDERATE FORCES AT THE BATTLE OF THE CRATER

ARMY OF NORTHERN VIRGINIA
Gen. Robert E. Lee

Aide de Camp & Assistant Military Secretary — Maj. Charles Marshall
Aide de Camp & Assistant Adjutant General — Col. Walter H. Taylor
Aide de Camp & Assistant Inspector General — Maj. Charles S. Venable
Chief of Artillery — Brig. Gen. William N. Pendleton
Chief Engineer — Col. Walter Husted Stevens
Chief of Ordnance — Lt. Col. Briscoe G. Baldwin

THIRD CORPS
Maj. Gen. Ambrose P. Hill

Anderson's Division
Brig. Gen. William Mahone

Appendix A: Organization of Engaged Forces

Mahone's (Virginia) Brigade — Col. David Weisiger [W]
    6th Virginia, Col. George Thomas Rogers
    12th Virginia, Capt. Richard W. Jones
    16th Virginia, Lt. Col. Richard Owen Whitehead
    41st Virginia, Maj. William H. Etheridge
    61st Virginia, Lt. Col. William H. Stewart

Wilcox (Alabama) Brigade — Col. John C.C. Sanders
    8th Alabama, Capt. M.W. Mordecai
    9th Alabama, Col. J. Horace King
    10th Alabama, Capt. W.L. Brewster
    11th Alabama, Lt. Col. George Edward Tayloe
    14th Alabama, Capt. Elias Folk [K]

Wright's (Georgia) Brigade — Lt. Col. Matthew R. Hall
    3rd Georgia, Lt. Col. Claiborne Snead
    22nd Georgia, Col. George H. Jones
    48th Georgia, Lt. Col. Reuben W. Carswell
    64th Georgia, Col. John W. Evans [K]

Army of Northern Virginia Artillery
Brig. Gen. William N. Pendleton

First Corps — Lt. Col. Frank Huger
    Haskell's Battalion — Maj. John C. Haskell
        Branch (NC) Battery, Capt. Henry G. Flanner
        Nelson (VA) Battery, Capt. James N. Lamkin

13th Battalion Virginia Light Artillery — Maj. Wade Hampton Gibbs [W]
    Company A, Otey Battery, Capt. David Norvell Walker
    Company B, Ringgold Battery, Capt. Crispin Dickinson
    Company C, Davidson's Battery, Lt. John H. Chamberlayne
    Mortar Battery, Lt. Jack Langhorne

Third Corps — Col. Reuben Lindsay Walker
    Pegram's Battalion, Lt. Col. William J. Pegram
        Crenshaw's (VA) Battery, Capt. Thomas Ellett
        Letcher (VA) Light Artillery, Capt. Thomas A. Brander

Dept. of North Carolina & Sourthern Virginia
Lt. Gen. P.G.T. Beauregard

Johnson's Division
Maj. Gen. Bushrod Rust Johnson

Ransom's (North Carolina) Brigade — Col. Lee M. McAfee
  24th North Carolina, Col. William J. Clarke
  25th North Carolina, Maj. William S. Grady [MW]
  35th North Carolina, Col. James T. Johnson
  49th North Carolina, Lt. Col. John A. Flemming [K]
  56th North Carolina, Capt. Lawson Harrill

Elliott's (South Carolina) Brigade — Brig. Gen. Stephen Elliott [W]
  17th South Carolina, Col. Fitz William McMaster
  18th South Carolina, Capt. R.H. Glenn
  22nd South Carolina, Col. David G. Fleming [K]
  23rd South Carolina, Capt. E.R. White [W]
  26th South Carolina, Col. Alexander D. Smith

Wise's (Virginia) Brigade — Col. J. Thomas Goode
  26th Virginia, Capt. Napoleon B. Street
  34th Virginia, Maj. John R. Bagby
  46th Virginia, Capt. George Norris
  59th Virginia, Capt. Henry Wood [W]

Hoke's Division
Maj. Gen. Robert F. Hoke

Clingman's (North Carolina) Brigade — Brig. Gen. Thomas L. Clingman
  61st North Carolina, Col. James D. Radcliffe

Colquitt's (Georgia) Brigade — Brig. Gen. Alfred H. Colquitt
  6th Georgia, Col. John T. Lofton
  19th Georgia, Col. James H. Neal
  23rd Georgia, Col. James H. Huggins
  27th Georgia, Maj. Hezekiah Bussey
  28th Georgia, Capt. John A. Johnson

DEPT. OF NORTH CAROLINA & SOUTHERN VIRGINIA ARTILLERY
Col. Hilary Polard Jones

Branch's Battalion — Maj. James C. Coit
  Halifax (VA) Battery, Capt. Samuel T. Wright
  Petersburg (VA) Battery, Capt. Richard G. Pegram

Appendix B: Casualties Incurred at the Battle of the Crater

	Total Strength (est.)	Killed & Mortally Wounded	Wounded	Captured & Missing	Total Casualties
Union	16,800	504	1,881	1,413	3,798
Confederate*	9,400	361 +	727 +	403 +	1,612

*Includes victims of the mine explosion. Existing records of Confederate casualties are incomplete.

Appendix C: Soldiers Decorated for Gallantry at the Battle of the Crater

UNITED STATES MEDAL OF HONOR

Ninth Corps

First Division

    Capt. Charles H. Houghton, 14th New York Heavy Artillery

    Color Sgt. Conrad Homan, 29th Massachusetts

    Sgt. James Hill, 14th New York Heavy Artillery

    Sgt. Benjamin F. McAlwee, 3rd Maryland

    Sgt. George Schneider, 3rd Maryland

Second Division

    Lt. Harlan J. Swift, 2nd New York Mounted Rifles

    Sgt. Maj. Abraham Cohn, 6th New Hampshire

    Sgt. William H. Matthews, 2nd Maryland

    Sgt. Charles Simons, 9th New Hampshire

    Sgt. Leander A. Wilkins, 9th New Hampshire

    Corp. Frank Hogan, 45th Pennsylvania

    Corp. Charles Knight, 9th New Hampshire

    Pvt. James Welsh, 4th Rhode Island

Third Division

    Col. Isaac S. Catlin, 109th New York

    Sgt. Charles H. De Puy, 1st Michigan Sharpshooters

    Corp. Sidney Haight, 1st Michigan Sharpshooters

    Pvt. Robert F. Dodd, 27th Michigan

Pvt. Nathaniel Gwynne, 13th Ohio Cavalry (Dismounted)
Pvt. Charles M. Thatcher, 1st Michigan Sharpshooters

Fourth Division
Col. Delevan Bates, 30th United States Colored Troops
Capt. Albert D. Wright, 43rd United States Colored Troops
Lt. Andrew Davidson, 30th United States Colored Troops
Sgt. Decatur Dorsey, 39th United States Colored Troops

Eighteenth Corps
First Division
Sgt. Walter Jamieson, 139th New York

CONFEDERATE ROLL OF HONOR

Anderson's Division (Mahone)
Mahone's Virginia Brigade (Weisiger)
Lt. Col. Richard Owen Whitehead, 16th Virginia
Capt. Leroy R. Kilby, 16th Virginia
Lt. Julius J. Billsoly, 61st Virginia
Lt. Joseph B. Goodwin, 16th Virginia
Lt. St. Julien Wilson, 61st Virginia
Corp. Solomon V. Butler, 16th Virginia
Corp. T.R. Collins, 61st Virginia
Corp. B.F. Martin, 61st Virginia
Pvt. David Barnes, 16th Virginia
Pvt. D.C. Cannou, 61st Virginia
Pvt. William H. Cooper, 61st Virginia
Pvt. C.J. Falk, 61st Virginia
Pvt. A. Jackson, 61st Virginia
Pvt. R.S. Jones, 61st Virginia
Pvt. W.F. Lane, 16th Virginia
Pvt. John W. Miles, 41st Virginia
Pvt. J.T. Rushing, 61st Virginia
Pvt. Addison J. Sadler, 16th Virginia
Pvt. Lemuel Tucker, 41st Virginia
Pvt. Walter B. Wellons, 6th Virginia

Wilcox Alabama Brigade (Sanders)
Sgt. John E. Deaton, 8th Alabama

Appendix C: Soldiers Decorated for Gallantry at the Battle of the Crater

Pvt. John M. Critcher, 9th Alabama
Pvt. James N. Keeton, 11th Alabama

Wright's Georgia Brigade (Hall)
  Corp. Furney I. Herndon, 3rd Georgia

Sources for Appendices

1. U.S. War Department. *War of the Rebellion: A Compilation of the Official Records of the Union and Confederate Armies.* 128 vols. Washington: Government Printing Office, 1880–1901.

2. Cavanaugh, Michael A. and Marvel, William. *The Petersburg Campaign: The Battle of the Crater: "The Horrid Pit" June 25–August 6, 1864.* Lynchburg, Virginia: H.E. Howard, Inc., 1989.

Notes

Introduction

1. Colonel Alexander K. McClure, ed., *Lincoln's Yarns and Stories* (Chicago: The J.C. Winston Company, n.d.).

2. Lee confided in General Jubal Early. Shelby Foote, *The Civil War: A Narrative: Red River to Appomattox* (New York: Random House, 1974), p. 428.

3. Noah Andre Trudeau, *The Last Citadel: Petersburg, Virginia, June 1864-April 1865* (Boston: Little, Brown and Company, 1991), p. 30.

1. Battleground Petersburg

1. Trudeau, *The Last Citadel*, p. 34.

2. *War of the Rebellion: A Compilation of the Official Records of the Union and Confederate Armies* (Washington: Government Printing Office, 1880–1901), Series 1, Volume XXXIV, Part 1, p. 17. (Hereafter cited as *O.R.*)

3. Trudeau, *The Last Citadel*, p. 8

4. Brigadier General R.E. Colston, "Repelling the First Assault on Petersburg," *Battles and Leaders of the Civil War* (New York: The Century Co., 1884–1888), Volume IV, pp. 535–537.

5. William C. Davis, *Death in the Trenches: Grant at Petersburg* (Alexandria, Virginia: Time-Life Books, 1986), p. 31.

6. Colston, "Repelling the First Assault on Petersburg," *Battles and Leaders of the Civil War.*

7. *Ibid.*

8. Major General August V. Kautz, "First Attempts to Capture Petersburg," *Battles and Leaders of the Civil War*, Volume IV, pp. 533–535.

9. *O.R.*, Series 1, Volume XXXVI, Part 1, p. 11.

10. Trudeau, *The Last Citadel*, p. 19. Comment made by Brigadier General Eppa Hutton.

11. *O.R.*, Series 1, Volume XL, Part 1, p. 12.

12. *O.R.*, Series 1, Volume XL, Part 2, p. 47.

13. Trudeau, *The Last Citadel*, p. 41. The enlisted man was George Ulmer of Maine.

14. General P.G.T. Beauregard, "Four Days of Battle at Petersburg," *Battles and Leaders of the Civil War*, Volume IV, pp. 540–544.

15. *O.R.*, Series 1, Volume XL, Part 2, p. 657.

16. Trudeau, *The Last Citadel*, p. 35.

17. *Ibid.*, p. 43.

18. Beauregard, "Four Days of Battle at Petersburg," *Battles and Leaders of the Civil War.*

19. *O.R.*, Series 1, Volume XL, Part 2, p. 117

20. *Ibid.*, p. 666.

21. *Ibid.*, p. 205.

22. Richard A. Sauers, editor, *The Civil War Journal of Colonel William J. Bolton, 51st Pennsylvania, April 20, 1861-August 2, 1865* (Pennsylvania: Combined Publishing, 2000), pp. 218–219.

23. Davis, *Death in the Trenches: Grant at Petersburg*, p. 50. Reminiscence by Captain A.C. Brown.

24. *Ibid.*, p. 51. Comment by Colonel Theodore Lyman.

25. *O.R.*, Series 1, Volume XL, Part 2, p. 157.

2. Unconventional Warfare

1. Trudeau, *The Last Citadel*, p. 56. Reminiscence by Major John Chester White.
2. W.A. Day, "The Breastworks at Petersburg," *Confederate Veteran*, Volume XXIX, Number 5, pp. 173–175.
3. *Ibid.*
4. Trudeau, *The Last Citadel*, p. 95. Comment by Colonel Hilary Herbert.
5. George S. Bernard, ed., *The Battle of the Crater* (Petersburg: Fenn & Owen Publishers, 1892), p. 66. Statement of Richard G. Pegram.
6. *O.R.*, Series 1, Volume XL, Part 2, p. 220.
7. The two other engineers were Captains George Gowen and Frank Farquhar. Oliver Christian Bosbyshell, *The 48th in the War*. (Philadelphia: Avil Printing Company, 1895), p. 165.
8. *O.R.*, Series 1, Volume XL, Part 2, p. 397.
9. Henry Pleasants, Jr. and George H. Straley, *Inferno at Petersburg* (Philadelphia: Chilton Company, 1961), p. 57. Also see *O.R.*, Series 1, Volume XL, Part 1, p. 59.
10. Foote, *The Civil War: A Narrative: Red River to Appomattox*, p. 443.
11. *Ibid.*
12. *Ibid.* The commander was General John Gibbon of Second Corps.
13. The commander who blamed Meade was General Francis Barlow of Second Corps. Trudeau, *The Last Citadel*, p. 70.
14. John Canaan, *The Crater: Burnside's Assault on the Confederate Trenches, July 30, 1864* (Cambridge, Massachusetts: Da Capo Press, 2002), p. 9.
15. *O.R.*, Series 1, Volume XL, Part 2, p. 417.
16. *Ibid.*, p. 608.
17. U.S. Congress, *Report of the Joint Committee on the Conduct of the War: Battle of Petersburg* (Washington: Government Printing Office, 1865), p. 113.
18. Trudeau, *The Last Citadel*, p. 102.

3. Tunneling Toward Destiny

1. Samuel P. Bates, *History of Pennsylvania Volunteers, 1861–5; Prepared in Compliance with Acts of the Legislature* (Harrisburg: B. Singerly, State Printer, 1869), p.1191. The attorney was John T. Werner.
2. Pleasants and Straley, *Inferno at Petersburg*, p. 41.
3. Bosbyshell, *The 48th in the War*, p. 163.
4. Pleasants and Straley, *Inferno at Petersburg*, p. 17.
5. U.S. Congress, *Report of the Joint Committee on the Conduct of the War: Battle of Petersburg*, p. 112.
6. *Ibid.*, p. 2.
7. *O.R.*, Series 1, Volume XL, Part 1, p. 557.
8. Asst. Surgeon J.B. Culver, "The Petersburg Mine," *The National Tribune*, September 4, 1919.
9. *O.R.*, Series 1, Volume XL, Part 1, p. 557.
10. *Ibid.*
11. *O.R.*, Series 1, Volume XL, Part 2, p. 591.
12. Colonel Byron M. Cutcheon, *The Story of the Twentieth Michigan Infantry, July 15, 1862 to May 30th, 1865* (Lansing, Michigan: R. Smith Printing Co., 1904), p. 138.
13. Warren Wilkinson, *Mother, May You Never See the Sights I Have Seen: The Fifty-Seventh Massachusetts Veteran Volunteers in the Army of the Potomac, 1864–1865* (New York: William Morrow and Company, Inc., 1990), p. 197.
14. Davis, *Death in the Trenches: Grant at Petersburg*, p. 68.
15. Michael A. Cavanaugh and William Marvel, *The Petersburg Campaign: The Battle of the Crater: "The Horrid Pit" June 25-August 6, 1864* (Lynchburg, Virginia: H.E. Howard, Inc., 1989), p. 11.
16. *O.R.*, Series 1, Volume XL, Part 3, p. 776.
17. *Ibid.*, p. 784.
18. *Ibid.*, p. 790.

4. Plan of Attack

1. Sauers, *Journal of Colonel William J. Bolton*, p. 223.
2. Journal of Col. William Hamilton Harris, Virginia Historical Society, Richmond, VA.
3. *O.R.*, Series 1, Volume XL, Part 1, pp. 34–36.

4. U.S. Congress, *Report of the Joint Committee on the Conduct of the War: Battle of Petersburg*, p. 2.

5. *Ibid.*, p. 115.

6. *O.R.*, Series 1, Volume XL, Part 3, p. 477.

7. E.B.Long, ed., *Personal Memoirs of U.S. Grant* (Cambridge, Massachusetts: Da Capo Press, 2001), p. 467.

8. Harris Journal, Virginia Historical Society, Richmond, VA.

9. U.S. Congress, *Report of the Joint Committee on the Conduct of the War: Battle of Petersburg*, p. 115.

10. Michael E. Stevens, ed., *As If It Were Glory: Robert Beecham's Civil War from the Iron Brigade to the Black Regiments* (Madison, Wisconsin: Madison House, 1998), p. 166.

11. U.S. Congress, *Report of the Joint Committee on the Conduct of the War: Battle of Petersburg*, p. 16.

12. *Ibid.*, p. 106.

13. *Ibid.*, p. 89.

14. Stevens, *As If It Were Glory*, p. 178.

15. Maj. Gen. Henry Goddard Thomas, "The Colored Troops at Petersburg," *Battles and Leaders of the Civil War*, Volume IV, pp. 563–567.

16. Stevens, *As if It Were Glory*, p. 179.

17. Bernard, *The Battle of the Crater*, p. 38.

18. *O.R.*, Series 1, Volume XL, Part 3, p. 476.

19. *Ibid.*, p. 252.

The University of North Carolina Press, 1991), p. 387.

9. Major William H. Powell, "The Battle of the Petersburg Crater," *Battles and Leaders of the Civil War*, Volume IV, pp. 545–560. Also see Canaan, *The Crater*, p. 49.

10. Harris Journal, Virginia Historical Society, Richmond, VA.

11. Chase, "The Charge at Daybreak," p. 13.

12. *O.R.*, Series 1, Volume XL, Part 3, p. 566.

13. U.S. Congress, *Report of the Joint Committee on the Conduct of the War: Battle of Petersburg*, p. 116.

14. Cutcheon, *The Story of the Twentieth Michigan Infantry*, p. 138.

15. *O.R.*, Series 1, Volume XL, Part 3, p. 596.

16. Thomas, "The Colored Troops at Petersburg," *Battles and Leaders of the Civil War*.

17. Trudeau, Noah Andre. *Like Men of War: Black Troops in the Civil War, 1862–1865* (Boston: Little, Brown and Company, 1998), p. 235.

18. Reminiscence of John W. Morrison, Petersburg National Battlefield, Petersburg, VA.

19. Francis Winthrop Palfrey, ed., *Memoir of William Francis Bartlett.* (Boston: Houghton, Osgood and Company, 1878), p. 118.

5. *Twelve Frantic Hours*

1. Day, "The Breastworks at Petersburg," *Confederate Veteran*.

2. James Judson Chase, "The Charge at Daybreak: Scenes and Incidents at the Battle of the Mine Explosion," (Lewiston, Maine: The Journal Office, 1875) p. 9.

3. Day, "The Breastworks at Petersburg," *Confederate Veteran*.

4. U.S. Congress, *Report of the Joint Committee on the Conduct of the War: Battle of Petersburg*, p. 18.

5. *Ibid.* Also see p. 89.

6. *Ibid.*

7. *Ibid.*, p. 110.

8. William Marvel, *Burnside* (Chapel Hill:

6. *"Muffled Thunder"*

1. Powell, "The Battle of the Petersburg Crater," *Battles and Leaders of the Civil War*.

2. Freeman S. Bowley, "The Battle of the Mine," *Overland Monthly and Out West Magazine*, Volume IV, Issue 4, (April 1870), pp. 319–327. Also see Cutcheon, *The Story of the Twentieth Michigan Infantry*, p. 139, and Chase, "The Charge at Daybreak," p. 16.

3. General Horace Porter, *Campaigning with Grant* (New York: The Century Company, 1897), p. 263. Also see Captain R.G. Richards, "The Forty-Fifth in the Battle of the Crater," *History of the Forty-Fifth Regiment Pennsylvania Veteran Volunteer Infantry, 1861–1865* (Williamsport, PA: Grit Publishing Company, 1912), pp. 149–159.

4. Thomas, "The Colored Troops at Petersburg," *Battles and Leaders of the Civil War*.

5. Major Charles H. Houghton, "In the Crater," *Battles and Leaders of the Civil War*, Volume IV, pp. 561–562.

6. Cutcheon, *The Story of the Twentieth Michigan Infantry*, p. 139. Sauers, *Journal of Colonel William J. Bolton*, p. 225. Bowley, "The Battle of the Mine," *Overland Monthly and Out West Magazine*.

7. John S. Wise, *The End of an Era*. (Boston: Houghton, Mifflin and Company, 1902), p. 355.

8. W.J. Andrews, "Sketch of Company K., 23rd South Carolina Volunteers," (Richmond: Whittet & Shepperson, Printers, n.d.)

9. Capt. John C. Featherston, "The Battle of the 'Crater' as I Saw It," *Confederate Veteran*, Volume XIV, Number 1, (January 1906), pp. 23–26.

10. Surgeon Hugh Toland, "Terrible Story of the Crater," Rutland Weekly Herald and Globe, October 3, 1878.

11. Colonel F.W. McMaster, "The Battle of the Crater, July 30, 1864," *Southern Historical Society Papers*, Volume X, pp. 119–123.

12. Houghton, "In the Crater," *Battles and Leaders of the Civil War*. The First Brigade captain was Stephen M. Weld. See Canaan, *The Crater*, p. 89.

13. Powell, "The Battle of the Petersburg Crater," *Battles and Leaders of the Civil War*.

14. Houghton, "In the Crater," *Battles and Leaders of the Civil War*.

15. Powell, "The Battle of the Petersburg Crater," *Battles and Leaders of the Civil War*.

16. Richards, "The Forty-Fifth in the Battle of the Crater," *History of the Forty-Fifth Regiment Pennsylvania Veteran Volunteer Infantry*.

17. Bosbyshell, *The 48th in the War*, p. 172.

18. Day, "The Breastworks at Petersburg," *Confederate Veteran*

19. Powell, "The Battle of the Petersburg Crater," *Battles and Leaders of the Civil War*. The captain from Massachusetts was Stephen M. Weld. Canaan, *The Crater*, p. 93.

20. U.S. Congress, *Report of the Joint Committee on the Conduct of the War: Battle of Petersburg*, p. 92.

21. *O.R.*, Series 1, Volume XL, Part 1, pp. 103–104, 118–119.

22. *O.R.*, Series 1, Volume XL, Part 3, p. 657.

7. Early Response

1. McMaster, "The Battle of the Crater, July 30, 1864," *Southern Historical Society Papers*.

2. Bernard, *The Battle of the Crater*, p. 53.

3. *Ibid.*

4. Major James C. Coit, "Letter from Major J.C. Coit, August 2, 1879," *Southern Historical Society Papers*, Volume X, pp. 123–130.

5. *Ibid.*

6. Memoir of Joseph William Eggleston, Virginia Historical Society, Richmond, VA.

7. *Ibid.*

8. *O.R.*, Series 1, Volume XL, Part 3, p. 658.

9. Chase, "The Charge at Daybreak," p. 19.

10. Davis, *Death in the Trenches*, p. 78. The officer was Major William H. Powell.

11. Canaan, *The Crater*, p. 102–103.

12. *O.R.*, Series 1, Volume XL, Part 1, p. 118. The captain from Massachusetts was John Anderson. Trudeau, *The Last Citadel*, p. 110.

13. Recollection of Frederick E. Cushman of the 58th Massachusetts. Cannan, *The Crater*, p. 106

14. Richards, "The Forty-Fifth in the Battle of the Crater," *History of the Forty-Fifth Regiment Pennsylvania Veteran Volunteer Infantry*.

15. General William Mahone, *The Battle of the Crater*, (Petersburg: The Franklin Press Co., n.d.), p. 5.

16. *Ibid.*

17. Wise, *The End of an Era*, p. 359.

18. Mahone, *The Battle of the Crater*, pp. 6–7.

19. *O.R.*, Series 1, Volume XL, Part 3, pp. 661–662. Also see *O.R.*, Series 1, Volume XL, Part 1, p. 157.

8. Charge of the USCT

1. See Marvel, *Burnside*, p. 403 and

Cavanaugh and Marvel, *The Battle of the Crater*, p. 24.

2. *O.R.*, Series 1, Volume XL, Part 1, p. 63.

3. *O.R.*, Series 1, Volume XL, Part 3, p. 659.

4. *Ibid.*

5. *Ibid.* See p. 660.

6. *Ibid.*

7. *Ibid.*

8. Thomas, "The Colored Troops at Petersburg," *Battles and Leaders of the Civil War*. Also see Porter, *Campaigning with Grant*, p. 265.

9. *Ibid.* Also see Bowley, "The Battle of the Mine," *Overland Monthly and Out West Magazine*.

10. U.S. Congress, *Report of the Joint Committee on the Conduct of the War: Battle of Petersburg*, p. 92.

11. *Ibid.*

12. Bowley, "The Battle of the Mine," *Overland Monthly and Out West Magazine*.

13. Thomas, "The Colored Troops at Petersburg," *Battles and Leaders of the Civil War*.

14. Bernard, *The Battle of the Crater*, p. 38.

15. Cutcheon, *The Story of the Twentieth Michigan Infantry*, p. 142.

16. Chase, *The Charge at Daybreak*, pp. 22–23.

17. *Ibid.*

18. Wise, *The End of an Era*, p. 363.

19. George S. Bernard, "The Battle of the Crater, July 30, 1864," *Southern Historical Society Papers*, Volume XVIII, pp. 3–38.

20. Lt. Col. William H. Stewart, "The Charge of the Crater," *Southern Historical Society Papers*, Volume XXV, pp. 77–90.

21. Bernard, *The Battle of the Crater*, p. 35.

22. Colonel George T. Rogers, "The Crater Battle, 30th July, 1864," *Confederate Veteran*, Volume III, No. 1, (January 1895), pp. 12–14.

9. Confederate Counterstrike

1. Thomas, "The Colored Troops at Petersburg," *Battles and Leaders of the Civil War*.

2. Stevens, *As if It Were Glory*, p. 184.

3. *Ibid.*

4. Mahone, *The Battle of the Crater*, pp. 7–8.

5. Bernard, *The Battle of the Crater*, p. 77.

6. George S. Bernard, "Great Battle of the Crater: The Work of Mahone and Weisiger at the Fight," *Southern Historical Society Papers*, Volume XXVIII, pp. 204–221.

7. Day, "The Breastworks at Petersburg," *Confederate Veteran*.

8. Bernard, "The Battle of the Crater, July 30, 1864," *Southern Historical Society Papers*.

9. *Ibid.*

10. Bowley, "The Battle of the Mine," *Overland Monthly and Out West Magazine*.

11. U.S. Congress, *Report of the Joint Committee on the Conduct of the War: Battle of Petersburg*, p. 121. Also see *O.R.*, Series 1, Volume XL, Part 1, p. 120. The Eighteenth Corps officer was Brigadier General J.B. Carr.

12. *O.R.*, Series 1, Volume XL, Part 3, p. 661.

13. Porter, *Campaigning with Grant*, p. 267.

14. Trudeau, *The Last Citadel*, p. 120. See also Cavanaugh and Marvel, *The Battle of the Crater*, p. 93.

15. Reminiscence of James E. Phillips, Virginia Historical Society, Richmond, VA.

16. Bernard, *The Battle of the Crater*, p. 86.

17. Bernard, "Great Battle of the Crater," *Southern Historical Society Papers*.

18. Lynda Lasswell Crist, ed., *The Papers of Jefferson Davis, Volume 10, October 1863-August 1864* (Baton Rouge: Louisiana State University Press, 1999), p. 577.

19. *Ibid.*

20. U.S. Congress, *Report of the Joint Committee on the Conduct of the War: Battle of Petersburg*, p. 10.

10. End Game

1. Powell, "The Battle of the Petersburg Crater," *Battles and Leaders of the Civil War*.

2. Bowley, "The Battle of the Mine," *Overland Monthly and Out West Magazine*.

3. Bernard, *The Battle of the Crater*, p. 63.

4. W.J.Andrews, *Sketch of Company K., 23rd South Carolina Volunteers* (Richmond: Whittet & Shepperson, Printers, n.d.). Also see Memoir of Joseph William Eggleston, Virginia Historical Society, Richmond, VA.

5. Bowley, "The Battle of the Mine," *Overland Monthly and Out West Magazine*. Also see Bernard, *The Battle of the Crater*, p. 37.

6. Houghton, "In the Crater," and Powell, "The Battle of the Petersburg Crater," *Battles and Leaders of the Civil War*.

7. Ervin T. Case, *Personal Narratives of the Battles of the Rebellion, No. 10: The Battle of the Mine* (Providence, Rhode Island: Sidney S. Rider, 1879), p. 31. Also see Cavanaugh and Marvel, *The Horrid Pit*, p. 96.

8. Featherston, "The Battle of the 'Crater' as I Saw It," *Confederate Veteran*.

9. *Ibid.*

10. Richards, "The Forty-Fifth in the Battle of the Crater," *History of the Forty-Fifth Regiment Pennsylvania Veteran Volunteer Infantry, 1861–1865*.

11. Featherston, "The Battle of the 'Crater' as I Saw It," *Confederate Veteran*. Bowley, "The Battle of the Mine," *Overland Monthly and Out West Magazine*.

12. Bowley, "The Battle of the Mine," *Overland Monthly and Out West Magazine*.

13. Featherston, "The Battle of the 'Crater' as I Saw It," *Confederate Veteran*.

14. Stewart, "The Charge of the Crater," *Southern Historical Society Papers*.

15. Andrews, *Sketch of Company K., 23rd South Carolina Volunteers*. Featherston, "The Battle of the 'Crater' as I Saw It," *Confederate Veteran*.

11. Aftershocks

1. U.S. Congress, *Report of the Joint Committee on the Conduct of the War: Battle of Petersburg*, p. 24.

2. Canaan, *The Crater*, p. 143.

3. Stewart, "The Charge of the Crater," *Southern Historical Society Papers*.

4. Trudeau, *The Last Citadel*, p. 125.

5. Featherston, "The Battle of the 'Crater' as I Saw It," *Confederate Veteran*.

6. Trudeau, *Like Men of War*, p. 248.

7. *O.R.*, Series 1, Volume XL, Part 1, p. 17.

8. *O.R.*, Series 1, Volume XL, Part 1, p. 558.

9. U.S. Congress, *Report of the Joint Committee on the Conduct of the War: Battle of Petersburg*, p. 117.

10. Wilkinson, *Mother, May You Never See the Sights I Have Seen*, p. 268.

11. Crist, *The Papers of Jefferson Davis*, p. 576.

12. *O.R.*, Series 1, Volume XLII, Part 2, p. 1155.

13. *O.R.*, Series 1, Volume XL, Part 1, p. 174.

14. *O.R.*, Series 1, Volume XL, Part 1, p. 171.

15. *Ibid.*

16. *O.R.*, Series 1, Volume XL, Part 1, pp. 531–532.

17. *Ibid.*

12. Censure and Commendation

1. *O.R.*, Series 1, Volume XL, Part 1, pp. 80–81.

2. *O.R.*, Series 1, Volume XL, Part 1, p. 129.

3. U.S. Congress, *Report of the Joint Committee on the Conduct of the War: Battle of Petersburg*, p. 76.

4. U.S. Congress, *Report of the Joint Committee on the Conduct of the War: Battle of Petersburg*, pp. 110–111.

5. *Ibid.*

6. U.S. Congress, *Report of the Joint Committee on the Conduct of the War: Battle of Petersburg*, pp. 1–12.

7. *Ibid.*

8. *Ibid.*

Epilogue

1. Case, *The Battle of the Mine*, p. 28.

2. Bernard, *The Battle of the Crater*, p. 90.

3. Bosbyshell, *The 48th in the War*, pp. 176–177.

4. Pleasants, Jr., and Straley, *Inferno at Petersburg*, pp 167–168.

Bibliography

Articles

Andrews, W.J. "Sketch of Company K., 23rd South Carolina Volunteers" (pamphlet), Richmond: Whittet & Shepperson, Printers, n.d.

Bausum, Daniel F. "Personal Reminiscences of Sergeant Daniel F. Bausum, Co. K, 48th Regt., Penna. Vol. Inf., 1861–1865," A Publication of the Historical Society of Schuylkill County, Volume IV, 1914, pp. 240–249.

Beauregard, General P.G.T. "Four Days of Battle at Petersburg," *Battles and Leaders of the Civil War*, New York: The Century Co., 1884–1888, Volume IV, pp. 540–544.

Bernard, George S. "The Battle of the Crater, July 30, 1864," *Southern Historical Society Papers*, Volume XVIII, pp. 3–38.

_____. "Great Battle of the Crater: The Work of Mahone and Weisiger at the Fight," *Southern Historical Society Papers*, Volume XXVIII, pp. 204–221.

Bowley, Freeman S. "The Battle of the Mine," *Overland Monthly and Out West Magazine*, Volume IV, Issue 4 (April 1870), pp. 319–327.

Chase, Lieutenant James Judson. "The Charge at Daybreak: Scenes and Incidents at the Battle of the Mine Explosion" (pamphlet), Lewiston, Maine: The Journal Office, 1875.

Coit, Major James C. "Letter from Major J.C. Coit, August 2, 1879," *Southern Historical Society Papers*, Volume X, pp. 123–130.

Colston, Brig. Gen. R.E. "Repelling the First Assault on Petersburg," *Battles and Leaders of the Civil War*, New York: The Century Co., 1884–1888, Volume IV, pp. 535–537.

Culver, Asst. Surgeon J.B. (48th PA). "The Petersburg Mine," *The National Tribune*, September 4, 1919.

Day, W.A. "The Breastworks at Petersburg," *Confederate Veteran*, Volume XXIX, Number 5 (May 1921), pp. 173–175.

Etheredge, Major William H. "Another Story of the Crater Battle," *Southern Historical Society Papers*, Volume XXXVII, pp. 203–207.

Featherston, Capt. John C. "The Battle of the 'Crater' as I Saw It," *Confederate Veteran*, Volume XIV, Number 1 (January 1906), pp. 23–26.

Flanner, Captain Henry G. "Flanner's North Carolina Battery at the Battle of the Crater," *Southern Historical Society Papers*, Volume V, pp. 247–248.

Guttman, Jon. "Had He Not Become a General, Posterity Might Have Remembered Ambrose Burnside for His Carbine," *America's Civil War*, Volume 13, Issue 3, July 2000, pp. 12–16.

Haas, James F. "The Famous 48th," *Schuylkill County in the Civil War*, A Publication of the Historical Society of Schuylkill County, Volume VII, Number 3, 1961, pp. 53–62.

Bibliography

Hauptman, Laurence M. "Into the Abyss," *Civil War Times Illustrated*, Volume 35, Issue 7, February 1997, pp. 46–55.

Houghton, Major Charles H. "In the Crater," *Battles and Leaders of the Civil War*, New York: The Century Co., 1884–1888, Volume IV, pp. 561–562.

Inners, Jon D. "Colonel Henry Pleasants and the Military Geology of the Petersburg Mine-June-July, 1864," *Pennsylvania Geology*, Volume 20, Number 5, October 1989, pp. 3–10.

Kautz, Maj. Gen. August V. "First Attempts to Capture Petersburg," *Battles and Leaders of the Civil War*, New York: The Century Co., 1884–1888, Volume IV, pp. 533–535.

Mahone, General William. "The Battle of the Crater" (pamphlet), Petersburg: The Franklin Press Co., n.d.

McCabe, Captain W. Gordon. "Defence of Petersburg," *Southern Historical Society Papers*, Volume II, pp. 257–305.

McMaster, Colonel F.W. "The Battle of the Crater, July 30, 1864," *Southern Historical Society Papers*, Volume X, pp. 119–123.

Powell, Major William H. "The Battle of the Petersburg Crater," *Battles and Leaders of the Civil War*, New York: The Century Co., 1884–1888, Volume IV, pp. 545–560.

Ray, Frederic. "Fiasco at Petersburg," *Civil War Times*, Volume II, Number 1, April 1960, pp. 4–7.

Razza, Michael S. "The Man Behind the Mine," *Civil War*, Issue 57 (June 1996), pp. 22–27.

Richards, Captain R.G. "The Forty-Fifth in the Battle of the Crater," *History of the Forty-Fifth Regiment Pennsylvania Veteran Volunteer Infantry, 1861–1865*, Williamsport, Pennsylvania: Grit Publishing Company, 1912, pp. 149–159.

Rogers, Colonel George T. "The Crater Battle, 30th July, 1864," Confederate Veteran, Volume III, No. 1 (January 1895), pp. 12–14.

Roulhac, Thomas R. "History of the Forty-Ninth N.C. Infantry, C.S.A., 1862-'65," *Southern Historical Society Papers*, Volume XXIII, pp. 58–78.

Stewart, Lt. Col. William H. "The Charge of the Crater," *Southern Historical Society Papers*, Volume XXV, pp. 77–90.

_____. "Field of Blood Was the Crater," *Southern Historical Society Papers*, Volume XXXIII, pp. 351–357.

Thomas, Maj. Gen. Henry Goddard. "The Colored Troops at Petersburg," *Battles and Leaders of the Civil War*, New York: The Century Co., 1884–1888, Volume IV, pp. 563–567.

Toland, Hugh (Surgeon, 18th SC). "Terrible Story of the Crater," *Rutland Weekly Herald and Globe*, October 3, 1878.

W.R.S. (full name unknown). "The Sharpshooters of Mahone's Old Brigade at the Crater," *Southern Historical Society Papers*, Volume XXVIII, pp. 307–308.

Books

Arnold, James R. *Grant Wins the War: Decision at Vicksburg*. New York: John Wiley & Sons, 1997.

Bates, Samuel P. *History of Pennsylvania Volunteers, 1861–5; Prepared in Compliance with Acts of the Legislature*. Harrisburg: B. Singerly, State Printer, 1869.

Bernard, George S., ed. *The Battle of the Crater*. Petersburg: Fenn & Owen Publishers, 1892.

Blake, Nelson Morehouse. *William Mahone of Virginia: Soldier and Political Insurgent*. Richmond: Garrett & Massie, 1935.

Bosbyshell, Major Oliver Christian. *The 48th in the War*. Philadelphia: Avil Printing Company, 1895.

Canaan, John. *The Crater: Burnside's Assault on the Confederate Trenches, July 30, 1864.* Cambridge, Massachusetts: Da Capo Press, 2002.

Case, Ervin T. *Personal Narratives of the Battles of the Rebellion, No. 10: The Battle of the Mine.* Providence, Rhode Island: Sidney S. Rider, 1879.

Cavanaugh, Michael A. and Marvel, William. *The Petersburg Campaign: The Battle of the Crater: "The Horrid Pit" June 25–August 6, 1864.* Lynchburg, Virginia: H.E. Howard, Inc., 1989.

Crist, Lynda Lasswell. *The Papers of Jefferson Davis, Volume 10, October 1863–August 1864.* Baton Rouge: Louisiana State University Press, 1999.

Cutcheon, Colonel Byron M. *The Story of the Twentieth Michigan Infantry, July 15, 1862 to May 30th, 1865.* Lansing, Michigan: R. Smith Printing Co., 1904.

Davis, William C. *Death in the Trenches: Grant at Petersburg.* Alexandria, Virginia: Time-Life Books, 1986.

Foote, Shelby. *The Civil War: A Narrative: Red River to Appomattox.* New York: Random House, 1974.

Gould, Joseph. *The Story of the Forty-eighth: A Record of the Campaigns of the Forty-eighth Regiment Pennsylvania Veteran Volunteer Infantry During the Four Eventful Years of Its Service in the War for the Preservation of the Union.* Philadelphia: Alfred M. Slocum, 1908.

Heidler, David S. and Heidler, Jeanne T., eds. *Encyclopedia of the American Civil War: A Political, Social, and Military History.* New York: W.W. Norton & Company, 2000.

Herek, Raymond J. *These Men Have Seen Hard Service: The First Michigan Sharpshooters in the Civil War.* Detroit: Wayne State University Press, 1998.

Horn, John. *The Petersburg Campaign: June 1864–April 1865.* Pennsylvania: Combined Publishing, 1993.

Long, E.B., ed. *Personal Memoirs of U.S. Grant.* Cambridge, Massachusetts: Da Capo Press, 2001.

Marvel, William. *Burnside.* Chapel Hill: The University of North Carolina Press, 1991.

Palfrey, Francis Winthrop, ed. *Memoir of William Francis Bartlett.* Boston: Houghton, Osgood and Company, 1878.

Pleasants, Jr., Henry and Straley, George H. *Inferno at Petersburg.* Philadelphia: Chilton Company, 1961.

Porter, General Horace. *Campaigning with Grant.* New York: The Century Company, 1897.

Sauers, Richard A., ed. *The Civil War Journal of Colonel William J. Bolton, 51st Pennsylvania, April 20, 1861–August 2, 1865.* Pennsylvania: Combined Publishing, 2000.

Stevens, Michael E., ed. *As If It Were Glory: Robert Beecham's Civil War from the Iron Brigade to the Black Regiments.* Madison, Wisconsin: Madison House, 1998.

Trudeau, Noah Andre. *The Last Citadel: Petersburg, Virginia, June 1864–April 1865.* Boston: Little, Brown and Company, 1991.

_____. *Like Men of War: Black Troops in the Civil War, 1862–1865.* Boston: Little, Brown and Company, 1998.

Wilkinson, Warren. *Mother, May You Never See the Sights I Have Seen: The Fifty-Seventh Massachusetts Veteran Volunteers in the Army of the Potomac, 1864–1865.* New York: William Morrow and Company, Inc., 1990.

Wise, John S. *The End of an Era.* Boston: Houghton, Mifflin and Company, 1902

Manuscripts

Richmond, VA: Virginia Historical Society

Eggleston, Joseph William, memoir
Harris, Col. William Hamilton, journal
Phillips, James E., papers

Petersburg, VA: Petersburg National Battlefield
Morrison, John W., reminiscence

Newspapers

The National Tribune (Washington D.C.)
The Rutland Weekly Herald and Globe (Vermont)
The Shamokin Herald (Pennsylvania)

Official Documents

U.S. Congress. *Report of the Joint Committee on the Conduct of the War: Battle of Petersburg.* Washington: Government Printing Office, 1865.
U.S. War Department. *War of the Rebellion: A Compilation of the Official Records of the Union and Confederate Armies.* 128 vols. Washington: Government Printing Office, 1880–1901.

Index

183

Index